Rogue State

A Guide to the World's Only Superpower

William Blum

Common Courage Press   Monroe, Maine

Library of Congress Cataloging-in-Publication Data

Blum, William.
    Rogue state : a guide to the world's only superpower / William
Blum.
        p. cm.
    Includes bibliographical references (p.) and index.
    ISBN 1-56751-195-3 -- ISBN 1-56751-194-5 (pbk.)
        1. United States--Foreign relations--1945-1989. 2. United
States--Foreign relations--1989- 3. United States--Military policy.
4. Intervention (International law) 5. Human rights--Foreign
countries. 6. Human rights--Government policy--United States.
I. Title

E840 .B596 2000
327.73--dc21

                                                    00-021558

Second printing

Common Courage Press
Box 702
Monroe, ME 04951

(207) 525-0900; FAX (207) 525-3068
orders-info@commoncouragepress.com

www.commoncouragepress.com

Never before in modern history has a country dominated the earth so totally as the United States does today…America is now the Schwarzenegger of international politics: showing off muscles, obtrusive, intimidating…The Americans, in the absence of limits put to them by anybody or anything, act as if they own a kind of blank check in their "McWorld."

Der Spiegel, Germany's leading newsmagazine, 1997[1]

The United States is good.
We try to do our best everywhere.

Madeleine Albright, 1999[2]

―――――――――――

A world once divided into two armed camps now recognizes one sole and preeminent power, the United States of America. And they regard this with no dread. For the world trusts us with power, and the world is right. They trust us to be fair, and restrained. They trust us to be on the side of decency. They trust us to do what's right.

George Bush, 1992[3]

How can they have the arrogance to dictate to us where we should go or which countries should be our friends? Gadhafi is my friend. He supported us when we were alone and when those who tried to prevent my visit here today were our enemies. They have no morals. We cannot accept that a state assumes the role of the world's policeman.

Nelson Mandela, 1997[4]

―――――――――――

When I came into office, I was determined that our country would go into the 21st century still the world's greatest force for peace and freedom, for democracy and security and prosperity.

Bill Clinton, 1996[5]

Throughout the world, on any given day, a man, woman or child is likely to be displaced, tortured, killed or "disappeared", at the hands of governments or armed political groups. More often than not, the United States shares the blame.

Amnesty International, 1996[6]

Update

As this new edition was being prepared for printing, on September 11, 2001, four planes were hijacked and terrorists proceeded to carry out the most devastating attack on American soil in the history of the United States. The physical destruction and personal suffering caused by the attacks has been immense. In addition to punishing the perpetrators who are still alive, we must not allow the event to pass without deriving important lessons from it. Clearly, the most important lesson to be learned is the answer to the question "Why?"

It happens that there is a chapter in this book entitled: "Why Do Terrorists Keep Picking on the United States?", which argues that "terrorists—whatever else they might be—might also be rational human beings; which is to say that in their own minds they have a rational justification for their actions. Most terrorists are people deeply concerned by what they see as social, political, or religious injustice and hypocrisy, and the immediate grounds for their terrorism is often retaliation for an action of the United States."

This is followed by a lengthy list of such US actions in the Middle East, which took many lives, from the bombing of Lebanon and Libya to the sinking of an Iranian ship; from the shooting down of an Iranian passenger plane and the massive bombing of the Iraqi people to the bombing of Sudan and Afghanistan and the habitual support of Israel despite the devastation and routine torture it commits against the Palestinian people.

The rest of the Third World and even parts of Europe have suffered the explosive fist of the most powerful nation in history as much as has the Middle East. Where once the United States felt immune to the kind of large scale terrorism that it has regularly carried out, and could afford to ignore the suffering its policies inflicted upon others, that is no longer the case. American foreign policy will have to undergo a great metamorphosis. Only then will anti-US terrorism cease, only then will Americans feel safe in their places of work and travel.

It was perhaps hoping for too much that after the attack American leaders, the media, or the public would look into the terrorism question from this angle with any kind of seriousness. Instead, as usual, the terrorists were depicted as little more than evil monsters, or insane, or motivated by religious fanaticism at best; with little or no hint that they were retaliating for things done to them. Instead of an outpouring of reflection upon what the United States does to the world to make it so hated, there was an outpouring of patriotism: Congress members stood on the steps of the Capitol and sang "God Bless America", stores quickly sold out their stocks of American flags, callers to radio shows spit out venom and bloodlust, and the only member of congress who voted against the "Authorization for use of Military Force", Barbara Lee, of California, received innumerable threats and hate mail.

A few years ago, journalist Alan Nairn wrote that with the end of the Cold War, the United States "wields powers that no nation should have. It can go anywhere and kill anyone. Only the American public can hold Washington back. Only the American people stand between the bombers and the bombed." If there's to be any hope of the American public ever performing this role, their consciences and intellects will have to be awakened. To this end, this book has gathered in one place the many deeds of American foreign policy of the past half century which increasingly have earned the US government the enmity of people in every corner of the world.

William Blum
September 19, 2001

Contents

A Rogue State versus the World

Introduction

This book could be entitled *Serial Chain-Saw Baby Killers and the Women Who Love Them.*

The women don't really believe that their beloved would do such a thing, even if they're shown a severed limb or a headless torso. Or if they believe it, they know down to their bone marrow that lover-boy really had the best of intentions; it must have been some kind of very unfortunate accident, a well-meaning blunder; in fact, even more likely, it was a humanitarian act.

For 70 years, the United States convinced much of the world that there was an international conspiracy out there. An *International Communist Conspiracy*, seeking no less than control over the entire planet, for purposes which had no socially redeeming values. And the world was made to believe that it somehow needed the United States to save it from communist darkness. "Just buy our weapons," said Washington, "let our military and our corporations roam freely across your land, and give us veto power over whom your leaders will be, and we'll protect you."

It was the cleverest protection racket since men convinced women that they needed men to protect them—if all the men vanished overnight, how many women would be afraid to walk the streets?

And if the people of any foreign land were benighted enough to not realize that they needed to be saved, if they failed to appreciate the underlying nobility of American motives, they were warned that they would burn in Communist Hell. Or a CIA facsimile thereof. And they would be saved nonetheless.

A decade after the fall of the Berlin Wall, America is still saving countries and peoples from one danger or another. The scorecard reads as follows: From 1945 to the end of the century, the United States attempted to overthrow more than 40 foreign governments, and to crush more than 30 populist-nationalist movements struggling against intolerable regimes. In the process, the US caused the end of life for several million people, and condemned many millions more to a life of agony and despair.

As I write this in Washington, DC, in April 1999, the United States is busy saving Yugoslavia. Bombing a modern, sophisticated society back to a pre-industrial age. And The Great American Public, in its infinite wisdom, is convinced that its government is motivated by "humanitarian" impulses.

Washington is awash with foreign dignitaries here to celebrate the 50th anniversary of the North Atlantic Treaty Organization, three days of unprecedented pomp and circumstance. The prime ministers, presidents and foreign ministers, despite their rank, are delighted to be included amongst the schoolyard bully's close friends. Private corporations are funding the opulent weekend; a dozen of them paying $250,000 apiece to have one of their executives serve as a director on the NATO Summit's host committee. Many of the same firms lobbied hard to expand NATO by adding the Czech Republic, Hungary and Poland, each of which will be purchasing plentiful quantities of military hardware from these companies.

This marriage of NATO and the transnationals is the foundation of the New World Order, the name George Bush gave to the American Empire. The credibility of the New World Order depends upon the world believing that the new world will be a better one for the multitude of humanity, not just for those for whom too much is not enough, and believing that the leader of the New World Order, the United States, means well.

Let's have a short look at some modern American history, which may be instructive. A congressional report of 1994 informed us that:

> Approximately 60,000 military personnel were used as human subjects in the 1940s to test two chemical agents, mustard gas and lewisite [blister gas]. Most of these subjects were not informed of the nature of the experiments and never received medical followup after their participation in the research. Additionally, some of these human subjects were threatened with imprisonment at Fort Leavenworth if they discussed these experiments with anyone, including their wives,

parents and family doctors. For decades, the Pentagon denied that the research had taken place, resulting in decades of suffering for many veterans who became ill after the secret testing.[1]

Now let's skip ahead to the 1990s. Many thousands of American soldiers came home from the Gulf War with unusual, debilitating ailments. Exposure to harmful chemical or biological agents was suspected, but the Pentagon denied that this had occurred. Years went by while the GIs suffered terribly: neurological problems, chronic fatigue, skin problems, scarred lungs, memory loss, muscle and joint pain, severe headaches, personality changes, passing out and much more. Eventually, the Pentagon, inch by inch, was forced to move away from its denials and admit that, yes, chemical weapon depots had been bombed; then, yes, there probably were releases of the deadly poisons; then, yes, American servicemen were indeed in the vicinity of these poisonous releases, 400 soldiers; then, it might have been 5,000; then, "a very large number", probably more than 15,000; then, finally, a precise number—20,867; then, "The Pentagon announced that a long-awaited computer model estimates that nearly 100,000 U.S. soldiers could have been exposed to trace amounts of sarin gas…"[2]

Soldiers were also forced to take vaccines against anthrax and nerve gas not approved by the FDA as safe and effective, and punished, sometimes treated like criminals, if they refused. (During World War II, US soldiers were forced to take a yellow fever vaccine, with the result that some 330,000 of them were infected with the hepatitis B virus.[3]) Finally, in late 1999, almost nine years after the Gulf War's end, the Defense Department announced that a drug given to soldiers to protect them against a particular nerve gas, "cannot be ruled out" as a cause of lingering illnesses in some veterans.[4]

The Pentagon brass, moreover, did not warn American soldiers of the grave danger of being in close proximity to expended depleted uranium weapons on the battlefield.

If the Pentagon had been much more forthcoming from the outset about what it knew all along about these various substances and weapons, the soldiers might have had a proper diagnosis early on and received appropriate care sooner. The cost in terms of human suffering was incalculable. One gauge of that cost may lie in the estimate that one-third of the homeless in America are military veterans.

And in the decades between the 1940s and 1990s, what do we find? A remarkable variety of government programs, either formally, or in effect, using soldiers as guinea pigs—marched to nuclear explosion sites, with pilots then sent through the mushroom clouds; subjected to chemical and biological weapons experiments; radiation experiments; behavior modification experiments that washed their brains with LSD; exposure to the dioxin of Agent Orange in Korea and Vietnam...the list goes on...literally millions of experimental subjects, seldom given a choice or adequate information, often with disastrous effects to their physical and/or mental health, rarely with proper medical care or even monitoring.[5]

The moral of this little slice of history is simple: If the United States government does not care about the health and welfare of its own soldiers, if our leaders are not moved by the prolonged pain and suffering of the wretched warriors enlisted to fight the empire's wars, how can it be argued, how can it be believed, that they care about foreign peoples? At all.

When the Dalai Lama was asked by a CIA officer in 1995: "Did we do a good or bad thing in providing this support [to the Tibetans]?", the Tibetan spiritual leader replied that though it helped the morale of those resisting the Chinese, "thousands of lives were lost in the resistance" and that "the U.S. Government had involved itself in his country's affairs not to help Tibet but only as a Cold War tactic to challenge the Chinese."[6]

"Let me tell you about the very rich," wrote F. Scott Fitzgerald. "They are different from you and me."

So are our leaders.

Consider Zbigniew Brzezinski, national security adviser to Jimmy Carter. In a 1998 interview he admitted that the official story that the US gave military aid to the Afghanistan opposition only *after* the Soviet invasion in 1979 was a lie. The truth was, he said, that the US began aiding the Islamic fundamentalist Moujahedeen six months *before* the Russians made their move, even though he believed—and told this to Carter—that "this aid was going to induce a Soviet military intervention".

Brzezinski was asked whether he regretted this decision.

Regret what? That secret operation was an excellent idea. It had the effect of drawing the Russians into the Afghan trap and you want me to regret it? The day that the Soviets officially crossed the border, I wrote to President Carter: We now have the opportunity of giving to the USSR its Vietnam War. Indeed, for almost 10 years, Moscow had to carry on a war unsupportable by the government, a conflict that brought about the demoralization and finally the breakup of the Soviet empire.[7]

Besides the fact that there is no demonstrable connection between the Afghanistan war and the breakup of the Soviet empire, we are faced with the consequences of that war: the defeat of a government committed to bringing the extraordinarily backward nation into the 20th century; the breathtaking carnage; Moujahedeen torture that even US government officials called "indescribable horror"[8]; half the population either dead, disabled or refugees; the spawning of thousands of Islamic fundamentalist terrorists who have unleashed atrocities in numerous countries; and the unbelievable repression of women in Afghanistan, instituted by America's wartime allies.

And for playing a key role in causing all this, Zbigniew Brzezinski has no regrets. Regrets? The man is downright proud of it! The kindest thing one can say about such a person—as about a sociopath—is that he's amoral. At least in his public incarnation, which is all we're concerned with here. In medieval times he would have been called Zbigniew the Terrible.

And what does this tell us about Jimmy Carter, whom many people think of as perhaps the only halfway decent person to occupy the White House since Roosevelt? Or is it Lincoln?

In 1977, when pressed by journalists about whether the US had a moral obligation to help rebuild Vietnam, President Carter responded: "Well, the destruction was mutual."[9] (Perhaps when he observed the devastation of the South Bronx later that year, he was under the impression that it had been caused by Vietnamese bombing.)

In the now-famous exchange on TV between Madeleine Albright and reporter Lesley Stahl, the latter was speaking of US sanctions against Iraq, and asked the then-US ambassador to the UN: "We have heard that a half million children have died. I mean, that's more children than died in Hiroshima. And—and you know, is the price worth it?"

Replied Albright: "I think this is a very hard choice, but the price—we think the price is worth it."[10]

One can give Albright the absolute full benefit of any doubt and say that she had no choice but to defend administration policy. But what kind of person is it who takes a job appointment knowing full well that she will be an integral part of such ongoing policies and will be expected to defend them without apology? Not long afterwards, Albright was appointed Secretary of State.

Lawrence Summers is another case in point. In December 1991, while chief economist for the World Bank, he wrote an internal memo saying that the Bank should encourage migration of "the dirty industries" to the less-developed countries because, amongst other reasons, health-impairing and death-causing pollution costs would be lower. Inasmuch as these costs are based on the lost earnings of the affected workers, in a country of very low wages the computed costs would be much lower. "I think," he wrote, "the economic logic behind dumping a load of toxic waste in the lowest-wage country is impeccable and we should face up to that."[11] Despite this memo receiving wide distribution and condemnation, Summers, in 1999, was appointed Secretary of the Treasury by President Clinton. This was a promotion from being Undersecretary of the Treasury—for international affairs.

We also have Clinton himself, who on day 33 of the aerial devastation of Yugoslavia—33 days and nights of destroying villages, schools, hospitals, apartment buildings, the ecology, separating people from their limbs, from their eyesight, spilling their intestines, traumatizing children for the rest of their days...destroying a life the Serbians will never know again—on day 33 William Jefferson Clinton, cautioning against judging the bombing policy prematurely, saw fit to declare: "This may seem like a long time. [But] I don't think that this air campaign has been going on a particularly long time."[12] And then the man continued it another 45 days.

Clinton's vice president, Albert Gore, appears eminently suitable to succeed him to the throne. In 1998, he put great pressure on South Africa, threatening trade sanctions if the government didn't cancel plans to use much cheaper generic AIDS drugs, which would cut into US companies' sales.[13] South Africa, it should be noted, has about three million HIV-positive persons among its largely impoverished population. When Gore, who at the time had significant ties to the drug industry[14], was heckled for what he had done during a speech in New York, he declined to respond in substance, but instead called out: "I love this country. I love the First Amendment."[15]

It's interesting to note that when Madeleine Albright was heckled in Columbus, Ohio in February 1998, while defending the administration's Iraq policy, she yelled: "We are the greatest country in the world!"

Patriotism is indeed the last refuge of a scoundrel, though Gore's and Albright's words don't quite have the ring of *"Deutschland über alles"* or "Rule Britannia".

In 1985, Ronald Reagan, demonstrating the preeminent intellect for which he was esteemed, tried to show how totalitarian the Soviet Union was by declaring: "I'm no linguist, but I've been told that in the Russian language there isn't even a word for 'freedom'."[16] In light of the above cast of characters and their declarations, can we ask if there's a word in American English for "embarrassment"?

No, it is not simply that power corrupts and dehumanizes.

Neither is it that US foreign policy is cruel because American leaders are cruel.

It's that our leaders are cruel because only those willing and able to be inordinately cruel and remorseless can hold positions of leadership in the foreign policy establishment; it might as well be written into the job description. People capable of expressing a full human measure of compassion and empathy toward faraway powerless strangers— let alone American soldiers—do not become president of the United States, or vice president, or secretary of state, or national security adviser or secretary of the treasury. Nor do they want to.

There's a sort of Peter Principle at work here. Laurence Peter wrote that in a hierarchy every employee tends to rise to his level of incompetence. Perhaps we can postulate that in a foreign policy establishment committed to imperialist domination by any means necessary, employees tend to rise to the level of cruelty they can live with.

A few days after the bombing of Yugoslavia had ended, the *New York Times* published as its lead article in the Sunday Week in Review, a piece by Michael Wines, which declared that "Human rights had been elevated to a military priority and a preeminent Western value...The war only underscored the deep ideological divide between an idealistic New World bent on ending inhumanity and an Old World equally fatalistic about unending conflict...there is also a yawning gap between the West and much of the world on the value of a single life."

And so on. A paean to the innate goodness of the West, an ethos unfortunately not shared by much of the rest of the world, who, Wines lamented, "just don't buy into Western notions of rights and responsibilities."[17] The *Times* fed us this morality tale after "the West" had just completed the most ferocious sustained bombing of a nation in the history of the planet, a small portion of whose dreadful consequences are referred to above.

During the American bombing of Iraq in 1991, the previous record for sustained ferociousness, a civilian air raid shelter was destroyed by a depleted-uranium projectile, incinerating to charred blackness many hundreds of people, a great number of them women and children. White House spokesman Marlin Fitzwater, reiterating US military statements that the shelter had been a command-and-control center, said: "We don't know why civilians were at that location, but we do know that Saddam Hussein does not share our value for the sanctity of human life."[18]

Similarly, during the Vietnam War, President Johnson and other government officials assured us that Asians don't have the same high regard for human life as Americans do. We were told this, of course, as American bombs, napalm, Agent Orange and helicopter gunships were disintegrating the Vietnamese and their highly regarded lives.

And at the same time, on a day in February 1966, David Lawrence, the editor of *US News & World Report*, was moved to put the following words to paper: "What the United States is doing in Vietnam is the most significant example of philanthropy extended by one people to another that we have witnessed in our times."

I sent Mr. Lawrence a copy of a well-done pamphlet entitled *American Atrocities in Vietnam*, which gave graphic detail of its subject. To this I attached a note which first repeated Lawrence's quotation with his name below it, then added: "*One* of us is crazy", followed by *my* name.

Lawrence responded with a full page letter, at the heart of which was: "I think a careful reading of it [the pamphlet] will prove the point

I was trying to make—namely that primitive peoples with savagery in their hearts have to be helped to understand the true basis of a civilized existence."

The American mind—as exemplified by that of Michael Wines and David Lawrence—is, politically, so deeply formed that to liberate it would involve uncommon, and as yet perhaps undiscovered, philosophical and surgical skill. The great majority of Americans, even the most cynical—who need no convincing that the words that come out of a politician's mouth are a blend of mis-, dis- and non-information, and should always carry a veracity health warning—appear to lose their critical faculties when confronted by "our boys who are risking their lives". If love is blind, patriotism has lost all five senses.

To the extent that the cynicism of these Americans is directed toward their government's habitual foreign adventures, it's to question whether the administration's stated interpretation of a situation is valid, whether the stated goals are worthwhile, and whether the stated goals can be achieved—but *not* to question the government's *motivation*. It is assumed *a priori* that our leaders *mean well* by the foreign people involved—no matter how much death, destruction and suffering their policies objectively result in.

Congressman Otis Pike (R.-NY) headed a committee in 1975 which uncovered a number of dark covert actions of US foreign policy, many of which were leaked to the public, while others remained secret. In an interview he stated that any member of Congress could see the entire report if he agreed not to reveal anything that was in it. "But not many want to read it," he added.

"Why?" asked his interviewer.

"Oh, they think it is better not to know," Pike replied. "There are too many things that embarrass Americans in that report. You see, this country went through an awful trauma with Watergate. But even then, all they were asked to believe was that their president had been a bad person. In this new situation they are asked much more; they are asked to believe that their country has been evil. And nobody wants to believe that."[19]

This has been compared to going to a counselor because your child is behaving strangely, and being told, "You have a problem of incest in your family." People can't hear that. They go to a different counselor. They grab at any other explanation. It's too painful.[20]

In *The History of the Peloponnesian War*, Thucydides, speaking of the practice of plundering villages, the main source of a warrior's livelihood, tells us that "no disgrace was yet attached to such an achievement, but rather credit".

Almost all of us grew up in an environment in which we learned that thou shalt not murder, rape, rob, probably not pay off a public official or cheat on your taxes—but not that there was anything wrong with toppling foreign governments, quashing revolutions or dropping powerful bombs on foreign people, if it served America's "national security".

Let us look at our teachers. During the bombing of Yugoslavia, CBS Evening News anchor, Dan Rather, declared: "I'm an American, and I'm an American reporter. And yes, when there's combat involving Americans, you can criticize me if you must, damn me if you must, but I'm always pulling for us to win."[21] (In the past, US journalists were quick to criticize their Soviet counterparts for speaking on behalf of the State.)

What does this mean? That he's going to support any war effort by the United States no matter the legal or moral justification? No matter the effect on democracy, freedom or self-determination? No matter the degree of horror produced? No matter *anything*? Many other American journalists have similarly paraded themselves as cheerleaders in modern times in the midst of one of the Pentagon's frequent marches down the warpath, serving a function "more akin to stenography than journalism".[22] During the Gulf War, much of the media, led by CNN, appeared to have a serious missile fetish, enough so to suggest a need for counseling.

The CEO of National Public Radio, Kevin Klose, is the former head of all the major, worldwide US government broadcast propaganda outlets, including Voice of America, Radio Free Europe, Radio Liberty and the anti-Castro Radio Marti, which broadcasts into Cuba from Florida. NPR, which can be thought of as the home service of the Voice of America, has never met an American war it didn't like. It was inspired to describe the war against Yugoslavia as Clinton's "most significant foreign policy success."[23]

And the head of the Corporation for Public Broadcasting, Robert Coonrod, has a résumé remarkably similar to that of Klose, from Voice of America to Radio Marti.

Is it any wonder that countless Americans—bearing psyches no less malleable than those of other members of the species—are only dimly conscious of the fact that they even have the *right* to be unequivocally opposed to a war effort and to question the government's real intentions for carrying it out, without thinking of themselves as (horror of horrors) "unpatriotic"? Propaganda is to a democracy what violence is to a dictatorship.

During the 1991 Gulf War, the Bush administration conducted three briefings a day with such telegenic figures as generals Colin Powell and Norman Schwarzkopf. Marlin Fitzwater later recalled that when ABC-TV interviewed a group of Kansans around a kitchen table, "every answer at that table reflected one of the reasons we had given for going in."[24]

In Spain, in the 16th century, the best minds were busy at work devising rationalizations for the cruelty its conquistadors were inflicting on the Indians of the New World. It was decided, and commonly accepted, that the Indians were "natural slaves", created by God to serve the conquistadors.

Twentieth-century America took this a step further. The best and the brightest have assured us that United States interventions—albeit rather violent at times—are not only in the natural order of things, but they're actually for the *good* of the natives.

The media and the public do in fact relish catching politicians' lies, but these are the small lies—lies about money, sex, drug use and other peccadillos, and the ritual doubletalk of campaignspeak. A certain Mr. A. Hitler, originally of Austria, though often castigated, actually arrived at a number of very perceptive insights into how the world worked. One of them was this:

> The great masses of the people in the very bottom of their hearts tend to be corrupted rather than consciously and purposely evil...therefore, in view of the primitive simplicity of their minds, they more easily fall a victim to a big lie than to a little one, since they themselves lie in little things, but would be ashamed of lies that were too big.[25]

How many Americans, after all, doubt the official rationale for dropping the A-bomb on Hiroshima and Nagasaki—to obviate the need for a land invasion of Japan, thus saving thousands of American lives? However, it's been known for years that the Japanese had been

trying for many months to surrender and that the US had consistently ignored these overtures. The bombs were dropped, not to intimidate
the Japanese, but to put the fear of the American god into the
Russians. The dropping of the A-bomb, it has been said, was not the
last shot of World War II, but the first shot of the Cold War.[26]

In 1964, Secretary of State Dean Rusk, when asked about US
involvement in the overthrow of the government of Brazil, declared:
"Well, there is just not one iota of truth in this. It's just not so in any
way, shape or form." Yet, the United States had been intimately
involved in the coup, its role being literally indispensable.[27]

In the 1980s, the Reagan administration declared that the
Russians were spraying toxic chemicals over Asia—the so-called "yellow rain"—and had caused thousands of deaths. So precise was
Washington's information they could state at one point that in
Afghanistan 3,042 had died in 47 separate incidents. President
Reagan denounced the Soviet Union for these atrocities more than 15
times in documents and speeches. The "yellow rain", it turned out,
was pollen-laden feces dropped by huge swarms of honeybees flying far
overhead.[28]

These are three examples, chosen virtually at random. Numerous
others could be given. But at the beginning of the 21st century do the
American people really need to be reminded that governments lie,
that great powers lie greater, that the world's only superpower has the
most to lie about, i.e., cover up? Do I have to descend to the banality
of telling this to my readers?

Apparently so, if we are to judge by all those who swallowed the
"humanitarian" excuse for the bombing of Yugoslavia without gagging,
including many on the left.

The idea of "altruism" has been a recurrent feature of America's
love affair with itself. From 1918 to 1920, the United States was a
major part of a Western invasion of the infant Soviet Union, an invasion that endeavored to "strangle at its birth", as Winston Churchill
put it, the Russian Revolution, which had effectively removed one-
sixth of the world's land surface from private capitalist investment. A
nation still recovering from a horrendous world war, in extreme chaos
from a fundamental social revolution, and in the throes of a famine
that was to leave many millions dead, was mercilessly devastated yet
further by the invaders, without any provocation.

When the smoke had cleared, the US Army Chief of Staff put out a report on the undertaking, which said: "This expedition affords one of the finest examples in history of honorable, unselfish dealings…to be helpful to a people struggling to achieve a new liberty."[29]

Seventy years later, the Chairman of the Joint Chiefs of Staff, General Colin Powell, was moved to tell an audience in California that the United States has "so many friends" in the Pacific because of "our values, our economic system and our altruism".[30]

Author Garry Wills has commented on this American benevolence toward foreigners: "We believe we can literally 'kill them with kindness', moving our guns forward in a seizure of demented charity. It is when America is in her most altruistic mood that other nations better get behind their bunkers."

What is it, then, that I mean to say here—that the US government does not care a *whit* about human life, human rights, humanity and all those other wonderful human things?

No, I mean to say that doing the right thing is not a *principle* of American foreign policy, not an ideal or a goal of policy in and of itself. If it happens that doing the right thing coincides with, or is irrelevant to, Washington's overriding international ambitions, American officials have no problem walking the high moral ground. But this is rarely the case. A study of the many US interventions— summarized numerically above, and detailed in the "Interventions" chapter—shows clearly that the engine of American foreign policy has been fueled not by a devotion to any kind of morality, nor even simple decency, but rather by the necessity to serve other masters, which can be broken down to four imperatives:

1) making the world open and hospitable for—in current terminology—globalization, particularly American-based transnational corporations

2) enhancing the financial statements of defense contractors at home who have contributed generously to members of Congress and residents of the White House

3) preventing the rise of any society that might serve as a successful example of an alternative to the capitalist model

4) extending political, economic and military hegemony over as much of the globe as possible, to prevent the rise of any regional power that might challenge American supremacy, and to create a world order in America's image, as befits the world's only superpower.

To American policymakers, these ends have justified the means, and all means have been available.[31]

In the wake of the 1973 military coup in Chile, which overthrew the socialist government of Salvador Allende, the Assistant Secretary of State for Inter-American Affairs, Jack Kubisch, was hard pressed to counter charges that the United States had been involved. "It was not in our interest to have the military take over in Chile," he insisted. "It would have been better had Allende served his entire term, taking the nation and the Chilean people into complete and total ruin. Only then would the full discrediting of socialism have taken place. The military takeover and bloodshed has confused the issue."[32]

Though based on a falsehood made up for the occasion—that Allende's policies were leading Chile to ruin—Kubisch's remark inadvertently expressed his government's strong fealty to the third imperative stated above.

During the Cold War, US foreign policy was carried out under the waving banner of fighting a moral crusade against what cold warriors persuaded the American people, most of the world, and usually themselves, was the existence of a malevolent International Communist Conspiracy. But it was always a fraud; there was never any such animal as the International Communist Conspiracy. There were, as there still are, people living in misery, rising up in protest against their condition, against an oppressive government, a government likely supported by the United States. To Washington, this was proof that the Soviet Union (or Cuba or Nicaragua, etc., functioning as Moscow's surrogate) was again acting as the proverbial "outside agitator".

In the final analysis, this must be wondered: What kind of omnipresent, omnipotent, monolithic, evil international conspiracy bent on world domination would allow its empire to completely fall apart, like the proverbial house of cards, without bringing any military force to bear upon its satellites to prevent their escaping? And without an invasion from abroad holding a knife to the empire's throat?

Enemies without number, threats without end

Now, of course, Washington spinmeisters can't cry "The Russians are coming, and they're ten feet tall!" as a pretext for intervention, so they have to regularly come up with new enemies. America cherishes her enemies. Without enemies, she is a nation without purpose and direction. The various components of the National Security State need enemies to justify their swollen budgets, to aggrandize their work, to protect their jobs, to give themselves a mission in the aftermath of the Soviet Union; ultimately, to reinvent themselves. And they understand this only too well, even painfully. Presented here is Col. Dennis Long, speaking in 1992, two years after the end of the Cold War, when he was director of "total armor force readiness" at Fort Knox:

> For 50 years, we equipped our football team, practiced five days a week and never played a game. We had a clear enemy with demonstrable qualities, and we had scouted them out. [Now] we will have to practice day in and day out without knowing anything about the other team. We won't have his playbook, we won't know where the stadium is, or how many guys he will have on the field. That is very distressing to the military establishment, especially when you are trying to justify the existence of your organization and your systems.[33]

The United States had postponed such a distressing situation for as long as it could. A series of Soviet requests during the Cold War to establish a direct dialogue with senior NATO officials were rejected as "inappropriate and potentially divisive". Longstanding and repeated Soviet offers to dissolve the Warsaw Pact if NATO would do the same were ignored. After one such offer was spurned, the *Los Angeles Times* commented that the offer "increases the difficulty faced by U.S. policy-makers in persuading Western public opinion to continue expensive and often unpopular military programs."[34]

In 1991, Colin Powell touched upon the irony of the profound world changes in cautioning his fellow military professionals: "We must not...hope that it [the changes] will disappear and let us return to comforting thoughts about a resolute and evil enemy."[35]

But the thoughts are indeed comforting to the military professionals and their civilian counterparts. So one month the new resolute and evil enemy is North Korea, the next month the big threat is Libya, then China, or Iraq, or Iran, or Sudan, or Afghanistan, or Serbia, or that old reliable demon, Cuba—countries each led by a Hitler-of-the-month, or at least a madman or mad dog, a degree of demonizing fit more for a theocratic society than a democratic one.

And in place of the International Communist Conspiracy, Washington now tells us, on one day or another, it's fighting a War Against Drugs, or military or industrial spying, or the proliferation of "weapons of mass destruction", or organized crime, or on behalf of human rights, or, most particularly, against terrorism. And they dearly want the American public to believe this. Here, for your terrorist-threat collection, are some of the headlines appearing in the *Washington Post* and *New York Times* in one 7-week period in early 1999:

Jan. 22:   "Clinton Describes Terrorism Threat for 21st Century"
Jan. 23:   "President Steps Up War on New Terrorism"
Jan. 23:   "Thwarting Tomorrow's Terrors"
Jan. 29:   "Anti-Terrorism Powers Grow"
Feb. 1:   "Pentagon Plans Domestic Terrorism Team"
Feb. 1:   "The Man Who Protects America From Terrorism"
Feb. 2:   "U.S. Targeting Terrorism With More Funds"
Feb. 16:   "Anti-Terrorism Military Drills Take Parts of Texas by Surprise"
Feb. 17:   "Has the U.S. Blunted Bin Laden?"
Feb. 19:   "Spending to Avert Embassy Attacks Assailed as Timid: Terrorist Threat Looms"
Feb. 19:   "Bangladesh: Bin Laden's Next Target?"
Feb. 23:   "Preparing for Invisible Killers"
Mar. 7:   "Muslim Militants Threaten American Lives"
Mar. 8:   "Reagan Building Vulnerable to Attack"
Mar. 14:   "2 Groups Appeal U.S. Designation as Terror Organizations"
Mar. 16:   "Clinton Plans Training for Firefighters on Terrorism"

And on January 20, Secretary of Defense William S. Cohen—a man who has written an ode to the F-15 fighter jet, literally[36]—announced that $6.6 billion was to be spent on a national missile defense system, a revival of President Reagan's Star Wars system. In explaining this expenditure, Mr. Cohen cited only one threat—from North Korea. North Korea! A country that can't feed its own people is going to wage a missile attack upon the United States? What possible reason—other than an overpowering, irresistible yearning for mass national suicide—could North Korea have for launching such an attack? Yet the average American, reading Cohen's announcement, must have found it very difficult to believe that one of their "leaders" could just step forward and publicly proclaim a crazy tale. They assume there must be *something* to what the man is saying.

That's how the man gets away with it.

Does the man believe it himself? No more likely than that President Clinton believes it. In 1993, while in South Korea, Clinton declared: "It is pointless for them [North Korea] to develop nuclear weapons. Because if they ever use them it would be the end of their country." This burst of honesty and common sense, which visits politicians occasionally, was prompted in this instance by a journalist's question about how likely it was that North Korea would comply with the Non-Proliferation Treaty.[37] Oddly enough, less than a year later, a survey showed that six times as many young South Koreans feared the United States as feared North Korea.[38]

Returning to 1999 and its new "threats"—in August a new National Security Council global strategy paper for the next century declared that "the nation is facing its biggest espionage threat in history."[39]

A remarkable statement. What ever happened to the KGB? Any Americans now past 30 had it drilled into their heads from the cradle on that there was a perpetual Soviet dagger aimed at our collective heart in the hand of the spy next door. Thousands lost their jobs and careers because of their alleged association to this threat, hundreds were imprisoned or deported, two were executed. Surely Senator Joe McCarthy and J. Edgar Hoover are turning over in their graves.

Meanwhile the drumbeat warnings of a possible chemical or biological attack upon the United States grow louder with each passing week. Police, fire and health agencies go through regular exercises with all manner of sophisticated equipment. Active-duty Army and Marine Corps personnel are engaged in the same. The FBI has an extensive hazardous materials unit ready to rush to the scene of an attack. And now the National Guard has joined the frenzy, outfitted in full-body protective suits with air tanks. The General Accounting

Office (GAO) has argued that the National Guard units are redundant and their mission poorly defined. The *Washington Post* reported that "In fact, some critics regard the [Guard] teams largely as an effort to find a new mission for the Guard and help it avoid deeper budget cuts in the post-Cold War era."[40] As noted, the same can be said about other elements of the National Security State.

In October 1999, ABC's "Nightline" program ran a five-part series in which it simulated a biological weapons attack on a large American city, featuring a squad of terrorists releasing anthrax spores into the subway system, complete with panic, death and rampant chaos. Ted Koppel made the explicit pronouncement that such an attack was bound to take place in the US at some future time. As one would expect, the programs were long on sensationalism and short on science. This was spelled out later by the director of the Johns Hopkins Center for Civilian Biodefense Studies.[41] Ironically, the fact that such a center exists is another sign of the ("threatening") times.

Shortly after this the FBI announced that the Washington area had become "the number one target in the world" for possible terrorist attacks. How did they know? Well, "downtown Washington receives three to six suspicious packages a day". Anything actually terroristic in any of these packages? Apparently not.[42]

All this in response to actual chemical, biological or radiological weapon attacks of—at last count—zero. But there have been many false anthrax reports, no doubt largely inspired by all the scare talk; talk which never gives the public a clue to how extremely difficult and unpredictable it actually would be to create and deliver a serious anthrax attack, particularly over a wide area; scare talk that also makes more credible and acceptable the US 1998 bombing of a Sudanese pharmaceutical plant on the (false) grounds that it was making chemical and biological weapons.

Air travel is another area where the "threat" mentality looms larger than life, and common sense. A flight from Atlanta to Turkey, August 4, 1999, that was about to take off was halted by the FBI; all 241 passengers were forced to leave the plane, some of them were questioned, one man was detained; all the luggage was unloaded and each piece painstakingly matched to a passenger; bomb-sniffing dogs and explosive experts were rushed in, and the flight was held up for more than four hours. The reason? The FBI had received word that one of the passengers might be "a potential threat to national security". And the reason for that? The man had paid for his ticket in cash.[43]

Three weeks later, at Chicago's O'Hare Airport, a man was seen running the wrong way into a passageway normally used by those exiting the terminal. He disappeared into the crowded concourse. Neither he nor anything suspicious was found. For all anyone knew, the man had simply forgotten something somewhere or had a very urgent need to get to what he thought was the closest bathroom. Whatever, as a result of this "threatening" situation, 6,000 passengers were evacuated, at least 120 flights were canceled, and air traffic was disrupted across the country for several hours.[44]

With all the scare talk, with all the "threats", what exactly has taken place in the real world? According to the State Department, in the period of 1993–1998 the number of actual terrorist attacks by region was as follows:

Western Europe 766, Latin America 569, Middle East 374. Asia 158, Eurasia 101, Africa 84, North America 14.[45]

It is now well known how during the Cold War the actual level of Soviet military and economic strength was magnified by the CIA and Defense Department, how data and events were falsified to exaggerate the Russian threat, how worst-case scenarios were put forth as if they were probable and imminent, even when they failed to meet the demands of plausibility.[46] One of the most enduring Soviet-threat stories—the alleged justification for the birth of NATO—was the coming Red invasion of Western Europe. If, by 1999, anyone still swore by this fairy tale, they could have read a report in *The Guardian* of London on newly declassified British government documents from 1968. Among the documents was one based on an analysis by the Foreign Office joint intelligence committee, which the newspaper summarized as follows:

> The Soviet Union had no intention of launching a military attack on the West at the height of the Cold War, British military and intelligence chiefs privately believed, in stark contrast to what Western politicians and military leaders were saying in public about the "Soviet threat".
>
> "The Soviet Union will not deliberately start general war or even limited war in Europe," a briefing for the British chiefs of staff—

marked Top Secret, UK Eyes Only, and headed The Threat: Soviet
Aims and Intentions—declared in June 1968.

"Soviet foreign policy had been cautious and realistic", the
department argued, and despite the Vietnam War, the Russians and
their allies had "continued to make contacts in all fields with the West
and to maintain a limited but increasing political dialogue with
NATO powers".[47]

Subtlety is not the order of the day. In 1998, the Pentagon created a new bureaucracy: the Defense Threat Reduction Agency, a budget already in the billions, personnel numbered in the thousands, and
"made up primarily of agencies founded to reduce the threat posed by
the Soviet Union".[48] It's called recycling.

The Soviet threat, the terrorist threat, the new enemies, the same
old same old, feverishly fostered at home and abroad, the mentality
that the Pentagon, the CIA, the FBI, et al. have had critical, life-sav-
ing, catastrophe-preventing missions thrust upon them, here, there,
and everywhere, and we rein these saviors in on pain of national and
world disaster...working the old protection racket again.

"I think we are already at war," CIA Director George Tenet told
the Senate in 1997. "We have been on a war footing for a number of
years now."[49]

*The whole aim of practical politics is to keep the populace alarmed
(and hence, clamorous to be led to safety) by menacing it with an
endless series of hobgoblins, most of them imaginary.*

                                            H.L. Mencken, 1920

*Our government has kept us in a perpetual state of fear—kept us
in a continuous stampede of patriotic fervor—with the cry of
grave national emergency. Always there has been some terrible
evil...to gobble us up if we did not blindly rally behind it by fur-
nishing the exorbitant funds demanded. Yet, in retrospect, these
disasters seem never to have happened, seem never to have been
quite real.*

                            General Douglas MacArthur, speaking
                                of large Pentagon budgets, 1957[50]

The political spectrum and conspiracies

It's ironic, but the far right in the United States is more open to believing the worst about American foreign policy than are most liberals. This may be because those on the far right, being extremists themselves, do not instinctively shy away from believing that the government is capable of extreme behavior, at home or abroad. The radical left and right share a profound cynicism about their government's very intentions. But those in between the two poles do not naturally come by such views.

To many of the latter, the statements here about the United States not meaning well may sound like an example of that frequent object of ridicule, the "conspiracy theory". They hear me saying (snicker) that our leaders have gotten together, covertly, in some secluded safehouse, to maliciously plan their next assault on everything holy, while throwing out signals intended to confuse and to obscure their real intentions.

But if our leaders strive for unambiguous *righteousness*, is it *not* a conspiracy? Don't they meet to plan how they're going to do nice things? Or perhaps they don't have to do this so formally because since they all mean nice to begin with, it thus happens quite automatically, naturally, built into the system—the government system, the corporate system, the military system, the intelligence system, the government-corporate-military-intelligence nexus.

But why, then, wouldn't it be the same with meaning bad?

It's not that Americans can't believe in *any* conspiracy theory. Witness the remarkably long shelf life of the International Communist Conspiracy. It's still a highly saleable commodity.

"Conspiracy" researcher and author Jonathan Vankin has observed:

> Journalists like to think of themselves as a skeptical lot. This is a flawed self-image. The thickest pack of American journalists are all too credulous when dealing with government officials, technical experts, and other official sources. They save their vaunted "skepticism" for ideas that feel unfamiliar to them. Conspiracy theories are treated with the most rigorous skepticism.
>
> Conspiracy theories *should* be approached skeptically. But there's no fairness. Skepticism should apply equally to official and unofficial information. To explain American conspiracy theories...I've had to

rectify this imbalance. I've opened myself to conspiracy theories, and applied total skepticism to official stories.[51]

Like the cover up in Waco. In August 1999 we finally received official confirmation that the FBI had fired incendiary devices into the Branch Davidian sect compound in 1993, where 76 people died in a fire the same day. This, after six years of categorical official denials, while "conspiracy theorists" and "conspiracy nuts", who insisted otherwise, were ridiculed, or—the more usual case—met by the media's most effective weapon: silence.

Can the truth about the "October Surprise", TWA800, Jonestown, and Mena, Arkansas under Governor Clinton be far behind? Yes, far behind. We'll likely never hear an official admission about those events until well into the new century.

The First Watergate Law of American Politics states: "No matter how paranoid or conspiracy-minded you are, what the government is actually doing is worse than you imagine."

The Second Watergate Law of American Politics states: "Don't believe anything until it's been officially denied."

Both laws are still on the books.

Cold War continuum

Though the putative "communist threat" has disappeared, the taxpayers still fill tractor-trailers to the bursting with cash and send them off to what had once been known as the War Department, then humorously renamed the Defense Department...That department's research into yet more futuristic weapons of the chemical dust and better ways to kill people en masse proceeds unabated, with nary a glance back at the body fragments littering the triumphant fields...Belief in an afterlife has been rekindled by the Clinton administration's new missile defense system, after universal certainty that Star Wars was dead and buried...NATO has also risen from the should-be-dead, more almighty than ever...Many hundreds of US military installations, serving a vast panoply of specialized warfaring needs, still dot the global map, including Guantanamo base in Cuba, and for the first time in Albania, Macedonia, Hungary, Bosnia and Croatia...Even as you read this, American armed forces and special operations forces, such as the Green Berets, are being deployed in well over 100 countries in every part of the world...Washington is supplying many of these nations with sizeable amounts of highly lethal military equipment, and training their armed forces and police in the brutal arts, regardless of how brutal they already are...American nuclear bombs are still stored in seven European countries, if not elsewhere...And American officials retain their unshakable belief that they have a god-given right to do whatever they want, for as long as they want, to whomever they want, wherever they want.

In other words, whatever the diplomats and policymakers at the time *thought* they were doing, the Cold War skeptics have been vindicated—it was not about containing an evil, expansionist communism after all; it was about American imperialism, with "communist" merely the name given to those who stood in its way.

In sum total, all these post-Cold War non-changes engender a scenario out of the 1950s and 1960s. And the 1970s and 1980s. John Foster Dulles lives! Has Ronald Reagan been faking illness as he lurks behind the curtain of Oz? Why has all this continued into the 21st century?

American foreign-policy makers are exquisitely attuned to the rise of a government, or a movement that might take power, that will not lie down and happily become an American client state, that will not look upon the free market or the privatization of the world known as "globalization" as the *summum bonum*, that will not change its laws to favor foreign investment, that will not be unconcerned about the effects of foreign investment upon the welfare of its own people, that will not produce primarily for export, that will not allow asbestos, banned pesticides and other products restricted in the developed world to be dumped onto their people, that will not easily tolerate the International Monetary Fund or the World Trade Organization inflicting a scorched-earth policy upon the country's social services or standard of living, that will not allow an American or NATO military installation upon its soil...To the highly-sensitive nostrils of Washington foreign-policy veterans, Yugoslavia smelled a bit too much like one of these governments.

Given the proper pretext, such bad examples have to be reduced to basket cases, or, where feasible, simply overthrown, like Albania and Bulgaria in the early 1990s; failing that, life has to be made impossible for these renegades, as with Cuba, still. As Michael Parenti has observed: "It has been noted that the cost of apprehending a bank robber may occasionally exceed the sum that is stolen. But if robbers were allowed to go their way, this would encourage others to follow suit and would put the entire banking system in jeopardy."[52]

And this was the foundation—the *sine qua non*—of American foreign policy for the entire twentieth century, both before and after the existence of the Soviet Union, from the Philippines, Panama and the Dominican Republic in the first decade of the century, to Peru, El Salvador and Colombia in the last decade.

Can we in fact say that the Cold War has actually ended? If the Cold War is defined as a worldwide contention between the United States and the Soviet Union for the hearts and minds of the Third World (for whatever motives), then certainly it is over. But if the Cold War is seen not as an East-West struggle, but rather a "North-South" struggle, as an American effort—as mentioned above—to prevent the rise of any society that might serve as a successful example of an alternative to the capitalist model, and to prevent the rise of any regional power that might challenge American supremacy, then that particular map with the pins stuck in it still hangs on the wall in the Pentagon's War Room. (Said a Defense Department planning paper in 1992: "Our first objective is to prevent the re-emergence of a new rival...we must maintain the mechanisms for deterring potential competitors from even *aspiring* to a larger regional or global role."[53] [emphasis added])

The current manifestation of this continuum, by whatever name, can be viewed as yet another chapter in the never-ending saga of the war of the rich upon the poor. And with the Soviet presence and influence gone, American interventions are more trouble-free than ever. (Consider that US friendliness toward Iraq and Yugoslavia lasted exactly as long as the Soviet Union and its bloc existed.)

There's a word for such a continuum of policy. Empire. The American Empire. An appellation that does not roll easily off an American tongue. No American has any difficulty believing in the existence and driving passion for expansion, power, glory and wealth of the Roman Empire, the Ottoman Empire, the Austro-Hungarian Empire or the British Empire. It's right there in their schoolbooks. But to the American mind, to American schoolbooks and to the American media, the history of empires has come to a grinding halt.

The American Empire? An oxymoron.

A compelling lust for political, economic and military hegemony over the rest of the world, divorced from moral considerations? Suggesting that to Americans is akin to telling them of one's UFO abduction, except that they're more likely to believe the abduction story.

Earth is not enough

Previous empires could not even imagine it. The American Empire is making detailed plans for it. Control of outer space. Not only control, but planning for wars there. Let us mark the words of the gentlemen of the Pentagon:

> US Space Command—dominating the space dimension of military operations to protect US interests and investment. Integrating Space Forces into warfighting capabilities across the full spectrum of conflict...During the early portion of the 21st century, space power will also evolve into a separate and equal medium of warfare...The emerging synergy of space superiority with land, sea and air superiority will lead to Full Spectrum Dominance...Development of ballistic missile defenses using space systems and planning for precision strikes from space offers a counter to the worldwide proliferation of WMD [weapons of mass destruction]...Space is a region with increasing commercial, civil, international and military interests and investments. The threat to these vital systems is also increasing...Control of Space is the ability to assure access to space, freedom of operations within the space medium and an ability to deny others the use of space, if required...Control of Space is a complex mission that casts USCINCSPACE [US Commander-in-Chief of space] in a classic warfighter role and mandates an established AOR [area of responsibility].[54]...With regard to space dominance, we have it, we like it, and we're going to keep it.[55]...We will engage terrestrial targets someday—ships, airplanes, land targets—from space...We're going to fight *in* space. We're going to fight *from* space and we're going to fight *into* space.[56]

In 1963, the UN General Assembly adopted by unanimous acclamation a resolution calling upon all States: "To refrain from placing in orbit around the earth any objects carrying nuclear weapons or any other kinds of weapons of mass destruction, installing such weapons on celestial bodies or stationing such weapons in outer space in any other manner."[57]

This expressed hope is still very much alive today. On January 26, 1999, United Nations Secretary-General Kofi Annan told the Conference on Disarmament in Geneva: "One concept which is now widely shared is that of maintaining outer space as a weapons-free environment."

The Madman philosophy

In March 1998, an internal 1995 study, "Essentials of Post-Cold War Deterrence", by the U.S. Strategic Command, the headquarters responsible for the U.S. strategic nuclear arsenal, was brought to light. The study stated:

> Because of the value that comes from the ambiguity of what the US may do to an adversary if the acts we seek to deter are carried out, it hurts to portray ourselves as too fully rational and cool-headed. The fact that some elements may appear to be potentially 'out of control' can be beneficial to creating and reinforcing fears and doubts within the minds of an adversary's decision makers. This essential sense of fear is the working force of deterrence. That the US may become irrational and vindictive if its vital interests are attacked should be a part of the national persona we project to all adversaries.[58]

The author of these words would have the world believe that the United States has only been *pretending* to be "out of control" or "irrational and vindictive". However, it can be argued—based on the objective facts of what Washington has inflicted upon the world, as described in this book—that for more than half a century American foreign policy has, *in actuality*, been clinically mad.

On the other hand, the desire for world hegemony, *per se*, is not necessarily irrational, whatever else one may think of it. Michael Parenti has pointed out that US foreign policy "may seem stupid because the rationales offered in its support often sound unconvincing, leaving us with the impression that policymakers are confused or out of touch. But just because the public does not understand what they are doing does not mean that national security leaders are themselves befuddled. That they are fabricators does not mean they are fools."[59]

A Truth Commission

In recent years, the people of South Africa, Guatemala and El Salvador have held official Truth Commissions to look squarely in the eyes of the crimes committed by their governments. There will never be any such official body to investigate and document the wide body of Washington's crimes, although several unofficial citizens' commissions have done so over the years for specific interventions, such as in Vietnam, Panama and Iraq; their findings were of course ignored by the establishment media (whose ideology is a belief that it doesn't have any ideology).

In the absence of an official Truth Commission in the United States, this book is offered up as testimony. Do not spend too much time looking for a review of it in the *New York Times*, *Washington Post* or *Los Angeles Times*.

Washington, DC, January 2000

PART I

Ours and Theirs: Washington's Love/Hate Relationship with Terrorists and Human-Rights Violators

CHAPTER 1

Why Do Terrorists Keep Picking on the United States?

Washington's war on terrorism is as doomed to failure as its war on drugs has been.

"I think the American people need to know that we live in a world where by virtue of America's leadership to some degree, by virtue of a degree of fanaticism by some people, we will be targeted," declared National Security Adviser Sandy Berger after the bombings of two US African embassies on August 7, 1998.[1]

When asked "What is it that these terrorists want from the United States?", Richard Haass, head of the foreign policy department at the Brookings Institution, replied: "Well, the answer is it's not anything we're simply doing. It is who we are. It's the fact that we're the most powerful country in the world. It's the fact that we're a secular country...It is simply who we are and it is our existence that really bothers them."[2]

Thomas Friedman of the *New York Times* would say amen. Terrorists, he wrote, "have no specific ideological program or demands. Rather, they are driven by a generalized hatred of the U.S., Israel and other supposed enemies of Islam."[3]

Finally, we have President Clinton: "Americans are targets of terrorism, in part, because we act to advance peace and democracy and because we stand united against terrorism."[4]

These are some of the platitudes our leaders and pundits feed us after each terrorist attack against an American installation.

> *...the image of America the beauteous on its hill, so envied by all that it is subject to attacks by terrorists who cannot bear so much sheer goodness to triumph in a world that belongs to **their** master, the son of morning himself, Satan.*   Gore Vidal[5]

What our leaders and pundits never let slip is that the terrorists—whatever else they might be—might also be *rational human beings*; which is to say that in their own minds they have a rational justification for their actions. Most terrorists are people deeply concerned by what they see as social, political or religious injustice and hypocrisy, and the immediate grounds for their terrorism is often retaliation for an action of the United States...

The shooting down of two Libyan planes in 1981; the bombardment of Beirut in 1983 and 1984; the bombing of Libya in 1986; the bombing and sinking of an Iranian ship in 1987; the shooting down of an Iranian passenger plane in 1988; the shooting down of two more Libyan planes in 1989; the massive bombing of the Iraqi people in 1991; the continuing sanctions and bombings against Iraq; the bombing of Sudan and Afghanistan in 1998; the habitual support of Israeli belligerence and torture, and condemnation of Arab resistance to it; the double standard applied to Israeli terrorism, such as the wilful massacre of 106 Lebanese at the UN base at Qana in 1996; the continued persecution of Libya, now nearing the end of its second decade; the abduction of wanted men from Muslim countries, such as Malaysia, Pakistan, Lebanon and Albania; the large military and hi-tech presence in Islam's holiest land, Saudi Arabia, and elsewhere in the Persian Gulf region...these are some of the American actions that can turn an Arab or a Muslim into a fanatic, into a terrorist, into a decrier of "America, the Great Satan".

But those who feed us the platitudes know this. They're merely performing the time-honored public dumbshow. Mir Aimal Kansi, the Pakistani who shot five people outside CIA headquarters in 1993, told the FBI that he had done so to protest US policies toward Muslims in the Middle East, including the bombing of Iraq.[6] Two days after Kansi's conviction in 1997, four Americans were gunned down in Karachi, Pakistan while driving in a car. "I think the linkage is quite evident," said a former CIA counter-terrorism expert about the Karachi slayings.[7]

The bombing of PanAm 103 in 1988 was clearly initiated by Iran as an act of retaliation for the shooting down of its own passenger plane by the United States a few months earlier, and American officials well know this. The bombing of the two US embassies in Africa in 1998 took place on the eighth anniversary, to the very day, of the arrival of the first US troops in Saudi Arabia, following the Iraqi invasion of Kuwait. And during the US bombing of Iraq in 1991, there were dozens of terrorist attacks against American institutions all over the Middle East and elsewhere. Did American officials and the media not pick up any hint of cause-and-effect? They did, but subsequently, when it's been platitude time, they suddenly become pre-Alzheimer.

> *When terrorists attack, they're terrorizing. When we attack, we're retaliating. When they respond to our retaliation with further attacks, they're terrorizing again. When we respond with further attacks, we're retaliating again.*   Norman Solomon, media critic

Good and bad terrorists

On March 13, 1996, the United States assembled 27 world leaders in Egypt at an "anti-terror" conference after a wave of suicide bombers had killed dozens of people in Israel. President Clinton asserted: "We must be clear in our condemnation of those who resort to terror. Violence has no place in the future we all seek in the Middle East."[8] At the very same time, in Iraq, the US was supporting with millions of dollars the Iraqi National Accord, which was using car bombs and other bombings in Baghdad and other cities, trying to destabilize Sadaam Hussein. It was estimated that the bombings had taken the lives of more than 100 civilians in Baghdad alone during the preceding few years. Two weeks after the Egyptian conference, the attending countries met in Washington for a follow-up on counter-terrorism. Among the topics discussed were the flow of funds to terrorist groups.[9]

The following month, President Clinton, with much fanfare, signed the Anti-terrorism Act, which bars financial transactions between American corporations and countries accused of supporting terrorism. Four months later, the administration quietly exempted

Sudan, to allow a US oil company to negotiate an oil deal. At the same time, Syria was granted an exemption, to encourage participation by Damascus in the Middle East peace process.[10]

In February 2000, there arose a new proposal for a major international conference to combat terrorism. On this occasion the United States was quick to throw cold water on the very idea, saying it would have no "practical benefits". The proposed conference was backed by the 119-member Non-Aligned Movement of Third World Nations. One of the issues the conference hoped to address was how to distinguish between a "terrorist" and a "freedom fighter", citing the examples of the Hizbollah and Hamas groups fighting Israel. The question of "state terrorism" also loomed as a possible conference issue—for example, should military attacks by armed forces of any State be deemed acts of terrorism when civilians are killed? The 1999 NATO bombing of Yugoslavia had been discussed as a case in point.[11]

FBI definition of terrorism

The FBI defines international terrorism as "the unlawful use of force or violence committed by a group or individual, who has some connection to a foreign power or whose activities transcend national boundaries, against persons or property to intimidate or coerce a government, the civilian population or any segment thereof, in furtherance of political or social objectives."[12]

The FBI definition, although meant to describe acts directed against the United States, would seem to cover rather well countless acts of the US government itself. Many of these acts will be found in the pages of this book, under the headings of bombings, interventions, torture, chemical and biological warfare, etc.

CHAPTER 2

America's Gift to the World—the Afghan Terrorist Alumni

Osama bin Laden—alleged to have been the mastermind behind the bombing of two US embassies in Africa in 1998—was not always on Washington's hate list. He, along with many other Islamic fundamentalists, were supremely useful during the 1980s in Washington's war which quashed the last chance the Afghan people had for desperately needed social and economic reform and a secular society. Because of their uninhibited, sadistic cruelty directed against government and Soviet soldiers in Afghanistan, the fundamentalists—the moujahedeen (Muslim holy warriors)—were *good* terrorists. They were *our* terrorists. After the success of their *jihad*, these forces roamed afar, carrying out grisly actions in numerous corners of the world, metamorphosing into really *bad* terrorists.

Forcing the Soviet Union to withdraw its military forces from Afghanistan truly went to the heads of the moujahedeen. They thought they were invincible and had a god-given mission. Allah Akbar! They seemed to place little weight upon the fact that it had been the United States, bringing its military, political and financial weight to bear, that had been the *sine qua non* of the victory.

In 1992, after 12 years of battle, the various factions of the moujahedeen could claim Afghanistan as all their own, albeit now fighting each other. The war had been a rallying point for Muslim zealots from throughout the world—an Islamic Abraham Lincoln Brigade—and

laid the groundwork for their future collaboration and support. Tens of
thousands of veterans of the war—young men from every Muslim
nation, battle-hardened and armed—dispersed to many lands to carry
out other *jihads* against the infidels and to inflame and train a new
generation of militant Islamists and terrorists, ready to drink the cup
of martyrdom: a virtual Islamic Foreign Legion.

In the midst of a wave of assault weapons and violence (dubbed a
"Kalashnikov culture"), Pakistan Prime Minister Benazir Bhutto complained in 1996 that her country got stuck with this air of frenzy as a
direct result of cooperation with the United States in forcing Soviet
troops from Afghanistan. "We are left on our own to cope with the
remnants of the Afghan war, which include arms smuggling…drugs
and…[religious] zealots who were leaders at the time of the Afghan
war."[1]

"Your government participated in creating a monster," complained
an Algerian sociologist to a *Los Angeles Times* correspondent in
Algiers. "Now it has turned against you and the world—16,000 Arabs
were trained in Afghanistan, made into a veritable killing machine."[2]
His figure may be rather low inasmuch as there are an estimated
15,000 veterans of the Afghanistan war—or "Afghans" as they've
come to be known all over, whether from Afghanistan or not—in
Saudi Arabia alone.[3]

Professor of Middle East Studies, Eqbal Ahmad, has observed:

> The propaganda in the West suggests that violence and holy war are
> inherent in Islam. The reality is that as a world-wide movement, *Jihad*
> International, Inc. is a recent phenomenon…Without significant
> exception during the 20th century, *jihad* was used in a national, secu-
> lar and political context until, that is, the advent of the anti-Soviet
> war in Afghanistan.[4]

Following are some of the highlights of the remarkable bloodlet-
ting of the "Afghans":

In the United States

Mir Aimal Kansi—the Pakistani who slew two CIA employees,
wounded two other employees of the Agency and one employee of a
CIA contractor outside CIA headquarters in Virginia in 1993—came

of age in the Pakistani province that borders Afghanistan, which was used as a key staging area for the moujahedeen. His father and other relatives had ties to the CIA-Pakistani intelligence operations of the war. Kansi, those who knew him said, was "one of the children of the C.I.A.'s jihad."[5]

Most of those involved in the 1993 bombing of the World Trade Center in New York—which killed six people, wounded more than 1,000 and caused half a billion dollars in damage—were veterans of the Afghan war.[6]

In October 1995, 10 men were convicted for a plot to bomb New York targets, including the UN building, an FBI office and the Lincoln and Holland tunnels. The spiritual leader of the group, and one of the defendants, was Sheik Omar Abdul Rahman, who had worked with the moujahedeen in the war in Afghanistan. He had obtained a US visa in 1990 from a CIA undercover agent[7], leading to speculation that at that time he (still) had CIA links. At least one of the other defendants—who came mainly from Egypt and Sudan—had fought in Afghanistan.

Three men were convicted in New York in 1996 of plotting to bomb 12 US jumbo jets and 4,000 passengers out of the sky over the Pacific Ocean. Ramzi Ahmed Yousef, the alleged mastermind of the World Trade Center bombing, who had been a fugitive, was one of the three defendants. He had been trained in explosives by the moujahedeen. Investigators found in his computer a manifesto pledging terror to punish Americans for their government's support of Israel.[8]

Elsewhere

Ramzi Ahmed Yousef was convicted in absentia in the Philippines in 1994 of bombing a Philippine Airlines jet, killing one passenger. He reportedly was involved in training activities with the extremist Muslim Abu Sayyaf Organization of the Philippines.[9]

March 1995, Karachi, Pakistan: Two US diplomats were killed and a third wounded in an assault upon the car they were driving in. The FBI, which arrived in Pakistan to investigate the crime, announced that it was treating the attack as a possible retaliation for the arrest of Ramzi Ahmed Yousef the previous month in Pakistan by US and Pakistani agents and his extradition to the United States.[10]

In November 1995, five Americans and two Indians died when a pickup truck stuffed with explosives detonated outside a US Army building in Riyadh, Saudi Arabia. Three of the four Saudis who confessed to the attack admitted to having received firearms and explosives training in Afghanistan and to having fought in combat there.[11]

The following June, 19 US airmen died in the bombing of their housing complex in Dhahran, Saudi Arabia. The same groups claimed credit for both attacks.

In summer 1995, France underwent a series of eight bomb attacks beginning with a blast in a train station which killed eight and wounded 160. "Almost all of the leaders of the people we have arrested for terrorism have passed by Afghanistan or Pakistan," said a French law enforcement official.[12]

The Chechnyan guerrillas, who have bedeviled the Russians for years with their insurrection to create a Muslim society, have had their ranks swelled by Middle East and African "Afghans", as well as their own people who received military instruction in Afghanistan.[13]

Russian officials estimate that 4,000 to 5,000 Muslim militants from Tajikistan alone passed through camps in northern Afghanistan, then returned to the former Soviet Central Asian republic in 1993 to do battle against the secular government.[14] Another former Soviet republic, Azerbaijan, has experienced a similar fate.[15]

In western provinces of China, Afghan veterans have armed and trained Chinese Muslims and fought alongside them against the Chinese authorities.[16]

Since 1992, Egypt has been swept by a wave of anti-government terrorism in which graduates of the military training camps in Afghanistan and Pakistan have played a major role. They are believed to have also been behind the attempted assassination of President Hosni Mubarak while he was visiting Ethiopia.[17]

In August 1994, three "Afghans" robbed a tourist hotel in Morocco, killing tourists in an effort to destabilize Morocco's vital tourism industry.[18]

Throughout much of the 1990s, Kashmiris and other nationals trained in Afghanistan, have been fighting against India in the mountains of Kashmir, waging "holy war" for secession from New Delhi.[19]

Since Algeria's cancellation of the 1992 election, Algerian veterans of the Afghanistan conflict have played a key role in the rise of the Armed Islamic Group, responsible for many thousands of gory murders in their crusade for an Islamic state.[20]

In Bosnia, beginning in 1992, Afghans fought ferociously alongside the predominantly Muslim Bosnian army for two years, attacking Serbian positions to liberate Muslim villages.[21] One of those who confessed to the November 1995 bombing in Saudi Arabia, referred to above, said that he had fought with the Bosnian Muslims.[22]

In a 1999 interview, Libyan leader Moammar Qaddafi told a London-based Arabic newspaper that his government had crushed an Islamic militant movement of "Afghans". "They returned desperate and destructive," he said, "and adopted killing and explosives as their profession, according to the training they received from the American intelligence."[23]

And more of the same in other places, from the men Ronald Reagan fancied as "freedom fighters".

"This is an insane instance of the chickens coming home to roost," said a US diplomat in Pakistan in 1996. "You can't plug billions of dollars into an anti-Communist jihad, accept participation from all over the world and ignore the consequences. But we did. Our objectives weren't peace and grooviness in Afghanistan. Our objective was killing Commies and getting the Russians out."[24]

CHAPTER 3

Assassinations

I don't want to wipe out everyone...Just my enemies.
Michael Corleone, "The Godfather, Part II"

On June 26, 1993, President Clinton went before the American people and announced that the United States had fired several missiles against Iraq that day. It turned out that the missiles killed eight people and injured many more. The attack, said the president, was in retaliation for an Iraqi plot to assassinate former president George Bush who was due to visit Kuwait. (This alleged plot remains no more than that...alleged.[1]) Clinton announced that the US attack "was essential to send a message to those who engage in state-sponsored terrorism and to affirm the expectation of civilized behavior among nations."[2]

Following is a list of prominent foreign individuals whose assassination (or planning for same) the United States has been involved in since the end of the Second World War. (CIA humorists have at times referred to this type of operation as "suicide involuntarily administered", to be carried out by the Agency's Health Alteration Committee.)

1949	Kim Koo, Korean opposition leader
1950s	CIA/Neo-Nazi hit list of more than 200 political figures in West Germany to be "put out of the way" in the event of a Soviet invasion
1950s	Zhou Enlai, Prime minister of China, several attempts on his life

1950s, 1962	Sukarno, President of Indonesia
1951	Kim Il Sung, Premier of North Korea
1953	Mohammed Mossadegh, Prime Minister of Iran
1950s (mid)	Claro M. Recto, Philippines opposition leader
1955	Jawaharlal Nehru, Prime Minister of India
1957	Gamal Abdul Nasser, President of Egypt
1959/63/69	Norodom Sihanouk, leader of Cambodia
1960	Brig. Gen. Abdul Karim Kassem, leader of Iraq
1950s–70s	José Figueres, President of Costa Rica, two attempts on his life
1961	Francois "Papa Doc" Duvalier, leader of Haiti
1961	Patrice Lumumba, Prime Minister of the Congo
1961	Gen. Rafael Trujillo, leader of Dominican Republic
1963	Ngo Dinh Diem, President of South Vietnam
1960s	Fidel Castro, President of Cuba, many attempts and plots on his life
1960s	Raúl Castro, high official in government of Cuba
1965	Francisco Caamaño, Dominican Republic opposition leader
1965–6	Charles de Gaulle, President of France
1967	Che Guevara, Cuban leader
1970	Salvador Allende, President of Chile
1970	Gen. Rene Schneider, Chief of Army, Chile
1970s, 1981	General Omar Torrijos, leader of Panama
1972	General Manuel Noriega, Chief of Panama Intelligence
1975	Mobutu Sese Seko, President of Zaire
1976	Michael Manley, Prime Minister of Jamaica
1980–1986	Moammar Qaddafi, leader of Libya, several plots and attempts upon his life
1982	Ayatollah Khomeini, leader of Iran
1983	Gen. Ahmed Dlimi, Moroccan Army commander
1983	Miguel d'Escoto, Foreign Minister of Nicaragua
1984	The nine comandantes of the Sandinista National Directorate

1985	Sheikh Mohammed Hussein Fadlallah, Lebanese Shiite leader (see note below)
1991	Saddam Hussein, leader of Iraq
1998	Osama bin Laden, leading Islamic militant
1999	Slobodan Milosevic, President of Yugoslavia

In case they run short of assassins

In 1975, a US Navy psychologist, Lt. Com. Thomas Narut, revealed that his naval work included establishing how to induce servicemen who may not be naturally inclined to kill, to do so under certain conditions. He referred to these men using the words "hitmen" and "assassin". Narut added that convicted murderers as well had been released from military prisons to become assassins. The training of the carefully-selected recruits ranged from dehumanization of the enemy, to acclimating them emotionally through special films showing people being killed and injured in violent ways.[3] The disclosure by Narut was pure happenstance. We can only speculate about what programs are taking place or being planned today in that five-sided building in Virginia.

Blasphemy American style

The Western world was shocked when Iran condemned author Salmon Rushdie to death because of his book they called "blasphemous". But the United States has also condemned blasphemers to death—Castro, Allende, Sukarno and a host of others mentioned above who didn't believe in the holy objectives of American foreign policy.

Aberrations?

The senate committee known as the Church Committee, in its Assassination Report in 1975, said: "The committee does not believe that the acts [of assassination] which it has examined represent the real American character. They do not reflect the ideals which have given the people of this country and the world hope for a better, fuller, fairer life. We regard the assassination plots as aberrations."[4]

At the time the committee wrote this, it knew of about a dozen CIA assassination plots and still could call them all aberrations. Would congressmen today, knowing of the more than 40 incidents listed above, call them all aberrations?

Could they explain how these "aberrations" have continued through each of the ten presidencies, from Truman through Clinton?

For some years following the Church Committee's report, American presidents made it a point to issue public statements on assassination, perhaps trying to convince the world that "we really don't mean it".

1976: Ford signed a presidential order which stated: "No employee of the United States, shall engage in, or conspire to engage in, political assassination."

1978: Carter also issued an executive order prohibiting assassinations.

1981, Dec. 4: Reagan issued an executive order with language almost identical to that of Ford's.

But on Nov. 13, 1984, Reagan, obsessed with fighting the "International Communist Conspiracy" on several fronts, canceled his executive order, creating what was actually called by the press, a "license to kill"—a license to kill anyone deemed a "terrorist".

On April 10, 1985, Reagan canceled the "license to kill" because the previous month, the CIA had paid some people in Beirut to kill a certain sheikh Fadlallah, who was not to Washington's liking; a car bomb had been used and 80 people were killed, the sheikh not being among their number.

August 11, 1985: The "license to kill" was reinstated because of a hijacking of a TWA plane in June.

May 12, 1986: A new executive order was signed without the controversial language, apparently in deference to congressional objections.[5]

Clearly, Reagan was not acting out of any principle for or against assassination—it was all public relations, and the actual American policy in the field over the years, in all likelihood, has never varied to speak of, whatever the "official" PR message of the day coming out of the White House was.

Oct. 13, 1989: Bush added a new PR twist. He issued a "memorandum of law" that would allow "accidental" killing if it was a byproduct of legal action: "A decision by the President to employ overt military force...would not constitute assassination if U.S. forces were employed against the combatant forces of another nation, a guerrilla force, or a terrorist or other organization whose actions pose a threat to the security of the United States."[6] In other words, assassination was okay as long as we said "oops!"

Clinton, it appears, has not issued any official statement concerning US government policy on assassination.

The Doolittle Report

A 1954 White House commission to study the CIA's covert activities included in its report the following now-famous passage, which is relevant to this discussion of assassination. It may be what psychologists call "projection".

> It is now clear that we are facing an implacable enemy whose avowed objective is world domination by whatever means and at whatever cost. There are no rules in such a game. Hitherto acceptable norms of human conduct do not apply. If the United States is to survive, long-standing American concepts of "fair play" must be reconsidered. We must develop effective espionage and counterespionage services and must learn to subvert, sabotage and destroy our enemies by more clever, more sophisticated, and more effective methods than those used against us. It may become necessary that the American people be made acquainted with, understand and support this fundamentally repugnant philosophy.[7]

Does it work both ways?

If the United States can bomb Iraqi intelligence headquarters—which was their target in the bombing referred to above—because of an alleged assassination plot against an American leader, and cite self-defense under the UN charter as Washington did (a claim at least as questionable as the alleged plot), think of the opportunities opened to countries like Panama, Libya and Cuba to name but a few. Cuba could claim the right to bomb CIA headquarters, many times, not to mention Miami. It's safe to say though, that neither the White House nor American courts would accept this legal argument; nor would they be able to see behind the Irony Curtain.

CHAPTER 4

Excerpts from US Army and CIA Training Manuals

CIA, "A Study of Assassination", written early 1950s[1]

"For secret assassinations...the contrived accident is the most effective technique. When successfully executed, it causes little excitement and is only casually investigated. The most efficient accident...is a fall of 75 feet or more onto a hard surface. Elevator shafts, stair wells, unscreened windows and bridges will serve...The act may be executed by sudden, vigorous grabbing of the ankles, tipping the subject over the edge. If the assassin immediately sets up an outcry, playing the 'horrified witness', no alibi or surreptitious withdrawal is necessary."

"Drugs can be very effective. If the assassin is trained as a doctor or nurse and the subject is under medical care, this is an easy and sure method. An overdose of morphine administered as a sedative will cause death without disturbance and is difficult to detect. The size of the dose will depend upon whether the subject has been using narcotics regularly. If not, two grains will suffice. If the subject drinks heavily, morphine or a similar narcotic can be injected at the passing out stage, and the cause of death will often be held to be acute alcoholism."

"Edge weapons: Any legally obtained edge device may be successfully employed. A certain minimum of anatomical knowledge is needed for reliability. Puncture wounds of the body cavity may not be reliable unless the heart is reached. The heart is protected by the rib cage and is not always easy to locate…Absolute reliability is obtained by severing the spinal cord in the cervical region. This can be done with the point of a knife or a light blow of an axe or hatchet. Another reliable method is the severing of both jugular and carotid vessels on both sides of the windpipe."

"Conference room technique: [Assassin] #1 Enters room quickly but quietly. #2 Stands in doorway. #2 Opens fire on first subject to react. Swings across group toward center of mass. Times burst to empty magazine at end of swing. #1 Covers group to prevent individual dangerous reactions; if necessary, fires individual bursts of 3 rounds. #2 Finishes burst. Commands 'Shift'. Drops back through door. Replaces empty magazine. Covers corridor. #1 On command 'Shift', opens fire on opposite side of target. Swings one burst across group. Leaves propaganda [to implicate the opposition]."

US Army, "Terrorism and the Urban Guerilla", 1960s[2]

"Measures of Controlling the Population and Resources:

1. ID Cards. An effective system of identification is fundamental to the program…

2. Registration. A program of registering families is used to supplement the system of ID cards. This is the system of inventorying all families by house, making a list of all members of the family who live in the house along with the family's resources. One can also note the presence of insurgent tendencies and affiliations among the population.

3. Control by block. The purpose of block-by-block control is to detect the individuals who are supporting or sympathizing with the insurgents and the type of support they are providing.

4. Police patrols. Their purpose is to detect sources of insurgent support, sympathizers, and routes used by the insurgent forces for intelligence, logistics, and routine activities…

Curfew: The purpose is to permit the authorities to identify violators and take actions based on the premise that anyone who violates
the curfew is an insurgent or sympathizes with the insurgents until he
can prove the contrary.

Checkpoints. It is of little use to establish a program of passes and
ID cards unless there is a system of verifying these official papers.
Therefore, establishing checkpoints in all travel routes is necessary
once the use of passes has started."

US Army, "Handling of Sources", 1960s[3]

"The CI [counterintelligence] agent should cause the arrest of the
employee's [paid government informant] parents, imprison the
employee or give him a beating as part of the placement plan of said
employee in the guerrilla organization." [It's not clear whether these
things were to be done to force the person to be an informer or to give
him credibility as such.]

"The employee's value could be increased by means of arrests, executions or pacification, taking care not to expose the employee as the
information source."

"To assure the promotion of an employee...eliminate a potential
rival among the guerrillas."

"[Employees are required because] the government is not able to
depend only on the information provided voluntarily by faithful citizens or information obtained involuntarily from insurgents who have
been captured."

The official Defense Department view of these manuals was that the
objectionable material in them had simply fallen through the cracks.
The DOD stated: "There was no evidence that there was a deliberate
attempt to violate Army or Defense Department policies in the
preparation or use of these manuals." However, the office of Rep.
Joseph Kennedy (D.-MA), which had followed the issue closely, said
that at the School of the Americas, where the manuals had been
used, at least two officers had raised questions about the objectionable material with their superiors in the early 1980s, but had been
rebuffed.[4]

CIA, "KUBARK Counterintelligence Interrogation-July 1963"[5]

"The effectiveness of most of the non-coercive techniques depends on their unsettling effect. The interrogation situation is in itself disturbing to most people encountering it for the first time. The aim is to enhance this effect...[and to create] a traumatic or sub-traumatic experience which explodes, as it were, the world that is familiar to the subject as well as his image of himself in that world."

"Usually his own clothes are taken away because familiar clothing reinforces identity and thus the capacity for resistance."

"The following are the principal coercive techniques of interrogation: arrest, detention, deprivation of sensory stimuli through solitary confinement or similar methods, threats and fear, debility, pain, heightened suggestibility and hypnosis, narcosis, and induced regression."

CIA, "Human Resource Exploitation Training Manual-1983"[6]

"Control—The capacity to cause or change certain types of human behavior by implying or using physical or psychological means to induce compliance. Compliance may be voluntary or involuntary."

"Subject is brought into the facility blindfolded and handcuffed and should remain so during the entire processing...Subject is completely stripped and told to take a shower. Blindfold remains in place while showering and guard watches throughout. Subject is given a thorough medical examination, including all body cavities."

"Allowing a subject to receive carefully selected letters from home can help create an effect desired by the 'questioner'; for example, the subject may get the idea that his relatives are under duress or suffering. A suggestion at the proper time that his cooperation or confession can help protect the innocent may be effective."

"Bedding should be minimal—cot and blanket—no mattress. (The idea is to prevent the subject from relaxing and recovering from shock.) There should be no built-in toilet facilities. The subject should have to ask to relieve himself. Then he should either be given a bucket or escorted by a guard to the latrine. The guard stays at his side the entire time he is in the latrine."

"Deprivation of sensory stimuli induces stress and anxiety. The more complete the deprivation, the more rapidly and deeply the subject is affected."

CIA, "Freedom Fighters' Manual", 1984[7]

A 16-page "comic book" for Nicaraguans; its more than 40 illustrations showed the reader how s/he could "liberate Nicaragua from oppression and misery" of "the Marxist tyranny" by "a series of useful sabotage techniques". Amongst these were:

Stop up toilets with sponges...pull down power cables...put dirt into gas tanks...put nails on roads and highways...cut and perforate the upholstery of vehicles...cut down trees over highways...telephone to make false hotel reservations and false alarms of fires and crimes...hoard and steal food from the government...leave lights and water taps on...steal mail from mailboxes...go to work late...call in sick...short circuit electricity...break light bulbs...rip up books...spread rumors...threaten supervisors and officials over the phone...

CIA, "Psychological Operations in Guerrilla Warfare", 1984[8]

A manual designed for the US-backed Contra forces (the guerrillas) fighting in Nicaragua against the leftist Sandinista government. It advised:

"Kidnap all officials or agents of the Sandinista government and place them in 'public places'."

"Shame, ridicule and humiliate the 'personal symbols' of the government of repression in the presence of the people and foster popular participation through guerrillas within the multitude, shouting slogans and jeers."

"If a guerrilla fires at an individual, make the town see that he was an enemy of the people" and "that if that citizen had managed to escape, he would have alerted the enemy that is near the town or city, and they could carry out acts of reprisal such as rapes, pillage, destruction, captures, etc...Make the population see that it was the repressive system of the regime that...really killed the informer, and that the weapon fired was one recovered in combat against the Sandinista regime."

"It is possible to neutralize carefully selected and planned targets, such as court judges, mesta judges [justices of the peace], police and State Security officials, CDS [Sandinista Defense Committees] chiefs, etc." [As writer Holly Sklar has noted: "A hit list that starts with court judges and ends with *etcetera* is a mighty broad license for murder."]

"The notification of the police, denouncing a target who does not want to join the guerrillas, can be carried out easily...through a letter with false statements of citizens who are not implicated in the movement."

"If possible, professional criminals will be hired to carry out specific selected 'jobs'."

"Specific tasks will be assigned to others, in order to create a 'martyr' for the cause, taking the demonstrators to a confrontation with the authorities, in order to bring about uprisings or shootings, which will cause the death of one or more persons, who would become the martyrs, a situation that should be made use of immediately against the regime, in order to create greater conflicts."

"Shock Troops. These men should be equipped with weapons (knives, razors, chains, clubs, bludgeons) and should march slightly behind the innocent and gullible participants."

Throughout, the manual reads like what the Western world was always taught was the way communists scheme and indoctrinate.

The World Court found that in producing and disseminating this manual, the United States "encouraged the commission...of acts contrary to general principles of humanitarian law," including the Geneva Conventions of 1949.[9]

CHAPTER 5

Torture

"The first jolt was so bad I just wanted to die."

> Gloria Esperanza Reyes, speaking of her torture in Honduras, where electric wires were attached to her breasts and vagina.

"They always asked to be killed. Torture is worse than death."

> José Barrera, Honduran torturer.[1]

Turkey, July 14, 1999, the police break into the home of a Kurdish family and announce they want to take the two daughters—Medine, 14, and her younger sister Devran—in for questioning. "I headed for the bedroom to get dressed," said Devran later, "but Medine...went straight to the window and jumped."

Medine's mother explained: "My daughter, you see, preferred death to being tortured once again."[2]

"Torture might last a short time, but the person will never be the same."

> Amnesty International report[3]

"No exceptional circumstances whatsoever, whether a state of war or a threat of war, internal political instability or any other public emergency, may be invoked as a justification for torture."

> The Convention Against Torture and Other Cruel, Inhuman or Degrading Treatment or Punishment, Article 2, S2[4]

"**P**hysical abuse or other degrading treatment was rejected, not only because it is wrong, but because it has historically proven to be ineffective," said Richard Stolz, Deputy Director of Operations of the Central Intelligence Agency in 1988.[5]

The CIA likes to say things like this because they think it sounds like good plausible denial. But who can believe that torture does not loosen up tongues, that for such purpose it is not exceedingly effective? Richard Stolz and the CIA would have us believe that Medine, in the above example, if denied the opportunity to kill herself, would not talk under torture. Torture's effectiveness extends yet further, for its purpose is frequently not so much to elicit information as it is to punish, to coerce the victims from any further dissident activity by gouging out the idealism from their very being, and as a warning to their comrades.

For these ends, the CIA has co-existed with torture for decades. (Turkey, it must be remembered, is one of Washington's very closest strategic allies; for Honduras, see below.) Sleeping with friendly tortur-ers has been a closely guarded secret at the Agency, and for that reason the actual painful details have been difficult to come by over the years. But here is some of the record that has made its way to the light of day:

Greece

During the late 1940s, the CIA was instrumental in the creation of a new internal security agency, KYP. Before long, KYP was carrying out all the endearing practices of secret police everywhere, including sys-tematic torture. It was most active during the military junta, 1967–74, a period of routine horrific torture. Amnesty International later reported that "American policy on the torture question as expressed in official statements and official testimony has been to deny it where possible and minimize it where denial was not possible. This policy flowed naturally from general support for the military regime."[6]

James Becket, an American attorney sent to Greece by Amnesty, wrote in 1969 that some torturers told prisoners that some of their equipment had come as US military aid. One item was a special "thick white double cable" whip that was "scientific, making their work eas-ier"; another was the head screw, known as an "iron wreath", which

was progressively tightened around the head or ears.[7] American support, reported Becket, was vital to the torturers:

> Hundreds of prisoners have listened to the little speech given by
> Inspector Basil Lambrou, who sits behind his desk which displays the
> red, white, and blue clasped-hand symbol of American aid. He tries to
> show the prisoner the absolute futility of resistance: "You make your-
> self ridiculous by thinking you can do anything. The world is divided
> in two. There are the communists on that side and on this side the
> free world. The Russians and the Americans, no one else. What are
> we? Americans. Behind me there is the government, behind the gov-
> ernment is NATO, behind NATO is the U.S. You can't fight us, we
> are Americans."[8]

Iran

The notorious Iranian security service, SAVAK, which employed torture routinely, was created under the guidance of the CIA and Israel
in the 1950s.[9] According to a former CIA analyst on Iran, Jesse J. Leaf,
SAVAK was instructed in torture techniques by the Agency.[10] After
the 1979 revolution, the Iranians found CIA film made for SAVAK on
how to torture women.[11]

Germany

In the 1950s, in Munich, the CIA tortured suspected infiltrators of
Soviet émigré organizations in Western Europe, which the Agency
was using in anti-Soviet operations. Amongst the techniques
employed by the CIA were such esoteric torture methods as applying
turpentine to a man's testicles or sealing someone in a room and playing Indonesian music at deafening levels until he cracked.[12] This
information probably surfaced because it's weird-sounding to the point
of being amusing; there was likely more of regular torture methods not
fit for conversation.

Vietnam

The Green Berets taught its members who were slated for duty in
Vietnam in the 1960s how to use torture as part of an interrogation.[13]

The notorious Operation Phoenix, set up by the CIA to wipe out the Vietcong infrastructure, subjected suspects to torture such as electric shock to the genitals of both men and women, and the insertion into the ear of a six-inch dowel, which was tapped through the brain until the victim died; suspects were also thrown out of airborne helicopters to persuade the more important suspects to talk, although this should probably be categorized as murder of the ones thrown out, and a form of torture for those not.[14] In violation of the Geneva Convention, the US turned prisoners over to their South Vietnamese allies in full knowledge that they would be tortured, American military personnel often being present during the torture.[15]

Bolivia

In 1967, anti-Castro Cubans, working with the CIA to find Che Guevara, set up houses of interrogation where Bolivians suspected of aiding Che's guerrilla army were brought for questioning and some-times tortured. When the Bolivian interior minister learned of the torture, he was furious and demanded that the CIA put a stop to it.[16]

Uruguay

In the late 1960s, Dan Mitrione, an employee of the US Office of Public Safety (part of the Agency for International Development), which trained and armed foreign police forces, was stationed in Montevideo, Uruguay. Torturing political prisoners in Uruguay had existed before Mitrione's arrival. However, in a surprising interview given to a leading Brazilian newspaper, *Jornal do Brasil* in 1970, the former Uruguayan Chief of Police Intelligence, Alejandro Otero, declared that US advisers, and Mitrione in particular, had instituted torture as a more routine measure; to the means of inflicting pain, they had added scientific refinement; and to that a psychology to create despair, such as playing a tape in the next room of women and children screaming and telling the prisoner that it was his family being tortured.[17]

The newspaper interview greatly upset American officials in South America and Washington. The director of OPS in Washington tried to explain it all away by asserting: "The three Brazilian reporters in

Montevideo all denied filing that story. We found out later that it was slipped into the paper by someone in the composing room at the *Jornal do Brasil*."[18]

Mitrione built a soundproofed room in the cellar of his house in Montevideo, in which he assembled Uruguayan police officers to observe a demonstration of torture techniques. Four beggars were rounded up to be the subjects upon whom Mitrione demonstrated the effects of different voltages on different parts of the body. The four of them died.

And in 1981, a former Uruguayan intelligence officer declared that US manuals were being used to teach techniques of torture to his country's military. He said that most of the officers who trained him had attended classes run by the United States in Panama. Among the niceties, the manual listed 35 nerve points where electrodes could be applied.[19]

Brazil

Before the Office of Public Safety assigned Dan Mitrione to Uruguay, he had been stationed in Brazil. There, he and other Americans worked with OPS, AID and CIA in supplying Brazilian security forces with the equipment and training to facilitate the torture of prisoners. The Americans also advised on how much electric shock could be administered without killing the person, if his or her death might prove awkward.[20]

Guatemala

From the 1960s through the 1980s, Guatemalan security forces, notably the Army unit called G-2, routinely tortured "subversives". One method was electric shock to the genital area, using military field telephones hooked up to small generators, equipment and instructions for use supplied by Uncle Sam. The US and its clients in various countries were becoming rather adept at this technique. The CIA advised, armed and equipped the G-2, which maintained a web of torture centers, whose methods reportedly included chopping off limbs and singeing flesh, in addition to electric shocks. The Army unit even had its own crematorium, presumably to dispose of any incriminating evidence. The CIA thoroughly infiltrated the G-2, with at least three G-

2 chiefs of the 1980s and early 90s, as well as many lower-level officers, being on the Agency's payroll.[21]

Also benefiting from the Agency's generosity was General Hector Gramajo Morales (see "Haven" chapter), who was Defense Minister during the armed forces' 1989 abduction of Sister Dianna Ortiz, an American nun. She was burned with cigarettes, raped repeatedly, and lowered into a pit full of corpses. Typically, torturers exult in demonstrating the power they hold over their victims—one of them put a large knife or machete into Ortiz's hand, put his own hands on top of hers, and forced her to stab another female prisoner. Ortiz thinks she may have killed the woman. A fair-skinned man, whom the others referred to as "Alejandro", and as their "boss", seemed to be in charge, she said. He spoke Spanish with an American accent and cursed in English. Later, Ortiz adds, when this man realized she was American, he ordered the torture stopped. Clearly, if his motivation had been humanitarian, and not simply trying to avoid a possible political flap, he would have stopped it regardless of her nationality.[22]

In 1996, in the United States, Ortiz received a number of documents from the State Department in response to a Freedom of Information Act request. Only one, dated 1990, contained a significant reference to Alejandro. It read as follows:

> VERY IMPORTANT: We need to close the loop on the issue of the "North American" named by Ortiz as being involved in the case...The EMBASSY IS VERY SENSITIVE ON THIS ISSUE, but it is an issue we will have to respond to publicly...[23]

The next two pages were completely redacted.

El Salvador

During the counter-insurgency period of the 1980s, there was widespread torture practiced by the various Salvadoran security forces, all of whom had close working relations with the CIA and/or the US military. In January 1982, the *New York Times* published an interview with a deserter from the Salvadoran Army who described a class where severe methods of torture were demonstrated on teenage prisoners. He stated that eight US military advisers, apparently Green Berets, were present. Watching "will make you feel more like a man," a Salvadoran officer apprised the army recruits, adding that they should "not feel pity of anyone" but only "hate for those who are enemies of our country."[24]

Another Salvadoran, a former member of the National Guard, later testified in a 1986 British television documentary: "I belonged to a squad of twelve. We devoted ourselves to torture, and to finding people whom we were told were guerrillas. I was trained in Panama for nine months by the [unintelligible] of the United States for anti-guerrilla warfare. Part of the time we were instructed about torture."[25]

Honduras

During the 1980s, the CIA gave indispensable support to the infamous Battalion 316, which kidnapped, tortured and killed hundreds of citizens, using shock and suffocation devices for interrogation, amongst other techniques. The CIA supplied torture equipment, torture manuals, and in both Honduras and the US, taught battalion members methods of psychological and physical torture. On at least one occasion, a CIA officer took part in interrogating a torture victim. The Agency also funded Argentine counter-insurgency experts to provide further training for the Hondurans. At the time, Argentina was famous for its "Dirty War", an appalling record of torture, baby kidnappings and disappearances. Argentine and CIA instructors worked side by side training Battalion 316. US support for the battalion continued even after its director, Gen. Gustavo Alvarez Martinez, told the US ambassador that he intended to use the Argentine methods of eliminating subversives. In 1983, the Reagan administration awarded Alvarez the Legion of Merit "for encouraging the success of democratic processes in Honduras". At the same time, the administration was misleading Congress and the American public by denying or minimizing the battalion's atrocities.[26]

Panama

During the occupation of Panama following the invasion of December 1989, some American soldiers engaged in torture of soldiers of the Panama Defense Forces. In one case, a metal cable was inserted into an open wound, producing intense pain. In another reported case, a

PDF soldier was hung up by one arm on which he already had an injury to the elbow, which had been stitched up.[27]

At home

For those readers who have difficulty believing that American government civilian and military personnel could be closely involved in the torture of foreigners, it is suggested that they consider what these Americans have done to other Americans.

At the US Navy's schools in San Diego and Maine during the 1960s and 1970s, students were supposedly learning about methods of "survival, evasion, resistance and escape" which they could use if they were ever a prisoner of war. There was in the course something of survival in a desert, where students were forced to eat lizards, but the naval officers and cadets were also subjected to beatings, jarring judo flips, "tiger cages"—hooded and placed in a 16-cubic-foot box for 22 hours with a coffee can for their excrement—and a torture device called the "water board": the subject strapped to an inclined board, head downward, a towel placed over his face, and cold water poured over the towel; he would choke, gag, retch and gurgle as he experienced the sensation of drowning.

A former student, Navy pilot Lt. Wendell Richard Young, claimed that his back was broken during the course and that students were tortured into spitting, urinating and defecating on the American flag, masturbating before guards, and, on one occasion, engaging in sex with an instructor.[28]

In 1992, a civilian oversight board revealed that over a 13-year period (1973–1986), Chicago police officers and commanders engaged in "systematic" torture and abuse of suspects, including electric shock to penises, testicles and other areas; beatings, suffocation (plastic bags secured over the heads, stopping the flow of oxygen; some subjects passed out, and when they recovered, the bag was placed over their head again); guns stuck in prisoners' mouths and triggers pulled; prisoners hung from hooks by handcuffs attached to their wrists and beaten on the bottoms of their feet and on their testicles; as well as much psychological torture. Some were released after being tortured and were never charged. More than 40 cases were collected. According to one of their attorneys, "All of the victims were black or Latino, so far as we've seen, and the people who were doing the torturing were white officers."[29]

A Human Rights Watch investigation of more than 20 US prisons and jails in New York, California, Florida and Tennessee, and a close look at prison litigation for a ten-year period, showed "extensive abuses of the U.N.'s minimum standards for the treatment of prisoners...amounting to torture"...a handcuffed prisoner forced into a tub of 145-degree water...prisoners dying after receiving repeated jolts of electricity from stun guns or stun belts (50,000 volt shock for 8 seconds)...prisoners held in outdoor cages, rain or shine...prisoners held in total isolation from other human beings for long periods of time with sensory deprivation...[30]

Amnesty International has released reports such as "Torture, Ill Treatment and Excessive Force by Police in Los Angeles, California" (1992), and "Police Brutality and Excessive Force in the New York City Police Department" (1996), as well as later reports dealing with Chicago and other cities. Amnesty states that US police forces have been guilty of "violating international human rights standards through a pattern of unchecked excessive force amounting to torture or other cruel, inhuman and degrading treatment".[31]

Lest any of the above give the impression that the United States government is not disturbed by the practice of torture, it should be pointed out that Congress passed a bill in 1996 allowing, for the first time, an American citizen to sue a foreign government in a US court for having been tortured in the foreign country. There was one small limitation imposed, however. The only countries that can be sued under this law are Washington's officially-designated enemies (ODE), those categorized as "terrorist states".[32]

For other states, the situation may be like the case in the early 1990s of Scott Nelson, an American who sued Saudi Arabia in a US court for torture. A Circuit Court of Appeals ruled that he had a right to sue, but the State Department helped the Saudis to get the case reversed in the Supreme Court.[33]

CHAPTER 6

The Unsavories

During the 1980s, there were a number of disclosures of past and present CIA involvement with torturers, death-squaders, drug traffickers and other types not fit for American schoolbooks. At some unrecorded moment, a government spinhead came up with the term "unsavory persons", implying that the government was as repulsed by these types as much as any decent American citizen ought to be.

The media obediently picked up on it. With each new revelation of the CIA's connection to human rights violations in the company of some despicable people abroad, who were on the Agency payroll, we were told—and told officially—that the CIA had no choice but to associate with "unsavory" persons if it wished to obtain certain important information in foreign countries; information, of course, vital to our "national security". A new whitewash cliché had been born, still very much alive.

Even when the media is critical of the CIA for working with unsavories, there's no indication that the relationship was ever anything more than paying for information while holding one's nose.

But it should be clearly understood that these unsavories have not been simply informants.

To the CIA and the US military these men are America's allies on the same side of a civil conflict.

US propaganda insists that the side these men are fighting on is the side of freedom and democracy.

We champion their cause, for it is our cause as well.

We select certain of them to attend American military schools and we bestow graduation certificates upon them.

We wine and dine them in the US, we give them gifts, we set them up with prostitutes.

We train them and give them their weapons and uniforms.

We teach them methods of bomb-making, methods of assassination and methods of interrogation (read torture).

We provide them with information about individuals from the CIA's mammoth international databases. Some of these individuals then wind up tortured and/or murdered.

We cover up their atrocities.

We facilitate and cover up their drug trafficking.

We socialize with them. They are our friends. They have often betrayed their own country for us.

The money paid to unsavories is of course available to them to finance their vile purposes. When someone like Qaddafi of Libya does this, it's called "supporting terrorism".

CIA payments and other support to these unsavories necessarily bring more than information—they bring influence and control. When one looks at the anti-democratic and cruelty levels of the recipients, one has to wonder what the CIA's influence was. And at the same time one has to ask the following question: If the United States must take sides in a foreign civil war, why must it repeatedly be on the same side as the unsavories?

Other unsavory skeletons in Washington's closet

In the post-World War II period, US foreign policy embraced many other unsavories—"former" Nazis (including war criminals like Klaus Barbie), Italian fascists, Japanese enemy armed forces, Japanese scientists who had carried out terrible experiments on prisoners, including Americans, and many thousands of others who had collaborated with these individuals during the war. In many parts of Europe and Asia, collaborators with the enemy were publicly disgraced, imprisoned, and/or executed by the post-war governments or citizens' groups. But in China, Italy, Greece, the Philippines, Korea, Albania, West Germany, Iran, Soviet Union, Vietnam and elsewhere, many of the fascists and collaborators who eluded punishment became American allies in setting up new governments, trying to overthrow governments, fighting civil wars, suppressing the left, gathering intelligence and in manipulating electoral politics; indeed, many of them eluded punishment *because* they became American allies.[1]

As late as 1988, there were a number of genuine pro-Nazi, anti-Semitic types from Eastern and Central Europe in the Republican Party's National Republican Heritage Groups Council. Several of these worthies were leaders of the George Bush presidential campaign's ethnic outreach arm, the Coalition of American Nationalities, despite the fact that their checkered past was not a big secret. One of them, Laszlo Pasztor (or Pastor) had served in the pro-Nazi Hungarian government's embassy in Berlin during the war. This had been revealed in a 1971 page-one story in the *Washington Post*.[2] When this past was again brought up in September 1988, the Republicans were obliged to dump Pasztor and four others of his ilk from Bush's campaign.[3]

When lying down with unsavories has such a long heritage, for Washington to pretend that it's no more than a temporary marriage of convenience to an (unfortunately) unattractive bride, is an exercise that fails to rise above simplistic propaganda. What has attracted the two sides to each other over the years has been a shared class consciousness, manifesting itself in an abhorrence of progressive movements, or something called "communism" or most anything or anyone seen as a threat to a mutually-desired status quo. The lowly, crude Guatemalan lieutenant relishes hanging around the American stage door more than gazing upon his country's Indian peasants. His Yankee drinking buddy is convinced it's an act of duty to help him kill them.

Chapter 7

Training New Unsavories

I have seen no evidence in my 24 years in Congress of one instance where because of American military involvement with another military that the Americans have stopped that foreign army from carrying out atrocities against their own people. No evidence, none.

—Senator Tom Harkin (D.-Iowa), 1999[1]

School of the Americas

The School of the Americas (SOA), an Army school at Fort Benning, Georgia, has been beleaguered for years by protestors because so many of its graduates have been involved in very serious human-rights abuses in Latin America, often involving torture and murder. SOA insists that it teaches its students to respect human rights and democracy. To examine this claim we must note that wars between nations in Latin America are extremely rare. The question which thus arises is: Who are these military men being trained to fight if not the army of another country? Who but their own citizens?

Over the years, SOA has trained tens of thousands of Latin American military and police in subjects like counter-insurgency, infantry tactics, military intelligence, anti-narcotics operations and commando operations. The students have also been taught to hate and fear something called "communism", later something called "terrorism", with little, if any, distinction made between the two, thus establishing the ideological justification to suppress their own people, to stifle dissent, to cut off at the knees anything bearing a likeness to a movement for social change which—although the military men might not think in such terms—might interfere with Washington's global agenda.

Those on the receiving end of anti-communist punishment would have a difficult time recognizing themselves from this piece of philosophy from an SOA class: "Democracy and communism clash with the firm determination of the Western countries to conserve their own traditional way of life."[2] This reads as if dissidents came from some faraway land, with alien values and no grievances that could be comprehended as legitimate by the "Western" mind.

On New Year's Day 1994, peasants in Mexico's state of Chiapas staged a bloodless takeover of nearby communities under the banner of the Zapatista National Liberation Army. It was the same day that NAFTA took effect, as the Zapatistas were careful to point out. The Mexican military responded brutally. As the conflict dragged on, to the NAFTA-powers-that-be in Washington the situation threatened to be an embarrassing impediment to the peaceful implementation of the trade agreement.

Whether by coincidence or not, as the Zapatista rebellion has continued to the present day, the Mexican enrollment at SOA has proceeded accordingly. Here are the figures for number of students: 1994 - 15; 1995 - 24; 1996 - 148; 1997 - 333; 1998 - 219. Presumably, by 1998, Mexico had sufficient trained officers to be able to cut back, although their number was still the highest of any country for that year. These newly-honed SOA "professionals" have formed an "army of occupation", which has militarized Chiapas, setting up camps from which they beat, terrorize, often murder, and dislocate the indigenous population and inhibit free movement with roadblocks.

In September 1996, under continual insistence from religious and grassroots groups, the Pentagon released seven Spanish-language training manuals used at the SOA until 1991. A *New York Times* editorial declared:

> Americans can now read for themselves some of the noxious lessons the United States Army taught to thousands of Latin American military and police officers at the School of the Americas during the 1980s. A training manual recently released by the Pentagon recom-

mended interrogation techniques like torture, execution, blackmail and arresting the relatives of those being questioned.[3]

SOA graduates have led a number of military coups—so many that the *Washington Post* reported in 1968 that the school was "known throughout Latin America as the 'escuela de golpes' or coup school"[4]—and are responsible for the murders of thousands of people, particularly in the 1980s, such as the Uraba massacre in Colombia; the El Mozote massacre, the assassination of Archbishop Oscar Romero, the rape and murder of four US churchwomen and the Jesuit massacre in El Salvador; the La Cantuta massacre in Peru; the torture and murder of a UN worker in Chile; and hundreds of other human-rights abuses.

In the village of El Mozote, El Salvador, in December 1981, from 700 to 1,000 persons were reported killed, mostly the elderly, women and children, in extremely cruel and gruesome ways.[5] Ten of the twelve soldiers cited for the massacre were SOA graduates. In the slaying of six Jesuit priests and two others in November 1989, the UN Truth Commission revealed that 19 of the 26 Salvadoran officers involved had been trained at the SOA.[6]

The full scope of atrocities committed by SOA graduates will likely never be known because members of Latin American militaries are generally above the law. It has been rare that crimes by members of these militaries have been investigated, and rarer still that the names of those suspected have been released.

The SOA has always claimed that it doesn't teach its students how to torture or how to commit other human-rights abuses. When the truth was revealed by the release of the training manuals, the SOA claimed that it had changed. But only one of 42 courses in the 1996 course catalogue—"Democratic Sustainment"—centers on issues of democracy and human rights. In 1997, only 13 students took this course, compared with 118 who took "Military Intelligence". The "mandatory human-rights component" of other courses comprises only a very small portion of the total course hours. Former SOA human-rights instructor Charles Call has reported that human-rights training is not taken seriously at the school, comprising an insignificant amount of students' overall training.[7]

Access

Why, in the face of decades of terrible publicity, increasingly more militant protests, thousands of arrests, and sharply decreasing Congressional support, has the Pentagon clung to the School of the Americas? What is it that's so vital to the military brass? The answer may lie in this: The school and its students, along with a never-ending supply of US military equipment to countries around the world, are part of a package that serves the US foreign policy agenda in a special way. The package is called "access". Along with the equipment come American technicians, instructors, replacement parts and more. Here is the testimony before Congress of General Norman Schwarzkopf, Commander in Chief, U.S. Central Command (CENTCOM), in 1990.

> Security assistance leads directly to access, and without access afforded by our friends we cannot project U.S. military forces into [an] area and stay there for any appreciable length of time...[If] our military assistance programs diminish, our influence will erode and we will come to the point where we will have little or no ability to control the use of the weapons or the escalation of hostilities...The second pillar of our strategy is presence. It is the symbol of America's continued interest in and commitment to stability in the region...The third pillar of CENTCOM's strategy is combined [military] exercises. They demonstrate our resolve and commitment to the region. They foster increased cooperation, and they enhance our ability to work with our friends in a coalition environment."[8]

Thus it is that military aid, military exercises, naval port visits, etc.—like the School of the Americas—means repeated opportunities to foster close ties, even camaraderie, between American officers and foreign military personnel; and, at the same time, the opportunity to build up files of information on many thousands of these foreigners, as well as acquiring language skills, maps and photos of the area. In sum total: personal connections, personal information, country data bases—indispensable assets in time of coup, counter-coup, revolution, counter-revolution or invasion.

US military presence has, in effect, served the purpose of "casing the joint"; it also facilitates selecting candidates, not just Latin Americans for SOA, but thousands of military and police personnel from other continents who come to the US for training at scores of other military schools; the process of access replenishes itself. It is not unusual for the military-to-military contacts to thrive even while diplomatic relations between Washington and the students' government are rather cool (in recent years, e.g., Algeria, Syria and Lebanon)—another indication of the priority given to the contacts.[9]

Historically, as shown in this chapter and others, strong military-to-military ties have tended to undermine civilian institutions and fuel human-rights abuses, particularly in Latin America, where fledgling democracies are now trying to keep their militaries in the barracks.

The equipment ale that access leads to ain't bad either.

The New Improved School of the Americas

When Congress came close to ending funding for the school in fall 1999, the Defense Department finally saw the writing on the wall. It announced in November that it was planning on making major changes by spring 2000—less strictly military focus and more academic; civilian students as well as military; teaching democratic principles, etc.; changing the name to the Center for Inter-American Security Cooperation.

The question remains: Why keep the school at all? Are there not enough academic schools here and in Latin America that fill the bill? Americans don't have free university education. Why should we provide it for foreigners?

The answer appears to be the factor that the changes wouldn't affect—access; perhaps new, improved access, inasmuch as in addition to military students, there will be access to present and future political and civilian leaders as students.[10]

In any event, there will still be the numerous other military training facilities for foreigners in the US, in addition to the extensive training the Pentagon carries out abroad.

Office of Public Safety schools

From the early 1960s until the mid 1970s, the US Office of Public Safety (part of AID), operated The International Police Academy, at first in Panama, then in Washington. It did for foreign police officers what the SOA did for the military. OPS provided training abroad for more than a million policemen in the Third World, ten thousand of whom were selected to come to Washington for advanced training. There may well have been more serious human-rights abusers amongst the OPS police students than amongst the SOA military graduates because of the former's closer and more frequent contact with the populace. Moreover, most of the classes were held abroad, where the instructors could feel less constrained than in Washington or Georgia about lecturing in a very militant manner on "the communist menace" and the use of any means necessary to combat it. Amongst the means sometimes taught was torture. (See "Torture" chapter.)

OPS provided the police with weapons, ammunition, radios, patrol cars, tear gas, gas masks, batons and other crowd control devices; a class on Assassination Weapons—"A discussion of various weapons which may be used by the assassin" is how OPS put it; and instruction on the design, manufacture and employment of bombs and incendiary devices, taught at the "bomb school" in Los Fresnos, Texas. The official OPS explanation for the bomb courses was that policemen needed such training in order to deal with bombs placed by terrorists. There was, however, no instruction in destroying bombs, only in making them.[11]

When Congress abolished the Public Safety Program in 1975 in response to rising criticism of this dark side of American foreign policy, the Drug Enforcement Administration, with help from the FBI and the Defense Department, quietly stepped in and continued the program.[12] In various reincarnations, the program continues, just as the School of the Americas made it to the 21st century.[13]

Brazil

The *Escola Superior de Guerra* (Higher War College), founded in Rio de Janeiro in 1949, allowed the United States to foster relationships with Brazilian officers similar to those with SOA students, while passing on a similar political mentality. Latin America historian Thomas E. Skidmore has observed:

> Under the U.S.-Brazilian military agreements of the early 1950s, the U.S. Army received exclusive rights to render assistance in the organization and operation of the college, which had been modeled on the National War College in Washington. In view of the fact that the

Brazilian War College became a rallying point for leading military opponents of civilian populist politicians, it would be worth examining the extent to which the strongly anti-Communist ideology—bordering on an anti-political attitude—was reinforced (or moderated?) by their frequent contacts with United States officers.[14]

There was, moreover, the ongoing US Military Assistance Program, which US Ambassador Lincoln Gordon described in a March 1964 cable to the State Department as a "major vehicle for establishing close relationships with personnel of the armed forces" and "a highly important factor in influencing [the Brazilian] military to be pro-US."[15]

Just weeks after this cable was sent, the Brazilian military overthrew a populist government which was on Washington's hate/hit list.

CHAPTER 8

War Criminals: Theirs and Ours

On December 3, 1996, the US Justice Department issued a list of 16 Japanese citizens who would be barred from entering the United States because of "war crimes" committed during the Second World War. Among those denied entry were some who were alleged to have been members of the infamous "Unit 731", which, said the Justice Department, "conducted inhumane and frequently lethal pseudo-medical experiments—on thousands of...prisoners and civilians," including mass dissections of living humans.[1] Oddly enough, after the war the man in charge of the Unit 731 program—whose test subjects included captured American soldiers—General Shiro Ishii, along with a number of his colleagues, had been granted immunity and freedom in exchange for providing the United States with details about their experiments, and were promised that their crimes would not be revealed to the world. The justification for this policy, advanced by American scientists and military officials, was, of course, the proverbial, ubiquitous "national security".[2]

Apart from the hypocrisy of the Justice Department issuing such a list, we are faced with the fact that any number of countries would be justified in issuing a list of Americans barred from entry because of "war crimes" and "crimes against humanity". Such a list might include the following:

William Clinton, president, for his merciless bombing of the people of Yugoslavia for 78 days and nights, taking the lives of many hundreds of civilians, and producing one of the greatest ecological catastrophes in history; for his relentless continuation of the sanctions and rocket attacks upon the people of Iraq; and for his illegal and lethal bombings of Somalia, Bosnia, Sudan and Afghanistan.

General Wesley Clark, Supreme Allied Commander in Europe, for his direction of the NATO bombing of Yugoslavia with an almost sadistic fanaticism..."He would rise out of his seat and slap the table. 'I've got to get the maximum violence out of this campaign—now!'"[3]

George Bush, president, for the murder of hundreds of thousands of innocent Iraqi civilians, including many thousands of children, the result of his 40 days of bombing and the institution of draconian sanctions; and for his unconscionable bombing of Panama, producing widespread death, destruction and homelessness, for no discernible reason that would stand up in a court of law.

General Colin Powell, Chairman of the Joint Chiefs of Staff, for his prominent role in the attacks on Panama and Iraq, the latter including destruction of nuclear reactors as well as plants making biological and chemical agents. It was the first time ever that live reactors had been bombed, and ran the risk of setting a dangerous precedent. Hardly more than a month had passed since the United Nations, under whose mandate the United States was supposedly operating in Iraq, had passed a resolution reaffirming its "prohibition of military attacks on nuclear facilities" in the Middle East.[4] In the wake of the destruction, Powell gloated: "The two operating reactors they had are both gone, they're down, they're finished."[5] He was just as cavalier about the lives of the people of Iraq. In response to a question concerning the number of Iraqis killed in the war, the good general replied: "It's really not a number I'm terribly interested in."[6]

And for his part in the cover up of war crimes in Vietnam by troops of the same brigade that carried out the My Lai massacre.[7]

General Norman Schwarzkopf, Commander in Chief, U.S. Central Command, for his military leadership of the Iraqi carnage; for continuing the carnage two days after the cease-fire; for continuing it against Iraqis trying to surrender.

Ronald Reagan, president, for eight years of death, destruction, torture and the crushing of hope inflicted upon the people of El Salvador, Guatemala, Nicaragua and Grenada by his policies; and for his bombings of Lebanon, Libya and Iran. He's forgotten all this, but the world shouldn't.

Elliott Abrams, Assistant Secretary of State under Reagan, for rewriting history, even as it was happening, by instituting lying as public policy. He was indispensable to putting the best possible face on the atrocities being committed daily by the Contras in Nicaragua and other Washington allies in Central America, thus promoting continued support for them; a spinmeister for the ages, who wrestled facts into ideological submission. "When history is written," he declared, "the Contras will be folk heroes."[8]

Casper Weinberger, Secretary of Defense for seven years under Reagan, for his official and actual responsibility for the numerous crimes against humanity perpetrated by the United States in Central America and the Caribbean, and for the bombing of Libya in 1986. George Bush pardoned him for Iran-Contra, but he should not be pardoned for his war crimes.

Lt. Col. Oliver North, assigned to Reagan's National Security Council, for being a prime mover behind the Contras of Nicaragua, and for his involvement in the planning of the invasion of Grenada, which took the lives of hundreds of innocent civilians.

Henry Kissinger (who has successfully combined three careers: scholar, Nobel peace laureate, and war criminal), National Security Adviser under Nixon and Secretary of State under Nixon and Ford, for his Machiavellian, amoral, immoral roles in the US interventions into Angola, Chile, East Timor, Iraq, Vietnam and Cambodia, which brought unspeakable horror and misery to the peoples of those lands.

Gerald Ford, president, for giving his approval to Indonesia to use American arms to brutally suppress the people of East Timor, thus setting in motion a quarter-century-long genocide.

Robert McNamara, Secretary of Defense under presidents Kennedy and Johnson, a prime architect of, and major bearer of responsibility for, the slaughter in Indochina, from its early days to its extraordinary escalations; and for the violent suppression of popular movements in Peru.

General William Westmoreland, Army Chief of Staff, for the numerous war crimes under his command in Vietnam. In 1971, Telford Taylor, the chief US prosecutor at the post-World War II Nuremberg Tribunal, cited the "Yamashita" case as grounds for indicting Westmoreland. Following the war, a US Army Commission had sentenced Japanese General Tomayuki Yamashita to be hung for atrocities committed by his troops in the Philippines. The Commission held that as the senior commander, Yamashita was responsible for not stopping the atrocities. The same ruling could of course apply to General Powell and General Schwarzkopf. Yamashita, in his defense, presented considerable evidence that he had lacked the communications to adequately control his troops; yet he was still hung. Taylor pointed out that with helicopters and modern communications, Westmoreland and his commanders didn't have this problem.[9]

The crime of bombing

As mentioned in the "bombing" chapter, the bombing of cities from airplanes goes not only unpunished but virtually unaccused. This is a legacy of World War II. The Nuremberg and Tokyo judgments are silent on the subject of aerial bombardment. Since both sides had played a terrible game of urban destruction—the Allies far more successfully—there was no basis for criminal charges against Germans or Japanese, and in fact no such charges were brought. But as Telford Taylor has asked: "Is there any significant difference between killing a babe-in-arms by a bomb dropped from a high-flying aircraft, or by an infantryman's point-blank gunfire?...The aviator's act [is described] as more 'impersonal' than the ground soldier's. This may be psychologically valid, but surely is not morally satisfactory."[10]

No one ever thinks they're guilty of anything...they're all just good ol' patriots

"Asked whether he wants to apologize for the suffering he caused, he looks genuinely confused, has the interpreter repeat the question, and answers 'No'...'I want you to know that everything I did, I did for my country.'" *Journalist Nate Thayer interviewing a dying Pol Pot, 1997*[11]

How to deal with the unthinkable

At the close of World War II, the International Military Tribunal for the Far East was held. At the trial in Tokyo of former Japanese prime minister Hideki Tojo, his lawyers asked why Tojo's crimes were any worse than dropping the A-bomb on Hiroshima and Nagasaki. At that moment, the prosecution interrupted the Japanese translation and ordered the removal of the remarks in the official trial record and in the press.[12]

Another unthinkable

The Convention on the Prevention and Punishment of the Crime of Genocide ("Genocide Convention"), adopted by the United Nations General Assembly in 1948..."The Contracting Parties confirm that genocide, whether committed in time of peace or in time of war, is a crime under international law which they undertake to prevent and to punish." The Convention then goes on to define genocide as certain acts, listed therein, "committed with intent to destroy, in whole or in part, a national, ethnical, racial or religious group, as such."

Missing from this list is perhaps the most significant manifestation of genocide in modern times: the extermination of people because of their political ideology. The Nazis became notorious for their slaughter of Jews and Gypsies, but German fascism, as in Italy, Spain, Greece, Chile, Indonesia, and elsewhere, was firstly and primarily directed against socialists and communists, regardless of any other characteristic. (Hitler, in any event, largely equated Jews and communists.)

As can be seen in the chapter on "Interventions" and in other chapters—from China and the Philippines in the 1940s to Colombia and Mexico in the 1990s, the United States has long been practicing this *politicide*. However, the CEOs of The World's Only Superpower can rest easy. There will be no international convention against it, and no American official will ever have to answer to a court for it.[13]

Yugoslavia—another war-crimes trial that will never be

Beginning about two weeks after the NATO bombing of Yugoslavia began in March 1999, international-law professionals from Canada, the United Kingdom, Greece and the American Association of Jurists began to file complaints with the International Criminal Tribunal for the Former Yugoslavia in The Hague, Netherlands, charging leaders of NATO countries and officials of NATO itself with crimes similar to those for which the Tribunal had issued indictments shortly before against Serbian leaders. Amongst the charges filed were: "grave violations of international humanitarian law", including "wilful killing, wilfully causing great suffering and serious injury to body and health, employment of poisonous weapons and other weapons to cause unnecessary suffering, wanton destruction of cities, towns and villages, unlawful attacks on civilian objects, devastation not necessitated by military objectives, attacks on undefended buildings and dwellings, destruction and wilful damage done to institutions dedicated to religion, charity and education, the arts and sciences."

The Canadian suit names 68 leaders, including William Clinton, Madeleine Albright, William Cohen, Tony Blair, Canadian Prime Minister Jean Chretien, and NATO officials Javier Solana, Wesley Clark and Jamie Shea. The complaint also alleges "open violation" of the United Nations Charter, the NATO treaty itself, the Geneva Conventions and the Principles of International Law Recognized by the International Military Tribunal at Nuremberg.

The complaint was submitted along with a considerable amount of evidence to support the charges. The evidence makes the key point that it was NATO's bombing campaign which had given rise to the bulk of the deaths in Yugoslavia, provoked most of the Serbian atrocities, created an environmental disaster and left a dangerous legacy of unexploded depleted uranium and cluster bombs.

In June, some of the complainants met in The Hague with the court's chief prosecutor, Louise Arbour of Canada. Although she cordially received their brief in person, along with three thick volumes of evidence documenting the alleged war crimes, nothing of substance came of the meeting, despite repeated follow-up submissions and letters by the plaintiffs. In November, her successor, Carla Del Ponte of Switzerland, also met with some of the complainants and received extensive evidence.

The complainants' brief in November pointed out that the prosecution of those named by them was "not only a requirement of law, it is a requirement of justice to the victims and of deterrence to powerful countries such as those in NATO who, in their military might and in their control over the media, are lacking in any other natural restraint such as might deter less powerful countries." Charging the war's victors, not only its losers, it was argued, would be a watershed in international criminal law.

In one of the letters to Arbour, Michael Mandel, a professor of law in Toronto and the initiator of the Canadian suit, stated:

> Unfortunately, as you know, many doubts have already been raised about the impartiality of your Tribunal. In the early days of the conflict, after a formal and, in our view, justified complaint against NATO leaders had been laid before it by members of the Faculty of Law of Belgrade University, you appeared at a press conference with one of the accused, British Foreign Secretary Robin Cook, who made a great show of handing you a dossier of Serbian war crimes. In early May, you appeared at another press conference with US Secretary of State Madeleine Albright, by that time herself the subject of two formal complaints of war crimes over the targeting of civilians in Yugoslavia. Albright publicly announced at that time that the US was the major provider of funds for the Tribunal and that it had pledged even more money to it.[14]

Arbour herself made little attempt to hide the pro-NATO bias she wore beneath her robe. She trusted NATO to be its own police, judge, jury and prison guard. In a year in which the arrest of General Pinochet was giving an inspiring lift to the cause of international law and international justice, the International Criminal Tribunal for the Former Yugoslavia, under Arbour's leadership, ruled that for the Great Powers it would be business as usual, particularly the Great Power that was most vulnerable to prosecution, and which, coincidentally, paid most of her salary. Here are her own words:

I am obviously not commenting on any allegations of violations of international humanitarian law supposedly perpetrated by nationals of NATO countries. I accept the assurances given by NATO leaders that they intend to conduct their operations in the Federal Republic of Yugoslavia in full compliance with international humanitarian law. I have reminded many of them, when the occasion presented itself, of their obligation to conduct fair and open-minded investigations of any possible deviance from that policy, and of the obligation of commanders to prevent and punish, if required.[15]

NATO Press Briefing, May 16, 1999:
Question: Does NATO recognize Judge Arbour's jurisdiction over their activities?
Jamie Shea: I think we have to distinguish between the theoretical and the practical. I believe that when Justice Arbour starts her investigation [of the Serbs], she will because we will allow her to...NATO countries are those that have provided the finance to set up the Tribunal, we are amongst the majority financiers.

The Tribunal—created in 1993, with the US as the father, the Security Council as the mother, and Madeleine Albright as the midwife—also relies on the military assets of the NATO powers to track down and arrest the suspects it tries for war crimes.

There appeared to be no more happening with the complaint under Del Ponte than under Arbour, but in late December, in an interview with *The Observer* of London, Del Ponte was asked if she was prepared to press charges against NATO personnel. She replied: "If I am not willing to do that, I am not in the right place. I must give up my mission."

The Tribunal then announced that it had completed a study of possible NATO crimes, which Del Ponte was examining, and that the study was an appropriate response to public concerns about NATO's tactics. "It is very important for this tribunal to assert its authority over any and all authorities to the armed conflict within the former Yugoslavia."

Was this a sign from heaven that the new millennium was going to be one of more equal justice? Could this really be?

No, it couldn't. From official quarters, military and civilian, of the United States and Canada, came disbelief, shock, anger, denials…"appalling"…"unjustified". Del Ponte got the message. Four days after *The Observer* interview appeared, her office issued a statement: "NATO is not under investigation by the Office of the Prosecutor of the International Criminal Tribunal for the former Yugoslavia. There is no formal inquiry into the actions of NATO during the conflict in Kosovo."[16] And there wouldn't be, it was unnecessary to add.

But the claim against NATO—heretofore largely ignored by the American media—was now out in the open. It was suddenly receiving a fair amount of publicity, and supporters of the bombing were put on the defensive. The most common argument made in NATO's defense, and against war-crime charges, has been that the death and devastation inflicted upon the civilian sector was "accidental". This claim, however, must be questioned in light of certain reports. For example, the commander of NATO's air war, Lt. Gen. Michael Short, declared at one point:

> If you wake up in the morning and you have no power to your house and no gas to your stove and the bridge you take to work is down and will be lying in the Danube for the next 20 years, I think you begin to ask, "Hey, Slobo, what's this all about? How much more of this do we have to withstand?"[17]

General Short, said the *New York Times*, "hopes that the distress of the Yugoslav public will undermine support for the authorities in Belgrade."[18]

At another point, NATO spokesman Jamie Shea added: "If President Milosevic really wants all of his population to have water and electricity all he has to do is accept NATO's five conditions and we will stop this campaign."[19]

After the April NATO bombing of a Belgrade office building—which housed political parties, TV and radio stations, 100 private companies and more—the *Washington Post* reported:

> Over the past few days, U.S. officials have been quoted as expressing the hope that members of Serbia's economic elite will begin to turn against Milosevic once they understand how much they are likely to lose by continuing to resist NATO demands.[20]

Before missiles were fired into this building, NATO planners spelled out the risks: "Casualty Estimate 50–100 Government/Party employees. Unintended Civ Casualty Est: 250—Apts in expected blast radius."[21] The planners were saying that about 250 civilians living in nearby apartment buildings might be killed in the bombing.

What do we have here? We have grown men telling each other: We'll do A, and we think that B may well be the result. But even if B does in fact result, we're saying beforehand—as we'll insist afterward—that it was *unintended.*

Following World War II there was an urgent need for a permanent international criminal court to prosecute those accused of war crimes, crimes against humanity and genocide, but the Cold War intervened. Finally, in 1998 in Rome, the nations of the world drafted the charter of The International Criminal Court. American negotiators, however, insisted on provisions in the charter that would, in essence, give the United States veto power over any prosecution through its seat on the Security Council. The American request was rejected, and primarily for this reason the US refused to join 120 other nations who supported the charter. The ICC is an instrument Washington can't control sufficiently to keep it from prosecuting American military and government officials. Senior US officials have explicitly admitted that this danger is the reason for their aversion to the proposed new court.[22] But this is clearly not the case with the International Criminal Tribunal for the Former Yugoslavia. It's Washington's kind of international court, a court for the New World Order.

Washington journalist Sam Smith observed in 1999: "It seems that the international war crimes tribunal has been taking selective enforcement lessons from the New Jersey State Police. The only war criminals it indicted this week were those with hard-to-spell foreign names. No one with a simple Anglican name—say like Clinton or Blair—was charged."

During its destructive military operations in Yugoslavia, the United States was supremely unconcerned about the possibility that anyone would even consider filing charges against NATO at the Hague, yet we now know that: "Midway through the war with Yugoslavia, the

Defense Department's top legal office issued guidelines warning that misuse of cyber attacks could subject U.S. authorities to war crimes charges." This was a reference to the Pentagon's considering hacking into Serbian computer networks to disrupt military operations and basic civilian services.[23]

CHAPTER 9

Haven for Terrorists

In 1998, the State Department issued its annual human-rights report, listing Cuba amongst those nations alleged to "sponsor terrorism". Curious about this, I called up the State Department and was connected to what they called "The Terrorism Desk", where a gentleman named Joe Reap told me that Cuba was included because "They harbor terrorists."

"So does the United States," I replied. "The Cuban exiles in Miami have committed hundreds of terrorist acts, in the US and abroad."

Mr. Reap exploded. "Sir," he cried in a rising voice, "that is a fatuous remark and I will not listen to such nonsense!" And he hung up.

Unrepentant trouble-maker that I am, the following year, May 4, 1999 to be exact, when the new human-rights report was issued (does the word "self-righteous" ring a bell with the folks at the State Department?), I again called 202-647-8682, and again 'twas Joe Reap who answered. I doubt he knew that I was the same caller as the year before but, in any event, we went through the same dance steps. When I repeated my comment about the Cuban terrorists being harbored in Miami, he became instantly indignant and said that they were not terrorists.

"But the FBI has labeled some of them just that," I said.

"Then take it up with the FBI," said Joe.

"But we're discussing a State Department report," I pointed out.

His voice rising…"I will not listen to people call this government a terrorist sponsor!" Phone slammed down. The intervening year had not mellowed ol' Joe any more than it had me.

It's always fascinating to observe how a True Believer reacts to a sudden, unexpected and unanswerable threat to his fundamental ideological underpinnings.

The Cuban exiles are in fact one of the longest lasting and most prolific terrorist groups in the world, and they're still at it. During 1997 they carried out a spate of hotel bombings in Havana, directed from Miami.[1]

Hijacking is generally regarded as a grave international crime, but although there have been numerous air and boat hijackings over the years from Cuba to the US, at gunpoint, knifepoint and/or with the use of physical force, including at least one murder, it's difficult to find more than a single instance where the United States brought criminal charges against the hijackers. In August 1996, three Cubans who hijacked a plane to Florida at knifepoint were indicted and brought to trial. In Florida. This is like trying someone for gambling in a Nevada court. Even though the kidnapped pilot was brought back from Cuba to testify against the men, the defense simply told the jurors that the man was lying, and the jury deliberated less than an hour before acquitting the defendants.[2]

Cubans are not the only foreign terrorists or serious human-rights violators who have enjoyed safe haven in the United States in recent years. Like the Cubans, the others listed below are fervent anti-communists, or in some other way are compatible with past or present US foreign-policy objectives. (For sources not indicated, see this note.[3])

There's former Guatemalan Defense Minister Hector Gramajo Morales. In 1995, a US court ordered Gramajo to pay $47.5 million in damages to eight Guatemalans and a US citizen for his responsibility in the torture of the American (Sister Dianna Ortiz—see "Torture" chapter) and the massacre of family members of the Guatemalans (among thousands of other Indians whose death he was responsible for). Gramajo had been served a court summons in 1991 as he graduated from the Kennedy School of Government at Harvard, where he had studied on a scholarship provided by the US government. The judge stated that "The evidence suggests that Gramajo devised and directed the implementation of an indiscriminate campaign of terror against civilians." It was only following the court judgment that the Defense Department withdrew Gramajo's invitation to speak at a military seminar.[4] Gramajo subsequently returned to Guatemala, without having paid any of the court judgment. In speaking of his previous residence in Guatemala, he said that he had carried out what he described as "a more humanitarian" means of dealing with perceived dissenters. "We instituted civil affairs [in 1982] which provides development for 70 percent of the population, while we kill 30 percent. Before, the strategy was to kill 100 percent."[5]

Florida is the retirement home of choice for serious human-rights violators seeking to depart from the scene of their crimes. Former general, José Guillermo Garcia, head of El Salvador's armed forces in the 1980s, when military-linked death squads killed thousands of people suspected of being "subversives", has lived in Florida since the early 1990s.

Garcia's successor, Gen. Carlos Eugenio Vides Casanova, who also served as the head of the much feared national guard, is now a resident of the sunshine state too. According to the U.N. Truth Commission for El Salvador, Vides covered up and protected those who raped and murdered three American nuns and a lay worker in 1980. He was physically present on at least two occasions when Dr. Juan Romagoza Arce was tortured; in the end, the injuries inflicted on Arce left him unable to perform surgery. (Interviewed in 1999, Vides was moved to declare: "I ask myself over and over if there is anything I have done wrong, and I can't find anything.")

During the time that Garcia and Vides have lived in the United States, US Immigration has been denying asylum status to many refugees from El Salvador even though they've claimed they were in fear of being tortured or losing their lives if sent back.

Numerous Haitian human-rights violators have resided in the United States in recent years, unmolested by the authorities. Their hands and souls are bloody from carrying out the repression of the Duvalier dynasty, or the overthrow of the democratically elected Father Jean-Bertrand Aristide in 1991, or the return to repression after the coup. Among their numbers are:

Luckner Cambronne, Haiti's minister of the interior and defense under Francois "Papa Doc" Duvalier and adviser to his son and successor, Jean Claude "Baby Doc" Duvalier.

Army Lt. Col. Paul Samuel Jeremie. After Baby Doc was forced to abdicate in 1986, Jeremie was convicted of torturing Duvalier opponents and sentenced to 15 years in prison. He escaped in 1988.

General Prosper Avril, another Haitian dictator, responsible for the torture of opposition activists, whom he then displayed, bloodied, on television. Forced out by angry mobs in 1990, he was flown to Florida by the US government, where he might have lived happily ever after except that some of his former torture victims brought suit against him. At one point in the process, he failed to make a court appearance and thus defaulted. He fled to several countries trying to find haven. Meanwhile, in 1994, a US federal judge awarded $41 million to six Haitians living in the US.

During the period of Aristide's exile, 1991–94, Colonel Carl Dorelien oversaw a 7,000-man force whose well-documented campaign of butchery included murder, rape, kidnapping and torture, leading to the deaths of some 5,000 Haitian civilians. The good colonel has found a home in Florida as well.

We also have leading Haitian death-squad leader, Emmanuel Constant, former head of FRAPH, the paramilitary group of thugs which spread deep fear amongst the Haitian people with its regular murders, torture, public beatings, arson raids on poor neighborhoods and mutilation by machete in the aftermath of the coup against Aristide. He was on the CIA payroll in Haiti and now lives in New York. The State Department refused a Haitian extradition request for Constant and stopped his deportation back to that country. Constant apparently knows of a lot of skeletons in the American closet.

Other Haitians of this ilk residing in the United States include Major General Jean-Claude Duperval, and Ernst Prud'homme, a high-ranking member of the Bureau du Information et Coordination, a notoriously violent propaganda unit.

Armando Fernández Larios, a member of a Chilean military squad responsible for the torture and execution of at least 72 political prisoners in the month following the 1973 coup, is now residing in the United States. Fernández has publicly acknowledged his service as a member of the military squad, as well as his role as an agent of Chile's notorious secret police, the DINA, during the Pinochet regime. He struck a plea bargain with US government prosecutors, pleading guilty to being an "accessory after the fact" in the DINA-sponsored 1976

Washington, DC bombing murder of former Chilean dissident official, Orlando Letelier. The Chilean government reportedly would like Fernández extradited from the US, but his lawyer in Miami has said that the 1987 plea-agreement between his client and the Department of Justice stipulated that Fernández would never be returned to Chile. Department of Justice officials have declined to comment on the degree of Fernández's protection under the terms of the agreement, which is under court seal.[6]

Michael Townley of Chile played an even more significant role in the Letelier assassination. He served some time in a US prison and is now in the Federal Witness Protection Program. So if you see him, you don't know him.

Argentine Admiral Jorgé Enrico, who was associated with *La Escuela Mecanica* in Buenos Aires, the infamous torture center of "The Dirty War" period (1976–83), now freely enjoys Hawaii when he wishes.

At least two former members of the Honduran army's Battalion 316 (see "Torture" chapter), a CIA-trained intelligence unit that murdered hundreds of suspected leftists in the 1980s, are also known to be living the good life in South Florida.

Kebassa Negawa of Ethiopia was a defendant in an Atlanta case for torture. When he lost the case and his wages began to be garnished, he disappeared.

Also a resident is Sintong Panjaitan, an Indonesian general responsible for the 1991 Santa Cruz massacre in East Timor that took hundreds of lives.

At Washington's insistence, Thiounn Prasith was the Cambodian envoy to the United Nations for Pol Pot's Khmer Rouge from 1979 to 1993, even though the Khmer Rouge were ousted from power in 1979. Prasith was a leading apologist for Pol Pot's horrendous crimes and played a major role in their cover up. (See "Pol Pot" chapter.) He resides in peace and comfort in Mount Vernon, New York.[7]

General Mansour Moharari, an Iranian who was in charge of prisons under the Shah, and thus is no stranger to the practice of torture, has lived in the US for many years despite a price being put on his head by the Iranian mullahs.

Twenty former South Vietnamese officers who have admitted to committing torture and other human-rights violations during the Vietnam War are residing legally in California.[8]

Throughout the 1980s and into the 90s, numerous other Vietnamese in California carried out a violent terrorist campaign against their countrymen who were deemed not sufficiently anti-communist, sometimes merely for calling for resumption of contacts with Hanoi; others were attacked simply for questioning the terrorists' actions. Under names such as "Anti-Communist Viets Organization" and "Vietnamese Organization to Exterminate Communists and Restore the Nation", on hundreds of occasions they assaulted and murdered, burned down businesses and vehicles, forced Vietnamese newspapers to cease publishing, issued death threats, engaged in extortion and many other aspects of organized crime...all with virtual impunity, even with numerous witnesses to some murders. In the few cases where arrests were made, suspects were generally released or acquitted; the few who were convicted had their wrists slapped.[9] This clear pattern of law-enforcement neglect suggests some kind of understanding with higher-ups in Washington. If there was indeed a "see-no-evil" federal policy, the most likely explanation would be the powerful, lingering antipathy toward any Vietnamese with a presumed leaning toward Hanoi.

Additionally, a number of persons from the former Yugoslavia who have been accused of war crimes by their fellow nationals are also living in the US, although in most cases it appears to be due to American bureaucratic failings, rather than knowingly offering haven to the henchmen of former allies.

The above doesn't include all the dictators *cum* terrorists whom the United States was kind enough to fly to safe havens in third countries (enabling them to be reunited with their bank accounts), such as those from Haiti who are still alive: Gen. Raoul Cédras and President Jean-Claude "Baby Doc" Duvalier; as well as the nefarious Police Chief Joseph Michel Francois.

In 1998 President Clinton went before the United Nations to speak about terrorism. "What are our global obligations?" he asked. "To give terrorists no support, no sanctuary."[10]

Extradite or prosecute

The system of international criminal prosecution covering genocide, terrorism, war crimes and torture makes all governments responsible for the criminal prosecution of offenders. Under this basic principle of "universal enforcement," countries where alleged offenders are found are obligated to either extradite them for prosecution by a more directly affected government (e.g., the country where the offenses were committed, or the country of citizenship of the victims or the abusers), or to initiate prosecution themselves. The Pinochet case in the UK had begun in 1998 as an example of this.

The US government strongly supports this principle of "extradite or prosecute" in theory, and in fact invoked it a few years ago in a proceeding before the International Court of Justice as the basis for seeking extradition from Libya of two men alleged to be responsible for the bombing of Pan Am flight 103. The US government also strongly supports the application of this principle to those indicted for war crimes by the International War Crimes Tribunals for former Yugoslavia and Rwanda. One of those indicted as a war criminal by the Rwanda tribunal was discovered in Texas, arrested, and bound over for criminal extradition by a federal court in that State.[11]

Yet, when it comes to the relics of the Cold War being given haven in the US, as listed above, Washington chooses to neither prosecute nor extradite, although Cuba, for one, has asked for the extradition of a number of individuals.

Zero tolerance for other havens

Presidential Decision Directive 39, signed by President Clinton in 1995, states:

> If we do not receive adequate cooperation from a state that harbors a terrorist whose extradition we are seeking, we shall take appropriate measures to induce cooperation. Return of suspects by force may be effected without the cooperation of the host government.[12]

So determined is the Clinton administration to punish other states that compete with the US in harboring terrorists, that in February 1999 it asserted the right to bomb government facilities in such nations. "We may not just go in a strike against a terrorist facility; we may choose to retaliate against the facilities of the host country, if that host country is a knowing, cooperative sanctuary," Richard Clarke, President Clinton's coordinator for counter-terrorism, declared.[13]

I tried to reach Mr. Clarke at his White House office to ask him what he thought of the proposition that Cuba could justifiably designate the United States as a "knowing, cooperative sanctuary" and bomb CIA headquarters or a Cuban exile office in Miami, amongst other sites. However, I was told that he was "not available to the general public to speak to". Pity. So I sent him a letter posing these questions, with little expectation of an answer. I was not disappointed.

CHAPTER 10

Supporting Pol Pot

The Killing Fields…the borders sealed, the cities emptied at gun-point, a forced march to the countryside…being a professional, know-ing a foreign language, wearing eyeglasses, almost anything, might be cause enough for persecution, execution…or the overwork will kill you, or a beating, or the hunger, or disease. For whatever reason: short-age of food, creation of an agrarian society impervious to the econom-ic world order, internal party power, security…well over a million dead at the hands of the Cambodian Communist Party, the Khmer Rouge, under Pol Pot, after ousting the US-supported regime of Lon Nol…the world is horrified, comparisons to the Nazi genocide mush-room, "worse than Hitler" is Pol Pot…

Four years later, January 1979, Vietnam—responding to years of attacks by the Khmer Rouge against ethnic Vietnamese in Cambodia and cross-border raids into Vietnam itself—invaded what was now called Kampuchea, overthrew Pol Pot's government, and installed a government friendly to Vietnam. The Khmer Rouge forces retreated to the western end of Cambodia, by the border with Thailand, and later some set up camp in Thailand itself.

Washington's reaction was not any kind of elation that the Cambodian nightmare had come to an end, but rather undisguised dis-pleasure that the hated Vietnamese were in control and credited with ousting the terrible Khmer Rouge. For years afterwards, the United States condemned Vietnam's actions as "illegal". A lingering bitter-ness by American cold warriors against the small nation which mon-umental US power could not defeat appears to be the only explana-tion for this attitude. Humiliation runs deep, particularly when you're the world's only superpower.

Thus it was that an American policy took root—to provide the Khmer Rouge with food, financial aid and military aid beginning soon after their ouster.[1] The aim, in conjunction with China and long-time American client state, Thailand, was to restore Pol Pot's troops to military capability as the only force which could make the Vietnamese withdraw their army, leading to the overthrow of the Cambodian government.

President Carter's National Security Adviser, Zbigniew Brzezinski, has stated that in the spring of 1979: "I encouraged the Chinese to support Pol Pot. I encouraged the Thai to help the [Khmer Rouge]. The question was how to help the Cambodian people.[sic] Pol Pot was an abomination. We could never support him. But China could."[2]

In November 1980, Ray Cline, former Deputy Director of the CIA, visited a Khmer Rouge enclave inside Cambodia in his capacity as senior foreign-policy adviser to President-elect Ronald Reagan. A Khmer Rouge press release said that Cline "was warmly greeted by thousands of villagers."[3] The Reagan administration was apparently preparing to continue the policy of opposition to the Vietnamese-supported Phnom Penh government.

Some of the relief organizations operating in Cambodia considered supporting the Khmer Rouge guerrillas inconsistent with their humanitarian goals, in addition to the fact that distributing aid to military personnel was impermissible for such organizations as UNICEF and the International Committee of the Red Cross. But as two American relief aid workers, Linda Mason and Roger Brown, later wrote: "Thailand, the country that hosted the relief operation, and the U.S. government, which funded the bulk of the relief operation, insisted that the Khmer Rouge be fed."[4]

In the 1979–81 period, the World Food Program, which was strongly under US influence, gave almost $12 million in food to the Thai Army to distribute to predominantly Khmer Rouge camps by the border.[5]

In 1982, trying to remove the smell from the Khmer Rouge, the United States put together a coalition composed of the Khmer Rouge and two "non-communist" groups also opposed to the Cambodian government, one headed by former Cambodian ruler, Prince Sihanouk.

The coalition became the recipient of much aid from the US and China, mainly funneled through Thailand. The American aid, by the late 1980s, reached $5 million officially, with the CIA providing between $20 and $24 million behind Congress's back.[6] The aid was usually referred to as "non-lethal" or "humanitarian", but any aid freed up other money to purchase military equipment in the world's arms markets. Officially, Washington was not providing any of this aid to the Khmer Rouge, but it knew full well that Pol Pot's forces were likely to be the ultimate beneficiaries. As one US official put it: "Of course, if the coalition wins, the Khmer Rouge will eat the others alive".[7] In any event, the CIA and the Chinese were supplying arms directly as well to the Khmer Rouge.[8]

From 1985 on, there was a Federal law prohibiting the government from providing any money to Cambodia which would have the effect of helping the Khmer Rouge's fighting capacity, either directly or indirectly.[9] After reports appeared in 1990 that aid to the coalition was getting into the hands of the Khmer Rouge, the Bush administration announced an official halt to the program.[10] Whether this was a serious effort to comply with the law, or simply an effort at damage control is not known; nor is it clear how long the halt lasted, if indeed it had been halted at all. The following February, the administration acknowledged to Congress that there may have been "tactical military cooperation" between US-backed non-communist forces and the Khmer Rouge during an unspecified period.[11]

The Khmer Rouge were meanwhile using this aid to regularly attack Cambodian villages, seed minefields, kill peasants and make off with their rice and cattle. But they never seriously threatened the Phnom Penh government.

The United States also successfully defended the right of the Khmer Rouge to the United Nations' Cambodian seat, although their government had ceased to exist in January 1979. They held the seat until 1993. Beginning in 1982, the seat ostensibly represented the coalition, but the chief UN representative, Thiounn Prasith, was a leading apologist for Pol Pot's horrendous crimes and played a major role in their cover up. When asked by *Newsweek* about reports that a million Cambodians had perished under Pol Pot's rule, he said: "We estimate between 10,000 and 20,000 persons were killed, 80 per cent of them by Vietnamese agents who infiltrated our government."[12]

During the late 1980s and the early 1990s, the United States pressed for the dismantling of the Cambodian government and the inclusion of the Khmer Rouge in an interim government and in elections[13], despite still-lingering revulsion against Pol Pot and his followers amongst the Cambodian people and the international community, and despite the fact that the Vietnamese withdrew virtually all their forces from Cambodia in September 1989.

The death of Khmer Rouge leader Pol Pot has again brought to international attention one of the most tragic chapters of inhumanity in the twentieth century—senior Khmer Rouge, who exercised leadership from 1975 to 1979, are still at large and share responsibility for the monstrous human rights abuses committed during this period. We must not permit the death of the most notorious of the Khmer Rouge leaders to deter us from the equally important task of bringing these others to justice.

President William Clinton, April 16, 1998[14]

PART II

United States' Use of
Weapons of Mass Destruction

Chapter 11

Bombings

It is a scandal in contemporary international law, don't forget, that while "wanton destruction of towns, cities and villages" is a war crime of long standing, the bombing of cities from airplanes goes not only unpunished but virtually unaccused. Air bombardment is state terrorism, the terrorism of the rich. It has burned up and blasted apart more innocents in the past six decades than have all the antistate terrorists who ever lived. Something has benumbed our consciousness against this reality. In the United States we would not consider for the presidency a man who had once thrown a bomb into a crowded restaurant, but we are happy to elect a man who once dropped bombs from airplanes that destroyed not only restaurants but the buildings that contained them and the neighborhoods that surrounded them. I went to Iraq after the Gulf War and saw for myself what the bombs did; "wanton destruction" is just the term for it.

C. Douglas Lummis, political scientist[1]

The above was written in 1994, before the wanton destruction begot by the bombing of Yugoslavia, the latest in a long list of countries the United States has bombarded since the end of World War II, which is presented below.

There appears to be something about launching bombs or missiles from afar onto cities and people that appeals to American military and political leaders. In part it has to do with a conscious desire to not risk American lives in ground combat. And in part, perhaps not entirely conscious, it has to do with not wishing to look upon the gory remains of the victims, allowing American GIs and TV viewers at home to cling to their warm fuzzy feelings about themselves and their government.

Washington officials are careful to distinguish between the explosives the US drops from the sky and "weapons of mass destruction" (WMD), which only the officially-designated enemies (ODE) are depraved enough to use. The US government speaks sternly of WMD, defining them as nuclear, chemical and biological in nature, and "indiscriminate" (meaning their use can't be limited to military objectives), as opposed to the likes of American "precision" cruise missiles. This is indeed a shaky semantic leg to stand on, given the well-known extremely extensive damage to non-military targets, including numerous residences, schools and hospitals, in the bombings of Iraq and Yugoslavia from American "smart" bombs.

Moreover, Washington does not apply the term "weapons of mass destruction" to other weapons the US has regularly used, such as landmines and cluster (anti-personnel) bombs, which are highly indiscriminate.

WMD are sometimes further defined as those whose effects linger in the environment, causing subsequent harm to people. This would certainly apply to landmines, cluster bombs and depleted uranium weapons, the latter remaining dangerously radioactive after exploding. It would apply less to "conventional" bombs, but even with those there are unexploded bombs lying around, and the danger of damaged buildings later collapsing. But more importantly, it seems highly self-serving and specious, not to mention exceptionally difficult, to try to paint a human face on a Tomahawk Cruise missile whose payload of a thousand pounds of TNT crashes into the center of a densely-populated city, often with depleted uranium in its warhead.

A terrorist is someone who has a
bomb but doesn't have an air force

China 1945–46
Korea and China 1950–53 (Korean War)
Guatemala 1954
Indonesia 1958
Cuba 1959–1961
Guatemala 1960
Congo 1964

Peru 1965
Laos 1964–73
Vietnam 1961–73
Cambodia 1969–70
Guatemala 1967–69
Grenada 1983
Lebanon 1983, 1984 (both Lebanese and Syrian targets)
Libya 1986
El Salvador 1980s
Nicaragua 1980s
Iran 1987
Panama 1989
Iraq 1991–2000
Kuwait 1991
Somalia 1993
Bosnia 1994, 1995
Sudan 1998
Afghanistan 1998
Yugoslavia 1999

Plus?

China, 1999—its heavily bombed embassy in Belgrade is legally Chinese territory, and it appears rather certain now that the bombing was no accident (see chapter 25).

Bulgaria and Macedonia, 1999—both hit by US missiles during the bombing of Yugoslavia.

Pakistan, 1998—at least one missile fell on it during the bombing of Afghanistan.

Philadelphia, Pennsylvania, May 13, 1985—A bomb dropped by a police helicopter burned down an entire block, some 60 homes destroyed, 11 dead, including several small children. The police, the mayor's office and the FBI were all involved in this effort to evict a black organization called MOVE from the house they lived in.

Them other guys are really shocking

"We should expect conflicts in which adversaries, because of cultural affinities different from our own, will resort to forms and levels of violence shocking to our sensibilities."

Department of Defense, 1999[2]

So is nature

What does the media call it when 10,000 persons in Central America die because of a hurricane? "A great human tragedy."

What does the Pentagon call it when 10,000 persons in Iraq die because of American bombing attacks? "A medium case scenario."

This was the estimate made during an internal discussion in 1998 by high-ranking Clinton administration officials on how to respond to Iraq's balking at the extent and nature of UN weapons inspections.[3]

The US vs. Osama bin Laden

Something fundamentally peculiar has happened when the US government fires cruise missiles at an individual, Osama bin Laden. When has a government ever declared war on an individual?

The survivors

A study by the American Medical Association: "Psychiatric disorders among survivors of the Oklahoma City bombing":

> Nearly half the bombing survivors studied had an active postdisaster psychiatric disorder, and full criteria for PTSD [posttraumatic stress disorder] were met by one third of the survivors. PTSD symptoms were nearly universal, especially symptoms of intrusive reexperience and hyperarousal.[4]

Martin Kelly, publisher of a nonviolence website:

> We never see the smoke and the fire, we never smell the blood, we never see the terror in the eyes of the children, whose nightmares will now feature screaming missiles from unseen terrorists, known only as Americans.

CHAPTER 12

Depleted Uranium

"The United States," wrote international environmental activist Dr. Helen Caldicott several years ago, "has conducted two nuclear wars. The first against Japan in 1945, the second in Kuwait and Iraq in 1991."

We can now add a third. Yugoslavia in 1999.

Depleted uranium (DU) is a by-product of the production of enriched fuel for nuclear reactors and weapons. It's used in the manufacture of armaments such as tank cartridges, bombs, rockets and missiles.

Because DU is denser than steel, shells containing it are capable of drilling a hole through the strongest of tank armors. But depleted uranium does have a drawback—it's radioactive. And like all heavy metals, uranium is chemically toxic. Upon impact with a target, DU aerosolizes into a fine mist of particles, which can be inhaled or ingested and then trapped in the lung, the kidneys or elsewhere in the body. This can lead to lung cancer, bone cancer, kidney disease, genetic defects and other serious medical problems. Or a person can be hit by DU shrapnel, and have a chunk of radioactive metal imbedded in their insides. One atomic scientist has asserted that DU particles thrown into the air by the round's impact, or by resultant fires and explosion, can be carried downwind for 25 miles or more.[1]

In the Gulf War, countless Iraqi and American soldiers breathed in the deadly DU dust, the product of tens of thousands of DU rounds fired by US aircraft and tanks. A study by the Operation Desert Shield/Desert Storm Association revealed that out of 10,051 Gulf War veterans who have reported mysterious illnesses, 82 percent had entered captured enemy vehicles, the main targets of DU weapons.

They did so in full innocence of even the existence of DU, let alone its danger.[2]

In 1991, a report of the United Kingdom Atomic Energy Authority warned that there was enough DU radioactive and toxic rubble left behind in Kuwait and southern Iraq to cause 500,000 deaths through increased cancer rates. This is not a realistic calculation because for it to happen all the DU munitions would have to be pulverized into dust and half a million people would have to line up in the desert and inhale equal quantities. But the fact remains that the DU debris was left lying there, in various states of smash-up, subject to any mishap, and with surface radioactivity that will last forever. Moreover, if DU gets into the food chain or water, the potential health problems would be multiplied.[3]

And now it may well be in the soil, the ground water, the air and the lungs of Yugoslavia.

In 1995, Iraqi health officials reported alarmingly high increases in rare and unknown diseases, primarily in children, and presented a study of this state of affairs to the United Nations. The increases occurred in leukemia, carcinoma, cancers of the lung and digestive system, late-term miscarriages, congenital diseases, and deformities in fetuses, such as anencephaly (absence of a brain), and fused fingers and toes, not unlike those found in the babies of Gulf War veterans. The Austrian president of the International Yellow Cross, Dr. Siegwart Gunther, stated that there was one significant common denominator: the allies' use of depleted uranium in the bombing of Iraq.[4]

In Scotland as well, DU has been linked to a leukemia cluster around the Ministry of Defense firing range at Dundrennan, near the Solway Firth. Communities close to the range, where 7,000 shells have been tested since 1983, reportedly show the highest rate of childhood leukemia in the UK.[5]

Victims at home

The United States radiates and poisons its own as well. In training exercises, DU is dropped on the island of San Clemente off the California coast, and perhaps only on some future day will we realize what the effects were of what drifted across to the mainland by air and sea. That island is at least uninhabited, unlike the island of Vieques in Puerto Rico, where over 9,000 American citizens dwell. They've had to endure almost 60 years of aerial target practice and war games, including dropping napalm, and in recent years, depleted uranium shells. Puerto Rican activists claim that Vieques has become contaminated with radioactivity, which contributes to a cancer rate among the island's inhabitants that is twice the national average. Studies have in fact shown that Vieques' cancer rate is by far the highest of any of Puerto Rico's 78 municipalities.[6] Moreover, the island's drinking water has reportedly been contaminated by the chemical soup formed by the myriad pieces of ordnance that have fallen from the sky over the years; a civilian security guard was killed and four others wounded in April 1999 by a bomb that missed its mark by three miles; the landscape is littered with bomb and shell casings, including some that the US Navy warns are still live; a container with three unexploded anti-tank rockets (presumably DU-tipped) was found in a civilian sector in 1997; and, amongst other mishaps, four years earlier five 500-pound bombs were dropped, and exploded, one-and-a-half miles from civilian homes.[7]

In response to rising protests, US military officials told members of the Puerto Rico Senate that they couldn't conduct the exercises on the US East Coast because population centers were too close. For obvious reasons, this remark served only to increase the rage of many in the country.[8] President Clinton, however, showed a bit more sensitivity. He announced that the Navy will abandon the Vieques bombing range. Within five years.[9] Subsequently, Washington offered $40 million in aid to the island, and a further $50 million if the people, in a scheduled referendum, would vote, in effect, to stop putting their health and safety ahead of "national security".

And while we were all quietly and unconsciously living our lives these past decades, the military-industrial complex was quietly paying off members of Congress and state legislatures, and anyone else who could wink and nod, to allow the acquisition of large tracts of public land, primarily in western states, and permit end-runs around existing environmental and other laws, as well as pesky environmental activists. These hundreds of thousands of acres were then turned into depleted-uranium-weapons testing grounds in California, Nevada, Washington, New Mexico and other states.

In New Mexico, open-air testing of DU has been going on in some parts since 1950. Los Alamos National Laboratory, White Sands Missile Range, New Mexico Institute of Mining and Technology in Socorro, Sandia National Laboratories in Albuquerque—these are some of the famous institutions that blast DU munitions into mountains and soil, contaminating the ground, water and air; at the same time, using their not-inconsiderable influence to convince the state's citizens that—even though they admit the contamination—radiation levels are no more than the proverbial "background level", or within EPA safety levels, etc. As the old saying goes, just don't breathe the air or drink the water. And don't raise your babies anywhere nearby.

In Socorro, the residents did not know until 1986 that DU testing had been taking place since 1972 less than two miles from the town square, downwind from the proving grounds. Over the years, there have been a few scattered surveys and anecdotal evidence of a high incidence of the congenital birth defect hydrocephalus, but the year 1999 saw an increasing movement of Socorro citizens demanding broad epidemiological and contamination surveys of the area.[10]

In April 1995, French general and military author Pierre-Marie Gallois observed, "If we equip these tanks with these sorts of munitions [DU], that means that chemical-nuclear war is morally allowable."[11] And legally allowable as well, perhaps, inasmuch as the United States is establishing precedents, albeit by the law of force rather than the force of law, as well as facilitating other precedents—Washington is doing a thriving business selling DU. As of late 1996, the Pentagon had already sold DU ammunition to Thailand, Taiwan, Bahrain, Israel, Saudi Arabia, Greece, Korea, Turkey, Kuwait and other countries.[12]

CHAPTER 13

Cluster Bombs

The Pentagon puts them in the category of "combined effects munition." The manufacturer describes them as an "all-purpose, air-delivered cluster weapons system." Human rights and anti-landmine campaigners say that cluster bombs are indiscriminate weapons of mass destruction, and they have requested that they be placed explicitly on the Geneva Convention list of banned weapons.

Cluster bombs are ingeniously designed. After being dropped from a plane, the heavy weapon breaks open in midair, scattering 200 or more "bomblets", the size of soda cans. The bomblets then explode, shooting out hundreds of high-velocity shards of jagged steel shrapnel, saturating a very wide area. One description of cluster bombs says "they can spray incendiary material to start fires, chunks of molten metal that can pierce tanks and other armor, or shrapnel that can slice with ease through 1/4-inch plate—or human flesh and bone."[1]

The yellow bomblets are aided by little parachutes which slow down their descent and disperse them so they hit plenty of what the manufacturer calls "soft targets"; i.e., people—military or civilian.

According to the Defense Department, US warplanes dropped 1,100 cluster bombs upon Yugoslavia in 1999, each carrying 202 bomblets. Thus, 222,200 of these weapons were propelled across the land. With a stated failure rate of 5 percent (other reports claim rates of 10 to 30 percent), this means that about 11,110 cluster bomblets were left lying unexploded[2], ready to detonate on contact, in effect becoming landmines. Some members of the US military oppose signing The International Treaty Banning the Use, Production, Stockpiling and Transfer of Anti-Personnel Landmines because the treaty's definition of land mines is broad enough to cover cluster bombs. Under the treaty, an anti-personnel mine is one "designed to be exploded by the presence, proximity or contact of a person and that will incapacitate, injure or kill one or more persons." Human-rights activists argue that since manufacturers of cluster bombs calculate "dud rates" into their design, the bombs can be included under the definition.[3] The treaty entered into force on March 1, 1999 without the United States being a signatory.

Unexploded bomblets are even more of a concern than regular landmines because children in particular are drawn to the colorful devices with the little parachutes. (On April 24, 1999, even before the bombing of Yugoslavia had come to an end, five young brothers playing with an unexploded cluster bomb were killed, and two cousins severely injured, near Doganovic in southern Kosovo.[4]) Landmines are usually laid down in more or less expected places, whereas unexploded bomblets can wind up in the back yards of homes, school playgrounds, anywhere. Moreover, the laying down of landmines is often tracked or mapped, the fields marked; not so with unexploded cluster bomblets. Some of them are designed to self-destruct after a set time period, but whether any of those scattered about Yugoslavia are of this type has not been reported. In any event, the Landmine Treaty does not recognize the distinction between "smart" and "dumb" landmines.

When the bombing ended in June, many areas of villages were left virtually uninhabitable, in desperate need of explosive experts who could find and incapacitate all the volatile live remnants. This will hinder agricultural and economic rehabilitation well into the future. Shortly after the end of the bombing, as people began to return to their villages and farms, more incidents involving the unexploded devices occurred, including one in which two British peacekeeping soldiers and three Albanians lost their lives in a Kosovo village.[5]

The words of a Yugoslav orthopedist: "Neither I nor my colleagues have ever seen such horrific wounds as those caused by cluster bombs. They are wounds that lead to disabilities to a great extent. The limbs are so crushed that the only remaining option is amputation. It's awful, awful."[6]

Unexploded ordnance—mainly cluster bombs—are still killing and maiming people in Laos a generation after the massive US carpet-bombing of 1965–73. It is estimated that up to 30 percent of the two million tons of bombs dropped by the United States failed to explode, and there have been 11,000 accidents so far. "More than half of the victims die almost immediately following the accident. If the victim survives, the explosion often causes severe wounding and trauma, especially to the upper half of the body."[7] Vietnam and Cambodia harbor similar dangers. As does the Persian Gulf. A 1999 Human Rights Watch report says that of an estimated 24 to 30 million bomblets dropped during the Gulf War, between 1.2 and 1.5 million did not explode, leading so far to 1,220 Kuwaiti and 400 Iraqi civilian deaths.[8]

The effects of the unexploded munitions from the bombing of Yugoslavia have reached beyond that country's borders. Two months after the war's end, 161 explosive devices, including 97 bomblets, had been recovered by NATO minesweepers in the Adriatic Sea. The munitions caused deaths and injuries to Italian fishermen and cost others the majority of their year's profits. A fishing ban was imposed in the Adriatic to allow minesweepers to collect more of the devices. In addition, tourists abandoned the beaches along the Adriatic coast during the summertime for fear of encountering unexploded bombs.[9]

Meanwhile, the Pentagon is working on the development of newer and better cluster bombs—higher tech, heat-seeking, spraying super-hot shrapnel, greater lethality...a cluster bomb suitable for the new millennium. America deserves nothing less.

CHAPTER 14

United States Use of Chemical and Biological Weapons Abroad

Poison gas and germ weapons turn civilization on its head. Diseases are not fought, but carefully cultivated; doctors use their knowledge of the functions of the human body to devise ever more effective means of halting those functions; agriculturalists deliberately induce fungi and develop crop destroyers...Modern nerve gases were originally designed to help mankind by killing beetles and lice: now, in the hands of the military, they are, literally, insecticides for people. Chemical and biological warfare, as one writer has put it, is "public health in reverse".[1]

Bahama Islands

From the late 1940s to sometime in the 1950s, a joint US-Canada-British team sprayed bacteria known to be dangerous in this area of the Caribbean. Thousands of animals died as a result of the tests. It is not known whether there were any human victims. Details of the test are still classified.[2]

Canada

In 1953, the US Army used air blowers atop trucks to disseminate potentially dangerous zinc cadmium sulfide through the city of Winnipeg as part of its chemical and biological weapons tests.[3]

China and Korea

In the early part of 1952, during the Korean War (1950–53), the Chinese claimed that the United States was dropping quantities of bacteria, insects, feathers, decaying animal and fish parts and many other strange objects that carried disease, over Korea and northeast China. The Chinese government declared that there had been casualties and quick deaths from plague, anthrax and encephalitis, amongst other diseases. They took testimony from some 36 captured American airmen who had purportedly flown the planes with the deadly cargo, and published 25 of these accounts. Many of the men went into voluminous detail about the entire operation: the kinds of bombs and other containers dropped, the types of insects, the diseases they carried, etc. Photographs of the alleged germ bombs and insects were also published. Then, in August, an "International Scientific Committee" was appointed, composed of scientists from Sweden, France, Great Britain, Italy, Brazil and the Soviet Union. After an investigation in China of more than two months, the committee produced a report of some 600 pages, many photos, and the conclusion that: "The peoples of Korea and China have indeed been the objectives of bacteriological weapons. These have been employed by units of the U.S.A. armed forces, using a great variety of different methods for the purpose."

However, some of the American airmen's statements contained so much technical biological information and were so full of communist rhetoric—"imperialist, capitalist Wall Street war monger" and the like—that their personal authorship of the statements must be seriously questioned. Moreover, it was later learned that most of the airmen had confessed only after being subjected to great mental and physical duress, and at least one case of a beating. And some did not necessarily know what they were dropping in their supposed explosive or leaflet bombs. When the pilots came home after the war, they retracted their confessions, but that was under threat of court martial, even "charges of treason", said the US Attorney General, and other threatened punishments—in short, great mental duress.[4]

It should be noted that it was revealed in 1979 that the US Army had experimented within the United States with the use of turkey feathers to conduct biological warfare.[5]

Moreover, in December 1951, the US Secretary of Defense had ordered that "actual readiness be achieved in the earliest practicable time" for offensive use of biological weapons. Within weeks, the chief of staff of the Air Force reported that such capabilities "are rapidly materializing".[6]

The United States also dropped huge amounts of napalm on Korea, an average of 70,000 gallons daily in 1952.[7]

And in 1980 it was disclosed for the first time that during the 1967–69 period, the US had sprayed Agent Orange over 23,607 acres of the southern boundary of the demilitarized zone between North and South Korea, in order to strip vegetation and discourage North Korean infiltration.[8]

Vietnam

For about a decade beginning in the early 1960s, the United States sprayed tens of thousands of tons of herbicides over three million acres of South Vietnam (as well as parts of Laos and Cambodia) to wipe out the foliage used as a cover by the enemy and to destroy crops. The herbicides, particularly the extensively-used Agent Orange, polluted Vietnam with some five hundred pounds of dioxin, a nearly indestructible pollutant that is regarded as one of the most toxic substances in the world; at least as toxic as nerve gas, and highly carcinogenic. Amongst other health effects associated with exposure to dioxin are metabolic disorders, immunological abnormalities, reproductive abnormalities, and neuro-psychiatric disorders.[9] Three ounces in the water supply is thought to be enough to wipe out the population of New York.[10]

As many as two million people were affected by these poisons in Vietnam (in addition to many thousands of American soldiers). There have been reports of high levels of birth defects in areas which were saturated with Agent Orange, and the Vietnam government estimates that the various chemicals have contributed to birth defects in

500,000 children, although this has not been documented.[11] No compensation has ever been paid by the United States to the Vietnamese people or government for any damage to health.

In addition, the US Army employed CS, DM and CN gasses, which, Washington officials insisted, did not constitute "gas warfare". They designated these gasses as "riot control" agents. The Army pumped CS gas—a violent purgative that causes uncontrollable vomiting—into Vietnamese tunnels and caves, causing many Vietcong to choke to death on their own vomit in the confined spaces.[12] The North Vietnamese branch of the International Red Cross and other international sources reported numerous deaths amongst women and children from these gasses, as well as injuries such as destroyed eye balls, blistered faces and scorched and erupted skin.[13] US Deputy Secretary of Defense Cyrus Vance admitted that cyanide and arsenic compounds were being used as well.[14] Other harmful chemicals employed by the US in Vietnam were napalm and Naphthalene flame throwers.

Laos

In September 1970, American forces in Laos, acting under "Operation Tailwind", used aerosolized sarin nerve gas (referred to also as CBU-15 or GB) to prepare their entry in an attack upon a Laotian village base camp, with the object of killing a number of American military defectors who were reported to be there. The operation succeeded in killing in excess of 100 people, military and civilian, including at least two Americans. How many died before the attack from the gas and how many from the attack itself is not known.

Sarin, which was developed in Germany in the 1930s, can kill within minutes after inhalation of its vapor. A tiny drop of it on the skin will do the same; it may even penetrate ordinary clothing. It works by inhibiting an enzyme needed to control muscle movements. Without the enzyme, the body has no means of stopping the activation of muscles, and any physical horror is possible.

When the invading Americans were making their getaway, they were confronted by a superior force of North Vietnamese and communist Pathet Lao soldiers. The Americans called for help from the air. Very shortly, US planes were overhead dropping canisters of sarin upon the enemy. As the canisters exploded, a wet fog enveloped the enemy soldiers, who dropped to the ground, vomiting and convulsing. Some of the gas spread towards the Americans, not all of whom were adequately protected. Some began vomiting violently. Today, one of them suffers from creeping paralysis, which his doctor diagnoses as nerve-gas damage.[15]

This story was reported on June 7, 1998, on the TV program "NewsStand: CNN & Time", and featured Admiral Thomas Moorer, who had been Chairman of the Joint Chiefs of Staff in 1970, as well as lesser military personnel, both on and off camera, who corroborated the incidents described above.

Then all hell broke loose. This was a story too much in conflict—painfully so—with American schoolbooks, Readers Digest, the flag, apple pie and mom. It was damage-control time. The big guns were called out—Henry Kissinger, Colin Powell, Green Beret veterans, the journalistic elite, the Pentagon itself. The story was wrong, absurd, slanderous, they all cried. CNN retracted, Moorer retracted, the show's producers were fired...lawsuits all over the place...[16]

Like the dissidents who became "non-persons" under Stalin, Operation Tailwind is now officially a "non-event".

Notwithstanding this, the program's producers, April Oliver and Jack Smith, put together a 77-page document supporting their side of the story, with actual testimony by military personnel confirming the use of the nerve gas.[17]

Panama

From the 1940s to the 1990s, the United States used various parts of Panama as a testing ground for all manner of chemical weapons, including mustard gas, VX, sarin, hydrogen cyanide and other nerve agents, in such forms as mines, rockets and shells; perhaps tens of thousands of chemical munitions in total. Some of the earlier tests used US troops as guinea pigs, with horrific results for some of the soldiers. When the US military vacated Panama at the end of 1999, it left behind many sites containing chemical and conventional weapons residue, including numerous chemical weapons dropped from planes which failed to detonate. Since 1979, 21 Panamanians have died from accidents with unexploded conventional weapons.[18]

The US military also conducted secret tests of Agent Orange and other toxic herbicides in Panama during the 1960s and 70s, potentially exposing many civilians and military personnel to these lethal chemicals. Hundreds of drums of dioxin-containing Agent Orange were shipped to Panama. Spraying was carried out in jungle areas and near popular outdoor sites in an effort to simulate the tropical battlefield conditions of Southeast Asia.[19]

During the invasion of Panama in December 1989 it was reported that the semi-mountainous village of Pacora, near Panama City, was bombed with a chemical substance by helicopters and aircraft from the US Southern Command in Panama. Residents complained to human-rights organizations and the press that the substances burned their skin, producing intense stinging and diarrhea. The bombing may have been carried out to keep the villagers from offering any assistance to the Panamanian soldiers who were camped in the nearby mountains.[20] What the long-term effects of the chemical exposure have been are not known.

Cuba

1) In August 1962, a British freighter under Soviet lease, having damaged its propeller on a reef, crept into the harbor at San Juan, Puerto Rico for repairs. It was bound for a Soviet port with 80,000 bags of Cuban sugar. The ship was put into dry dock and 14,135 sacks of sugar were unloaded to a warehouse to facilitate the repairs. While in the warehouse, the sugar was contaminated by CIA agents with a substance that was allegedly harmless but unpalatable. When President Kennedy learned of the operation he was furious because it had taken place in US territory and if discovered could provide the Soviet Union with a propaganda field day and set a terrible precedent for chemical sabotage in the Cold War. He directed that the sugar not be returned to the Russians, although what explanation was given to them is not publicly known.[21] Similar undertakings were apparently not canceled. A CIA official, who helped direct worldwide sabotage efforts against Cuba, later revealed that "There was lots of sugar being sent out from Cuba, and we were putting a lot of contaminants in it."[22]

2) The same year, a Canadian agricultural technician working as an adviser to the Cuban government was paid $5,000 by "an American military intelligence agent" to infect Cuban turkeys with a virus which would produce the fatal Newcastle disease. Subsequently, 8,000 turkeys died. The technician later claimed that although he had been to the farm where the turkeys had died, he had not actually administered the virus, but had instead pocketed the money, and that the turkeys had died from neglect and other causes unrelated to the virus. This may have been a self-serving statement. The *Washington Post* reported that "According to U.S. intelligence reports, the Cubans—and some Americans—believe the turkeys died as the result of espionage."[23]

3) According to a participant in the project:

> During 1969 and 1970, the CIA deployed futuristic weather modification technology to ravage Cuba's sugar crop and undermine the economy. Planes from the China Lake Naval Weapons Center in the California desert, where high tech was developed, overflew the island, seeding rain clouds with crystals that precipitated torrential rains over non-agricultural areas and left the cane fields arid (the downpours caused killer flash floods in some areas).[24]

This said, it must be pointed out while it's not terribly surprising that the CIA would have attempted such a thing, it's highly unlikely that it would have succeeded except through a great stroke of luck; i.e., heavy rains occurring at just the right time.

4) In 1971, also according to participants, the CIA turned over to Cuban exiles a virus which causes African swine fever. Six weeks later, an outbreak of the disease in Cuba forced the slaughter of 500,000 pigs to prevent a nationwide animal epidemic. The outbreak, the first ever in the Western hemisphere, was called the "most alarming event" of the year by the United Nations Food and Agricultural Organization.[25]

5) Ten years later, the target may well have been human beings, as an epidemic of dengue hemorrhagic fever (DHF) swept across the Cuban island. Transmitted by blood-eating insects, usually mosquitos, the disease produces severe flu symptoms and incapacitating bone pain.

Between May and October 1981, over 300,000 cases were reported in Cuba with 158 fatalities, 101 of which were children under 15.[26]

The Center for Disease Control later reported that the appearance in Cuba of this particular strain of dengue, DEN-2 from Southeast Asia, had caused the first major epidemic of DHF ever in the Americas.[27] Castro announced that Cuba had asked the United States for a pesticide to help eradicate the fever-bearing mosquito, but had not been given any.[28]

In 1956 and 1958, declassified documents have revealed, the US Army loosed swarms of specially bred mosquitos in Georgia and Florida to see whether disease-carrying insects could be weapons in a biological war. The mosquitos bred for the tests were of the *Aedes Aegypti* type, the precise carrier of dengue fever as well as other diseases.[29]

In 1967 it was reported by *Science* magazine that at the US government center in Fort Detrick, Maryland, dengue fever was amongst those "diseases that are at least the objects of considerable research and that appear to be among those regarded as potential BW [biological warfare] agents."[30] Then, in 1984, a Cuban exile on trial in New York on an unrelated matter testified that in the latter part of 1980 a ship traveled from Florida to Cuba with:

> a mission to carry some germs to introduce them in Cuba to be used against the Soviets and against the Cuban economy, to begin what was called chemical war, which later on produced results that were not what we had expected, because we thought that it was going to be used against the Soviet forces, and it was used against our own people, and with that we did not agree.[31]

It's not clear from the testimony whether the Cuban man thought that the germs would somehow be able to confine their actions to only Russians, or whether he had been misled by the people behind the operation.

6) On a clear day, October 21, 1996, a Cuban pilot flying over Matanzas province observed a plane releasing a mist of some substance about seven times. It turned out to be an American crop-duster plane operated by the US State Department, which had permission to fly over Cuba on a trip to Colombia via Grand Cayman Island.

Responding to the Cuban pilot's report, the Cuban air controller asked the US pilot if he was having any problem. The answer was "no". On December 18, Cuba observed the first signs of a plague of *Thrips palmi*, a plant-eating insect never before detected in Cuba. It severely damages practically all crops and is resistant to a number of pesticides. Cuba asked the US for clarification of the October 21 incident. Seven weeks passed before the US replied that the State Department pilot had emitted only smoke, in order to indicate his location to the Cuban pilot.[32] By this time, the *Thrips palmi* had spread rapidly, affecting corn, beans, squash, cucumbers and other crops.

In response to a query, the Federal Aviation Administration stated that emitting smoke to indicate location is "not an FAA practice" and that it knew of "no regulation calling for this practice".[33]

In April 1997, Cuba presented a report to the United Nations which charged the US with "biological aggression" and provided a detailed description of the 1996 incident and the subsequent controversy.[34] In August, signatories of the Biological Weapons Convention convened in Geneva to consider Cuba's charges and Washington's response. In December, the committee reported that due to the "technical complexity" of the matter, it had not proven possible to reach a definitive conclusion. There has not been any further development on the issue since that time.[35]

The full extent of American chemical and biological warfare against Cuba will never be known. Over the years, the Castro government has in fact blamed the United States for a number of other plagues which afflicted various animals and crops.[36] In 1977, newly-released CIA documents disclosed that the Agency "maintained a clandestine anti-crop warfare research program targeted during the 1960s at a number of countries throughout the world."[37]

The US military abroad—a deadly toxic legacy

It's not quite chemical or biological weaponry, but it's toxic, it sickens and it kills. It's what thousands of American military installations in every corner of the world (hundreds in Germany alone) have left behind: serious environmental damage. The pollution is remarkably widespread, the record too extensive to offer more than a taste here, such as this snippet from a lengthy piece in the *Los Angeles Times*:

> U.S. military installations have polluted the drinking water of the Pacific island of Guam, poured tons of toxic chemicals into Subic Bay in the Philippines, leaked carcinogens into the water source of a German spa, spewed tons of sulfurous coal smoke into the skies of Central Europe and pumped millions of gallons of raw sewage into the oceans.[38]

The military has done the same in the United States at countless installations.[39]

CHAPTER 15

United States Use of Chemical and Biological Weapons at Home

In a January 1999 interview, President Clinton said that what keeps him awake some nights is the fear of germ warfare.[1] It is safe to say that he did not have the Department of Defense or the CIA in mind as the purveyor of the source of his fear. Yet for two decades these two institutions conducted tests in the open air in the United States, exposing millions of Americans to large clouds of possibly-dangerous bacteria and chemical particles. They did so without informing the potentially affected populations, without taking any precautions to protect the health and safety of these people, and with no follow-up monitoring of the effects.

Government officials have consistently denied that the biological agents used could be harmful despite a plentitude of expert and objective scientific evidence that exposure to heavy concentrations of even apparently innocuous organisms can cause illness, at a minimum to the most vulnerable segments of the population—the elderly, children and those suffering from a variety of ailments. "There is no such thing as a microorganism that cannot cause trouble," George Connell, assistant to the director of the Centers for Disease Control and Prevention, testified before the Senate in 1977. "If you get the right concentration at the right place, at the right time and in the right person, something is going to happen."[2]

The Army has acknowledged that between 1949 and 1969, 239 populated areas from coast to coast were blanketed with various organisms during tests designed to measure patterns of dissemination in the air, weather effects, dosages, optimum placement of the source and other factors. Testing over such areas was supposedly suspended after 1969, but there is no way to be certain of this. In any event, open air spraying continued at Dugway Proving Ground in Utah.[3]

Following is a small sample of the tests carried out in the 1949–69 period:

Watertown, N.Y. area and Virgin Islands

1950: The Army used aircraft and homing pigeons to drop turkey feathers dusted with cereal rust spores to contaminate oat crops, to prove that a "cereal rust epidemic" could be spread as a biological warfare weapon.[4]

San Francisco Bay Area

September 20–27, 1950: Six experimental biological warfare attacks by the US Army from a ship, using *Bacillus globigii* and *Serratia marcescens*, at one point forming a cloud about two miles long as the ship traveled slowly along the shoreline of the bay. One of the stated objectives of the exercise was to study "the *offensive* possibilities of attacking a seaport city with a BW [biological warfare] aerosol" from offshore. (emphasis added). Beginning on September 29, patients at Stanford University's hospital in San Francisco were found to be infected by *Serratia marcescens*. This type of infection had never before been reported at the hospital. Eleven patients became infected, and one died.[5] According to a report submitted to a Senate committee by a professor of microbiology at the State University of New York at Stony Brook: "an increase in the number of *Serratia marcescens* can cause disease in a healthy person and…serious disease in sick people."[6]

Between 1954 and 1967, other tests were carried out in the Bay Area, including some with a base of operations at Fort Cronkhite in Marin County.[7]

Minneapolis

1953: 61 releases of zinc cadmium sulfide in four sections of the city, involving massive exposure of people at home and children in school. The substance was later described by the EPA as "potentially hazardous because of its cadmium content", and a former Army scientist, writing in the professional journal *Atmosphere Environment*, in 1972, said that cadmium compounds, including zinc cadmium sulfide, are "highly toxic and the use of them in open atmospheric experiments presents a human health hazard". He stated that the symptoms produced by exposure to zinc cadmium sulfide include lung damage, acute kidney inflammation and fatty degeneration of the liver.[8]

St. Louis

1953: 35 releases of zinc cadmium sulfide over residential, commercial and downtown areas, including the Medical Arts Building, which presumably contained a number of sick people whose illnesses could be aggravated by inhaling toxic particles.[9]

Washington, DC area

1953: Aerial spraying from a height of 75 feet of zinc cadmium sulfate combined with *lycopodium* spores. The areas sprayed included the Monocacy River Valley in Maryland and Leesburg, Virginia, 30 miles from the capital.[10]

In 1969, the Army conducted 115 open-air tests of zinc cadmium sulfate near Cambridge, Maryland.[11]

Earlier in the 1960s, the Army covertly disseminated a large number of bacteria in Washington's National Airport to evaluate how easy it would be for an enemy agent to scatter smallpox through the entire country by infecting air travelers. The bacterium used, *Bacillus subtilis*, is potentially harmful to the infirm and the elderly, whose immune system is impaired, and to those with cancer, heart disease or a host of other ailments, according to a professor of microbiology at the Georgetown University Medical Center. A similar experiment was carried out at the Washington Greyhound bus terminal.

Sometime during Richard Nixon's time in office (apparently 1969), the Army "assassinated" him with germs via the White House air conditioning system.[12]

And at a building used by the Food and Drug Administration, the Army surreptitiously placed a (supposedly harmless) colored dye into the water system. Whether anyone suffered harm from drinking a certain quantity of that water is not known.[13]

Florida

1955: The CIA conducted at least one open-air test with whooping-cough bacteria around the Tampa Bay area. The number of whooping cough cases recorded in Florida jumped from 339 and one death in 1954 to 1080 and 12 deaths in 1955. The Tampa Bay area was one of three places that showed a sharp increase in 1955.[14]

Savannah, Georgia and Avon Park, Florida

1956–58: The Army, wishing to test "the practicality of employing *Aedes aegypti* mosquitos to carry a BW agent", released over wide areas hundreds of thousands, if not millions, of this mosquito, which can be a carrier of yellow fever and dengue fever, both highly dangerous diseases. The Army stated that the mosquitos were uninfected, but prominent scientists said that, for several reasons, the experiment was not without risk, and was a "terrible idea".[15] The actual effects upon the targeted population will probably never be known.

New York City

Feb. 11–15, 1956: A CIA-Army team sprayed New York streets and the Holland and Lincoln tunnels, using trick suitcases and a car with a dual muffler.[16]

June 6–10, 1966: The army report of this test was called "A Study of the Vulnerability of Subway Passengers in New York City to Covert Attack with Biological Agents". Trillions of *Bacillus subtilis variant niger* were released into the subway system during rush hours. One method was to use light bulbs filled with the bacteria; these were unobtrusively shattered at sidewalk level on subway ventilating grills or tossed onto the roadbeds inside the stations. Aerosol clouds were momentarily visible after a release of bacteria from the light bulbs. The report noted that "When the cloud engulfed people, they brushed their clothing, looked up at the grating apron and walked on."[17] The wind of passing trains spread the bacteria along the tracks; in the time it took for two trains to pass, the bacteria were spread from 15th Street to 58th Street.[18] It will never be known how many people later became ill from being unsuspecting guinea pigs, for the United States Army exhibited not the slightest interest in this question.

Chicago

1960s: The Chicago subway system was the scene of a similar Army experiment.[19]

Stockyards

November 1964 to January 1965: The Army conducted aerosol tests over stockyards in Texas, Missouri, Minnesota, South Dakota, Iowa and Nebraska, using "anti-animal non-biological simulants".[20] It's not clear why stockyards were chosen, or what effect this might have had upon the meat consumed by the public.

Nuremberg

The International Military Tribunal at Nuremberg, Germany, 1946–1949, revealed many details of the Nazi medical experiments on involuntary subjects, leading the judges to formulate a set of principles that came to be called The Nuremberg Code; in effect, a bill of rights for people selected for medical experimentation. The Code's first tenet states: "The voluntary consent of the human subject is absolutely essential." Very shortly thereafter, the US Army-CIA testing program began, and although the tests were of course nowhere near as gruesome as those of the Nazis, and the subjects of the tests were not humans as such, but rather the behavior of certain substances released in the air, the fact remains that the testers knew that untold numbers of humans were being directly contaminated by the tests, and none of the reports of the tests mentions a word about obtaining the consent of any of these humans. If the testers did not "know" that the contaminating substances were potentially dangerous, it can only be because they didn't investigate this question, which is the same as saying that they didn't know because they didn't *want* to know.

Not to mention radiating the environment

During the period of 1948–1952, the government conducted many *deliberate* releases of radioactive material, mainly from airplanes, which carried as much as 10 miles over populated areas, in order to study fallout patterns and the rate at which radioactivity decayed, and to study the feasibility of creating "an offensive radiation warfare device".[21]

And the face-to-face human experimentation

In terms of sheer numbers, there can not be any parallel in all of history...a government conducting innumerable medically dangerous and medically unethical experiments on its own people. For decades after the end of World War II, the US government conducted experiments with literally millions of human subjects, both civilian humans and military humans, for the purpose of measuring the effects upon them of: a)sundry chemical and biological materials, including nerve agents; b)nuclear radiation, including injecting many with plutonium; c)a host of mind-control drugs: LSD and other hallucinogens, as well as various other exotic chemical concoctions.[22]

For the human experimentation, the various government agencies appear to have chosen as their subjects primarily those who had the least political clout, such as servicemen and women, conscientious objectors, prison inmates, blacks, the poor, the retarded, the elderly, the young, mental patients...

> "It's a little cocktail. It'll make you feel better," Helen Hutchison recalled the doctor telling her in July 1946, during a visit to the Vanderbilt University Hospital Prenatal Clinic. It didn't make her feel better at all. It contained radioactive iron. She was one of 829 women to receive various doses of the potion over a two-year period. Both Hutchison and the daughter she carried went on to suffer a lifetime of strange ailments. Hutchison's hair fell out at one point, she suffers from pernicious anemia, and she is highly sensitive to sunlight. Her daughter, now grown, suffers from an immune system disorder and skin cancer.[23]

By 1999, perhaps the American public had learned something. When it was disclosed that the federal government's Los Alamos National Laboratory in New Mexico planned to release a strain of bacteria into the atmosphere to test new biowarfare detectors, the public outcry was such that the test was canceled. At a public hearing aimed at easing the public's fear, a Santa Fe resident asked a Laboratory representative: "If it's so safe, why don't you release it into the office of someone in Washington, DC?"[24]

A final thought...What if?

On June 9, 1969, Dr. Donald M. MacArthur, Deputy Director, Research and Engineering, Department of Defense, testified before Congress.

> Within the next 5 to 10 years, it would probably be possible to make a new infective microorganism which could differ in certain important aspects from any known disease-causing organisms. Most important of these is that it might be refractory [resistant] to the immunological and therapeutic processes upon which we depend to maintain our relative freedom from infectious disease.[25]

CHAPTER 16

US Encouraging the Use of CBW by Other Nations

Egypt

It was reported in 1969 that for some years the US Army had been instructing foreign specialists in chemical and biological warfare. A total of 550 foreigners from 36 nations, including Egypt, Israel, Iraq, Jordan, Lebanon, Saudi Arabia, Yugoslavia and South Vietnam, had taken courses at the Army's Chemical School at Ft. McClellan, Alabama. The Egyptian specialists reportedly used their new American know-how to help plan the poison-gas attacks upon Yemen in 1967. The International Red Cross verified that Egyptian pilots dropped canisters of poison gases from planes over Yemen. Subsequently, the US Defense Intelligence Agency also confirmed this. Some 150 villagers gagged, coughed and bled to death.[1]

South Africa

According to testimony before the Truth and Reconciliation Commission in 1998, the United States encouraged South Africa's apartheid regime to develop a CBW program that was aimed at the country's black population. Dr. Wouter Basson, the South African general who headed the project from its inception in 1981, testified from notes he made of a meeting with US Maj. Gen. William Augerson: "He [Augerson] feels that chemical warfare is an ideal strategic weapon because infrastructure is preserved together with facilities, and only living people are killed. The warm climate of Africa is ideal for this type of weapon because the diffusion of the poison is better and the absorption is increased by perspiration and increased blood flow in the persons who are targets."[2]

South Africa's CBW program did in fact work on a number of projects that echoed US programs: using black soldiers as guinea pigs for experimental drugs; developing a toxin to cause a heart attack, which would appear to be the "natural" cause of death; contaminating drinking water with disease pathogens; using a variety of poisonous gases to paralyze and kill opponents in South Africa and neighboring states.[3]

Iraq

In his January 1998 State of the Union address, President Clinton spoke of how we must "confront the new hazards of chemical and biological weapons, and the outlaw states, terrorists and organized criminals seeking to acquire them." He castigated Iraq for "developing nuclear, chemical and biological weapons" and called for strengthening the Biological Weapons Convention. Who among his listeners knew, who among the media reported, that the United States had been the supplier to Iraq of much of the source biological materials Saddam Hussein's scientists required to create a biological warfare program?

According to reports of a US Senate Committee in 1994: From 1985, if not earlier, through 1989, a veritable witch's brew of biological materials were exported to Iraq by private American suppliers pursuant to application and licensing by the US Department of Commerce. Amongst these materials, which often produce slow, agonizing deaths, were:

Bacillus anthracis, cause of anthrax.

Clostridium botulinum, a source of botulinum toxin.

Histoplasma capsulatam, cause of a disease attacking lungs, brain, spinal cord and heart.

Brucella melitensis, a bacteria that can damage major organs.

Clostridium perfringens, a highly toxic bacteria causing systemic illness.

Clostridium tetani, highly toxigenic.

Also, *Escherichia coli* (*E.coli*); genetic materials; human and bacterial DNA. Dozens of other pathogenic biological agents were shipped to Iraq during the 1980s. The Senate Report pointed out that "These biological materials were not attenuated or weakened and were capable of reproduction."

"It was later learned," the committee stated, "that these microorganisms exported by the United States were identical to those the United Nations inspectors found and removed from the Iraqi biological warfare program."

The report noted further that US exports to Iraq included the precursors to chemical-warfare agents, plans for chemical and biological warfare production facilities and chemical-warhead filling equipment.

These exports continued to at least November 28, 1989 despite the fact that Iraq had been reported to be engaging in chemical warfare and possibly biological warfare against Iranians, Kurds and Shiites since the early 1980s as part of its war with Iran.[4] Presumably, Iraq's use of these weapons against Iran is what Washington expected would happen.

Hypocrisy of this magnitude has to be respected

For the better part of six years, 1992–98, following the Gulf War, the United States, acting through the United Nations, forced Iraq to open up its country to inspection for "weapons of mass destruction"—no building or structure was exempted. The wishes of the Iraqi government to place certain sites off limits were dismissed out of hand by US officials and the American media, who had a lot of fun with the issue. "What does Saddam have to hide?" was the prevailing attitude.

Then, in May 1997, the US Senate passed an act to implement the "Convention on the Prohibition of the Development, Production, Stockpiling and Use of Chemical Weapons and on Their Destruction" ["Chemical Convention"], an international treaty which had been ratified by more than 100 nations in its four-year life. But the Senate insisted on adding an amendment before it would ratify the Convention.

The Senate amendment, Section 307, stipulates that "the President may deny a request to inspect any facility in the United States in cases where the President determines that the inspection may pose a threat to the national security interests of the United States."

Saddam Hussein had asked for no more than this for Iraq.

It can be surmised that under the Senate amendment the White House, Pentagon, etc. would be off limits, as Saddam had insisted his presidential palaces should be, as well as the military unit responsible for his personal security, which an American colonel had demanded to inspect.

Moreover, we now know that in closing off certain places to the inspectors, Saddam was not being entirely paranoid or arbitrary, inasmuch as it was later revealed that for some time the United States had been supplying certain inspectors with the means of planting recording devices wherever they could gain access.

It may be further relevant that a detailed study of the first one-and-a-half years of the Chemical Convention's life has shown that Washington's record in complying with the Convention has been remarkably dismal, setting a rather bad example for other nations.[5]

PART III

A Rogue State versus the World

CHAPTER 17

A Concise History of United States Global Interventions, 1945 to the Present

P resented here is the most extensive compilation ever of serious post-World War II American interventions into the life of other nations, covering many more cases than found in the author's book, *Killing Hope: U.S. Military and CIA Interventions Since World War II.* (Please see this book for further details of some of the interventions and for sources not indicated below.)

The Roman Empire

There was no corner of the known world where some interest was not alleged to be in danger or under actual attack. If the interests were not Roman, they were those of Rome's allies; and if Rome had no allies, the allies would be invented. When it was utterly impossible to con-trive such an interest—why, then it was the national honor that had been insulted. The fight was always invested with an aura of legality. Rome was always being attacked by evil-minded neighbors...The whole world was pervaded by a host of enemies, it was manifestly Rome's duty to guard against their indubitably aggressive designs...Even less than in the cases that have already been discussed, can an attempt be made here to comprehend these wars of conquest from the point of view of concrete objectives. Here there was neither a warrior nation in our sense, nor, in the beginning, a military despotism or an aristocracy of specifically military orientation. Thus there is but one way to an understanding: scrutiny of domestic class interests, the question of who stood to gain.

Joseph Schumpeter, 1919[1]

America is today the leader of a world-wide anti-revolutionary movement in the defense of vested interests. She now stands for what Rome stood for. Rome consistently supported the rich against the poor in all foreign communities that fell under her sway; and, since the poor, so far, have always and everywhere been far more numerous than the rich, Rome's policy made for inequality, for injustice, and for the least happiness of the greatest number.

Arnold Toynbee, 1961[2]

The American Empire:
COMING SOON TO A COUNTRY NEAR YOU

China, 1945–51

At the close of World War II, the US intervened in a civil war, taking the side of Chiang Kai-shek's Nationalists against Mao Tse-tung's Communists, even though the latter had been a much closer ally of the United States in the war. To compound the irony, the US used defeated Japanese soldiers to fight for its side. After their defeat in 1949, many Nationalist soldiers took refuge in northern Burma, where the CIA regrouped them, brought in other recruits from elsewhere in Asia, and provided a large supply of heavy arms and planes. During the early 1950s, this army proceeded to carry out a number of incursions into China, involving at times thousands of troops, accompanied by CIA advisers (some of whom were killed), and supplied by air drops from American planes.

France, 1947

Communist Party members had fought in the wartime resistance, unlike many other French who had collaborated with the Germans. After the war the Communists followed the legal path to form strong labor unions and vie for political office. But the United States was determined to deny them their place at the table, particularly since some unions were taking steps to impede the flow of arms to French forces seeking to reconquer their former colony of Vietnam with US aid. The US funneled very large amounts of money to the Socialist Party, the Communists' chief rival; sent in American Federation of Labor (AFL) experts to subvert the CP's union dominance and import scabs from Italy; supplied arms and money to Corsican gangs to break up Communist strikes, burn down party offices and beat up and murder party members and strikers; sent in a psychological warfare team to complement all of these actions and used the threat of a cutoff of food aid and other aid...all to seriously undermine Communist Party support and prestige. It worked.

A portion of the financing for these covert operations came from the funds of the Marshall Plan, which also helped finance the corruption of the Italian elections of 1948 (see below), and set up a special covert operations agency which later melded into the CIA.[3] These are a few of the hidden sides of the Marshall Plan, which has long been held up to the world as a shining example of America's unselfish benevolence.

At the same time, Washington was forcing the French government to dismiss its Communist ministers in order to receive American economic aid. Said Premier Paul Ramadier: "A little of our independence is departing from us with each loan we obtain."[4]

Marshall Islands, 1946–58

Driven by perceived Cold War exigencies, the United States conducted dozens of ICBM, nuclear bomb and other nuclear tests on this trust territory in the Pacific, after forcing the residents of certain islands, notably Bikini Atoll, to relocate to other, uninhabited islands. In 1968, the former residents of Bikini were told by the Johnson administration that their island had been cleaned and was safe for habitation. Many went back, only to be told later that they had been subjected to massive doses of radiation and would have to leave again. In 1983, the US Interior Department declared that the islanders could return to their homes immediately—provided they ate no home-grown food until the late 21st century.[5] They have never returned.

Italy, 1947–1970s

In 1947, the US forced the Italian government to dismiss its Communist and Socialist cabinet members in order to receive American economic aid. The following year and for decades there-after, each time a combined front of the Communists and Socialists, or the Communists alone, threatened to defeat the US-supported Christian Democrats in national elections, the CIA used every (dirty) trick in the book and trained its big economic, political and psycho-logical-warfare guns on the Italian people, while covertly funding the CD candidates. And it worked. Again and again. This perversion of democracy was done in the name of "saving democracy" in Italy. American corporations also contributed many millions of dollars to help keep the left from a share of power.

Greece, 1947–49

The United States intervened in a civil war, taking the side of the neo-fascists against the Greek left, who had fought the Nazis coura-geously. The neo-fascists won and instituted a highly brutal regime, for which the CIA created a suitably repressive internal security agency. For the next 15 years, Greece was looked upon much as a piece of real estate to be developed according to Washington's needs.

Philippines, 1945–53

The US military fought against the leftist Huk forces even while the Huks were still fighting against the Japanese invaders in the world war. After the war, the US organized Philippine armed forces to continue the fight against the Huks, finally defeating them and their reform movement. The CIA interfered grossly in elections, installing a series of puppets as president, culminating in the long dictatorship of Ferdinand Marcos, for whom torture was *la spécialité de la maison* (see Elections chapter).

Korea, 1945–53

After World War II, the United States suppressed popular progressive organizations, who had been allies in the war—at times with brutal force—in favor of the conservatives who had collaborated with the Japanese. As a result, the best opportunities to unify North and South were derailed. This led to a long era of corrupt, reactionary and ruthless governments in the South and the huge, war-crime filled American military intervention of 1950–53 in the "Korean War", which was far from the simple affair of North Korea invading South Korea on a particular day, which the world has been led to believe.

In 1999, we learned that shortly after the war began, American soldiers machine-gunned hundreds of helpless civilians; amongst many other such incidents, hundreds were killed when the US purposely blew up bridges they were crossing.[6]

Albania, 1949–53

By infiltrating émigré guerrillas into the country, the US and Britain tried to overthrow the communist government and install a new one that would have been pro-Western, albeit composed largely of monarchists and collaborators with Italian fascists and Nazis. Hundreds of the émigrés lost their lives or were imprisoned.

Eastern Europe, 1948–56

Allen Dulles, Director of the CIA, in a remarkable chess game, instigated a high Polish security official, Jozef Swiatlo, to use a controversial American, Noel Field, to spread paranoia amongst the security establishments of Eastern Europe, leading to countless purge trials, hundreds of thousands of imprisonments and at least hundreds of deaths.[7]

Germany, 1950s

The CIA orchestrated a wide-ranging campaign of sabotage, terrorism, dirty tricks and psychological warfare against East Germany. This was one of the factors which led to the building of the Berlin Wall in 1961.

The United States also created a secret civilian army in Germany, which drew up a list of 200 leading Social Democrats, 15 Communists and various others who were to be "put out of the way" if the Soviet Union invaded.

This secret army had its counterparts all over Western Europe as part of "Operation Gladio", developed by the CIA and other intelligence services, and not answerable for its actions under the laws of any state. After NATO was formed in 1949, Gladio came under its discreet aegis. "Gladiators" were responsible for numerous acts of terrorism in Europe, foremost of which was the bombing of the Bologna railway station in 1980, claiming 86 lives. The purpose of the terrorism was to place the blame for these atrocities on the left and thus heighten public concern about a Soviet invasion and at the same time discredit leftist electoral candidates. NATO feared that if the left came to power in the government of any of its members, they might pass legislation that would be a threat to the NATO installations or operations in that country.[8]

Iran, 1953

Prime Minister Mossadegh was overthrown in a joint US-British operation. Mossadegh had been elected to his position by a large majority of parliament, but he had made the fateful mistake of spearheading the movement to nationalize a British-owned oil company, the sole oil company operating in Iran. The coup restored the Shah to absolute power, initiating a period of 25 years of repression and torture, while the oil industry was restored to foreign ownership, with the US and Britain each getting 40 percent.

Guatemala, 1953–1990s

Humorist Dave Barry boils the Monroe Doctrine down to three simple precepts: 1)Other nations are not allowed to mess around with the internal affairs of nations in this hemisphere. 2)But we are. 3) Ha ha ha.

A CIA-organized coup overthrew the democratically-elected and progressive government of Jacobo Arbenz, initiating 40 years of military-government death squads, torture, disappearances, mass executions and unimaginable cruelty, totaling more than 200,000 victims—

indisputably one of the most inhumane chapters of the 20th century. The justification for the coup that has been put forth over the years is that Guatemala had been on the verge of the proverbial Soviet takeover. In actuality, the Russians had so little interest in the country that it didn't even maintain diplomatic relations. The real problem was that Arbenz had taken over some of the uncultivated land of the US firm, United Fruit Company, which had extremely close ties to the American power elite. Moreover, in the eyes of Washington, there was the danger of Guatemala's social-democracy model spreading to other countries in Latin America.

Despite a 1996 "peace" accord between the government and rebels, respect for human rights remains as only a concept in Guatemala; death squads continue to operate with a significant measure of impunity against union activists and other dissidents; torture still rears its ugly head; the lower classes are as wretched as ever; the military endures as a formidable institution; the US continues to arm and train the Guatemalan military and carry out exercises with it; and key provisions of the peace accord concerning military reform have not been carried out.[9]

Costa Rica, mid-1950s, 1970–71

To liberal American political leaders, President José Figueres was the quintessential "liberal democrat", the kind of statesman they liked to think, and liked the world to think, was the natural partner of US foreign policy rather than the military dictators who somehow kept popping up as allies. Yet the United States tried to overthrow Figueres (in the 1950s, and perhaps also in the 1970s, when he was again president), and tried to assassinate him twice. The reasons? Figueres was not tough enough on the left, led Costa Rica to become the first country in Central America to establish diplomatic relations with the Soviet Union and Eastern Europe, and on occasion questioned American foreign policy, like the Bay of Pigs invasion.

Middle East, 1956–58

The Eisenhower Doctrine stated that the United States "is prepared to use armed forces to assist" any Middle Eastern country "requesting assistance against armed aggression from any country controlled by international communism". The English translation of this was that no one would be allowed to dominate, or have excessive influence over, the Middle East and its oil fields except the United States, and that anyone who tried would be, by definition, "communist". In keeping with this policy, the United States twice attempted to overthrow the Syrian government, staged several shows-of-force in the Mediterranean to intimidate movements opposed to US-supported governments in Jordan and Lebanon, landed 14,000 troops in Lebanon, and conspired to overthrow or assassinate Nasser of Egypt and his troublesome Middle-East nationalism.

Indonesia, 1957–58

Sukarno, like Nasser, was the kind of Third World leader the United States could not abide by: a nationalist who was serving the wrong national interest. He took neutralism in the Cold War seriously, making trips to the Soviet Union and China as well as to the White House. He nationalized many private holdings of the Dutch, the former colonial power. And he refused to crack down on the Indonesian Communist Party, which was walking the legal, peaceful road and making impressive gains electorally. Such policies could easily give other Third World leaders "wrong ideas". Thus it was that the CIA began throwing money into the elections, plotted Sukarno's assassination, tried to blackmail him with a phoney sex film, and joined forces with dissident military officers to wage a full-scale war against the government, including bombing runs by American pilots. Sukarno survived it all.

Haiti, 1959

The US military mission, in Haiti to train the troops of noted dictator Francois Duvalier, used its air, sea and ground power to smash an attempt to overthrow Duvalier by a small group of Haitians, aided by some Cubans and other Latin Americans.

Western Europe, 1950s–1960s

For two decades, the CIA used dozens of American foundations, charitable trusts and the like, including a few of its own creation, as conduits for payments to all manner of organizations in Western Europe. The beneficiaries of this largesse were political parties, magazines, news agencies, journalists' and other unions, labor organizations, student and youth groups, lawyers' associations and other enterprises, all ostensibly independent, but nonetheless serving Washington's Cold-War, anti-communist, anti-socialist agenda—an agenda which also included a militarized and united Western Europe, allied to (and dominated by) the United States, and support for the Common Market and NATO, all part of the bulwark against the supposed Soviet threat.

British Guiana/Guyana, 1953–64

The United States and Great Britain made life extremely difficult for the democratically elected leader, Cheddi Jagan, finally forcing him from office (see Elections chapter). Jagan was another Third World leader who incurred Washington's wrath by trying to remain neutral and independent. Although a leftist—more so than Sukarno or Arbenz—his policies in office were not revolutionary. But he was still targeted, for he represented Washington's greatest fear: building a society that might be a successful example of an alternative to the capitalist model. John F. Kennedy had given a direct order for his ouster, as, presumably, had Eisenhower.

One of the better-off countries in the region under Jagan, Guyana, by the 1980s, was one of the poorest. Its principal export had become people.

Iraq, 1958–63

In July 1958, Gen. Abdul Karim Kassem overthrew the monarchy and established a republic. Though somewhat of a reformist, he was by no means any kind of radical. His action, however, awakened revolutionary fervor in the masses and increased the influence of the Iraqi Communist Party. By April of the following year, CIA Director Allen Dulles, with his customary hyperbole, was telling Congress that the Iraqi Communists were close to a "complete takeover" and the situation in that country was "the most dangerous in the world today".[10] In actuality, Kassem aimed at being a neutralist in the Cold War and pursued rather inconsistent policies toward the Iraqi Communists, never allowing them formal representation in his cabinet, nor even full legality, though they strongly desired both. He tried to maintain power by playing the Communists off against other ideological groups.[11]

A secret plan for a joint US-Turkish invasion of the country was drafted by the United States Joint Chiefs of Staff shortly after the 1958 coup. Reportedly, only Soviet threats to intercede on Iraq's side forced Washington to hold back. But in 1960, the United States began to fund the Kurdish guerrillas in Iraq who were fighting for a measure of autonomy[12] and the CIA undertook an assassination attempt against Kassem, which was unsuccessful.[13] The Iraqi leader made himself even more of a marked man when, in that same year, he began to help create the Organization of Petroleum Exporting Countries (OPEC), which challenged the stranglehold Western oil companies had on the marketing of Arab oil; and in 1962 he created a national oil company to exploit the nation's oil.

In February 1963, Kassem told the French daily, Le Monde, that he had received a note from Washington—"in terms scarcely veiled, calling upon me to change my attitude, under threat of sanctions against Iraq...All our trouble with the imperialists [the US and the UK] began the day we claimed our legitimate rights to Kuwait."[14] (Kuwait was a key element in US and UK hegemonic designs over mid-east oil.) A few days after Kassem's remarks were published, he was overthrown in a coup and summarily executed; thousands of communists were killed. The State Department soon informed the press that it was pleased that the new regime would respect international agreements and was not interested in nationalizing the giant Iraq Petroleum Co., of which the US was a major owner.[15] The new government, at least for the time being, also cooled its claim to Kuwait.

Papers of the British cabinet of 1963, later declassified, disclose that the coup had been backed by the British and the CIA.[16]

Soviet Union, 1940s–1960s

The US infiltrated many hundreds of Russian émigrés into the Soviet Union to gather intelligence about military and technological installations; commit assassinations; obtain current samples of identification documents; assist Western agents to escape; engage in sabotage, such as derailing trains, wrecking bridges, actions against arms factories and power plants; or instigate armed political struggle against

Communist rule by linking up with resistance movements. There was also a mammoth CIA anti-Soviet propaganda campaign, highlighted by the covert publishing of well over a thousand books in English, a number by well-known authors, which were distributed all over the world, as well as hundreds in foreign languages.

Vietnam, 1945–73

"What we're doing in Vietnam is using the black man to kill the yellow man so the white man can keep the land he took from the red man."—Dick Gregory

The slippery slope began with the US siding with the French, the former colonizers, and with collaborators with the Japanese, against Ho Chi Minh and his followers, who had worked closely with the Allied war effort and admired all things American. Ho Chi Minh was, after all, some kind of "communist" (one of those bad-for-you label warnings). He had written numerous letters to President Truman and the State Department asking for America's help in winning Vietnamese independence from the French and finding a peaceful solution for his country. All his entreaties were ignored. For he was some kind of communist. Ho Chi Minh modeled the new Vietnamese declaration of independence on the American, beginning it with "All men are created equal. They are endowed by their Creator with…" But this would count for nothing in Washington. Ho Chi Minh was some kind of communist.

More than twenty years and more than a million dead later, the United States withdrew its military forces from Vietnam. Most people believe that the US lost the war. But by destroying Vietnam to its core, by poisoning the earth, the water and the gene pool for generations, Washington had in fact achieved its primary purpose: preventing what might have been the rise of a good development option for Asia. Ho Chi Minh was, after all, some kind of communist.

Cambodia, 1955–73

Prince Sihanouk, yet another leader who did not fancy being an American client. After many years of hostility toward his regime, including assassination plots and the infamous Nixon/Kissinger secret "carpet bombings" of 1969–70, Washington finally overthrew

Sihanouk in a coup in 1970. This was all that was needed to impel Pol Pot and his Khmer Rouge forces to enter the fray. Five years later, they took power. But the years of American bombing had caused Cambodia's traditional economy to vanish. The old Cambodia had been destroyed forever.

Incredibly, the Khmer Rouge were to inflict even greater misery upon this unhappy land. And to multiply the irony, the United States supported Pol Pot and the Khmer Rouge after their subsequent defeat by the Vietnamese (See "Pol Pot" chapter).

Laos, 1957–73

The Laotian left, led by the Pathet Lao, tried to effect social change peacefully, making significant electoral gains and taking part in coalition governments. But the United States would have none of that. The CIA and the State Department, through force, bribery and other pressures, engineered coups in 1958, 1959 and 1960. Eventually, the only option left for the Pathet Lao was armed force. The CIA created its famous *Armeé Clandestine*—totaling 30,000, from every corner of Asia—to do battle, while the US Air Force, between 1965 and 1973, rained down more than two million tons of bombs upon the people of Laos, many of whom were forced to live in caves for years in a desperate attempt to escape the monsters falling from the sky. After hundreds of thousands had been killed, many more maimed, and countless bombed villages with hardly stone standing upon stone, the Pathet Lao took control of the country, following on the heels of events in Vietnam.

Thailand, 1965–73

While using the country to facilitate its daily bombings of Vietnam and Laos, the US military took the time to try to suppress insurgents who were fighting for economic reform, an end to police repression and in opposition to the mammoth US military presence, with its huge airbases, piers, barracks, road building and other major projects, which appeared to be taking the country apart and taking it over. Eventually, the American military personnel count in Thailand reached 40,000, with those engaged in the civil conflict—including

365 Green Beret forces—officially designated as "advisers", as they were in Vietnam.

To fight the guerillas, the US financed, armed, equipped and trained police and military units in counter-insurgency, significantly increasing their numbers; transported government forces by helicopter to combat areas; were present in the field as well, as battalion advisers and sometimes accompanied Thai soldiers on anti-guerrilla sweeps. In addition, the Americans instituted considerable propaganda and psychological warfare activities, and actually encouraged the Thai government to adopt a more forceful response.[17] However, the conflict in Thailand, and the US role, never approached the dimensions of Vietnam.

In 1966, the *Washington Post* reported that "In the view of some observers, continued dictatorship in Thailand suits the United States, since it assures a continuation of American bases in the country and that, as a US official put it bluntly, "is our real interest in this place."[18]

Ecuador, 1960–63

Infiltrating virtually every department of the government, up to and including the second and third positions of power, along with an abundant use of dirty tricks, enabled the CIA to oust President José María Velasco because of his refusal to go along with US Cuba policy and not clamping down hard on the left domestically; and when his replacement also refused to break relations with Cuba, a military leader in the pay of the CIA gave him an ultimatum, which he acceded to.

The Congo/Zaire, 1960–65, 1977–78

In June 1960, Patrice Lumumba—legally and peacefully—became the Congo's first prime minister after independence from Belgium. At Independence Day ceremonies before a host of foreign dignitaries, Lumumba called for the nation's economic as well as its political liberation, recounting a list of injustices against the natives by the white owners of the country. The man was obviously a "communist". And obviously doomed, particularly since Belgium retained its vast mineral wealth in Katanga province, and prominent Eisenhower administration officials had financial ties to the same wealth.

Eleven days later, Katanga seceded; in September Lumumba was dismissed by the president at the instigation of the United States; and in January 1961 he was assassinated, with CIA involvement, after Eisenhower had requested that Lumumba should depart from this life. There followed several years of civil conflict and chaos and the rise to power in 1965 of Mobutu Sese Seko, a man not a stranger to the CIA. Mobutu went on to rule the country (which he renamed Zaire) for more than 30 years, with a level of corruption and cruelty that shocked even his CIA handlers. The Zairian people lived in abject poverty despite the country's extraordinary natural wealth, while Mobutu became a multibillionaire.

In both 1977 and 1978, the Carter administration rushed extensive military aid to Zaire, including airlifting Moroccan troops, to help Mobutu quell rebel uprisings and remain in power. President George Bush was later to remark that Mobutu was "our best friend in Africa".[19]

France/Algeria, 1960s

The CIA apparently supported a French military coup in Algeria to block that country's independence in the face of French president Charles de Gaulle's determination to grant independence. The US was concerned that an independent Algeria would have a "communist" government. Washington also hoped that the repercussions would topple de Gaulle, who was a major obstacle to American hegemonic plans for NATO. A few years later, evidence indicates, the CIA was involved in an aborted plot to assassinate the French president.

Brazil, 1961–64

President João Goulart was guilty of the usual crimes: He took an independent stand in foreign policy, resuming relations with socialist countries and opposing sanctions against Cuba; his administration passed a law limiting the amount of profits multinationals could transmit outside the country; a subsidiary of ITT was nationalized; he promoted economic and social reforms. And Attorney General Robert Kennedy was uneasy about Goulart allowing "communists" to hold positions in government agencies. Yet the man was no radical. He was a millionaire land owner and a Catholic who wore a medal of the Virgin around his neck. That, however, was not enough to save him. In 1964, he was overthrown in a military coup which had covert American involvement and indispensable support. The official Washington line was...yes, it's unfortunate that democracy has been overthrown in Brazil...but still, the country has been saved from communism.

For the next 15 years, all the features of military dictatorship which Latin America has come to know and love were instituted: Congress was shut down, political opposition was reduced to virtual extinction, habeas corpus for "political crimes" was suspended, criticism of the president was forbidden by law, labor unions were taken over by government interveners, mounting protests were met by police and military firing into crowds, peasants' homes were burned down, priests were brutalized...disappearances, death squads, a remarkable degree and depravity of torture...the government had a name for its program: the "moral rehabilitation" of Brazil.

Washington was very pleased. Brazil broke relations with Cuba and became one of the United States' most reliable allies in Latin America.

Peru, 1965

The US military set up "a miniature Fort Bragg" in the Peruvian jungle and proceeded to wipe out several guerrilla groups, which had arisen in response to the deep-seated poverty of the Peruvian masses.

Dominican Republic, 1963–65

In February 1963, Juan Bosch took office as the first democratically elected president of the Dominican Republic since 1924. Here at last was John F. Kennedy's liberal anti-communist, to counter the charge that the US supported only military dictatorships. Bosch's government was to be the long sought "showcase of democracy" that would put the lie to Fidel Castro. He was given the grand treatment in Washington shortly before he took office.

To Washington's dismay, however, Bosch was true to his beliefs. He called for land reform; low-rent housing; modest nationalization of business; foreign investment provided it was not excessively exploitative of the country and other policies making up the program of any liberal Third World leader serious about social change. He was likewise serious about the thing called civil liberties: communists, or those labeled as such, were not to be persecuted unless they actually violated the law.

A number of American officials and congressmen expressed their discomfort with Bosch's plans, as well as his stance of independence from the United States. Land reform and nationalization are always touchy issues in Washington, the stuff that "creeping socialism" is made of. In several quarters of the US press Bosch was red-baited.

In September, the military boots marched. Bosch was out. The United States, which could discourage a military coup in Latin America with a frown, did nothing. (The most recent demonstration of this was in Ecuador in January 2000, where a military coup was rescinded almost immediately after a few calls from Washington officials.)[20]

Nineteen months later, April 1965, a widespread popular revolt broke out, which promised to put the exiled Bosch back into power. The United States sent in 23,000 troops to help crush it.

Cuba, 1959 to present

The motto of the CIA: "Proudly overthrowing Fidel Castro since 1959."[21]

Castro came to power at the beginning of 1959. As early as March 10, a US National Security Council meeting included on its agenda the feasibility of bringing "another government to power in Cuba". There followed 40 years of terrorist attacks, bombings, full-scale military invasion, sanctions, embargos, isolation, assassinations...Cuba had carried out The Unforgivable Revolution, a very serious threat of setting a "good example" in Latin America.

The saddest part of this is that the world will never know what kind of society Cuba could have produced if left alone, if not constantly under the gun and the threat of invasion, if allowed to relax its control at home. The idealism, the vision, the talent, the internationalism were all there. But we'll never know. And that of course has been the idea.

The Cuban government, its critics claim, sees the CIA behind every problem. In actuality, the CIA is behind only half of the problems. The problem is, the Cuban government can't tell which half.

Indonesia, 1965

A complex series of events, involving a supposed coup attempt, a counter-coup, and perhaps a counter-counter-coup, with American fingerprints apparent at various points, resulted in the ouster from power of Sukarno and his replacement by General Suharto and the Indonesian military, which was very closely tied to the US military. The massacre that then began immediately—of communists, communist sympathizers, suspected communists, suspected communist sympathizers and none of the above—was called by the *New York Times* "one of the most savage mass slayings of modern political history". The estimates of the number killed in the course of a few years begin at half a million and go above a million.

It was later learned that the US embassy had compiled lists of "communists", from top echelons down to village cadres, as many as 5,000 names, and turned them over to the army, which then hunted those persons down and killed them. The Americans would then check off the names of those who had been killed or captured. "It really was a big help to the army," said one US diplomat. "They probably killed a lot of people, and I probably have a lot of blood on my hands. But that's not all bad. There's a time when you have to strike hard at a decisive moment."

Ghana, 1966

When Kwame Nkrumah tried to lessen his country's dependence on the West by strengthening economic and military ties to the Soviet Union, China and East Germany, he effectively sealed his fate. A CIA-backed military coup sent the African leader into exile, from which he never returned. A CIA document, declassified in 1977, revealed that the Agency was in close contact with the military plotters and had been reporting to Washington for a year on the military's plans to oust Nkrumah; the last such report was the day before the coup. There is no indication that the CIA ever informed Nkrumah of any of these plots.[22]

Uruguay, 1969–72

The 1960s was the era of the Tupamaros, perhaps the cleverest, most resourceful, most sophisticated, least violent, Robin-Hood-like urban guerrillas the world has ever seen. They were too good to be allowed to endure. A team of American experts arrived, to supply the police with all the arms, vehicles, communications gear, etc. they needed, to train them in assassination and explosives techniques, to teach methods of interrogation *cum* torture, to set up an intelligence service *cum* death squad. It was all-out war against the Tupamaros and any suspected sympathizers. The Tupamaros lost.

In 1998, Eladio Moll, a retired Uruguayan Navy rear admiral and former intelligence chief, testifying before a commission of the Uruguayan Chamber of Deputies, stated that during Uruguay's "dirty war" (1972–1983), orders came from the United States concerning captive Tupamaros. "The guidance that was sent from the U.S.," said Moll, "was that what had to be done with the captured guerrillas was to get information, and that afterwards they didn't deserve to live."[23]

Chile, 1964–73

Salvador Allende was the worst possible scenario for the Washington power elite, who could imagine only one thing worse than a Marxist in power—an *elected* Marxist in power, one who honored the constitution, and became increasingly popular. This shook the very foundation stones upon which the anti-communist tower was built: the doctrine, painstakingly cultivated for decades, that "communists" can take power only through force and deception, that they can retain that power only through terrorizing and brainwashing the population.

After sabotaging Allende's electoral endeavor in 1964, and failing to do so in 1970, despite their best efforts, the CIA and the rest of the American foreign policy machine left no stone unturned in their attempt to destabilize the Allende government over the next three years, paying particular attention to undermining the economy and building up military hostility. Finally, in September 1973, the military, under General Pinochet, overthrew the government, Allende dying in the process.

Thus it was that they closed the country to the outside world for a week, while the tanks rolled and the soldiers broke down doors; the stadiums rang with the sounds of execution and the bodies piled up along the streets and floated in the river; the torture centers opened for business, dogs trained to sexually molest female prisoners were set loose; the subversive books were thrown to the bonfires; soldiers slit the trouser legs of women, shouting that "In Chile women wear dresses!"; the poor returned to their natural state; and the men of the world in Washington and in the halls of international finance opened up their checkbooks. In the end, more than 3,000 had been executed, thousands more disappeared, tens of thousands tortured.[24]

The FBI accommodated the new government by trying to track down Chilean leftists in the United States, while Secretary of State Henry Kissinger assured Pinochet that "In the United States, as you know, we are sympathetic with what you are trying to do here...We wish your government well."[25]

Greece, 1967–74

A military coup took place in April 1967, just two days before the campaign for national elections was to begin, elections which appeared certain to bring the veteran liberal leader George Papandreou back as prime minister. The operation had been a joint effort of the Royal Court, the Greek military, the CIA and the American military stationed in Greece, and was followed immediately by the traditional martial law, censorship, arrests, beatings and killings, the victims totaling some 8,000 in the first month. This was accompanied by the equally traditional declaration that this was all being done to save the nation from a "communist takeover". Torture, inflicted in the most gruesome of ways, often with equipment supplied by the United States, became routine.

George Papandreou was not any kind of radical. He was a liberal anti-communist type. But his son Andreas, the heir-apparent, while only a little to the left of his father, had not disguised his wish to take Greece out of the Cold War, and had questioned remaining in NATO, or at least as a satellite of the United States.

Andreas Papandreou had been arrested at the time of the coup and held in prison for eight months. Shortly after his release, he and his wife Margaret visited the American ambassador, Phillips Talbot, in Athens. Papandreou related the following:

I asked Talbot whether America could have intervened the night of the coup, to prevent the death of democracy in Greece. He denied that they could have done anything about it. Then Margaret asked a critical question: What if the coup had been a Communist or a Leftist coup? Talbot answered without hesitation. Then, of course, they would have intervened, and they would have crushed the coup.

South Africa, 1960s–1980s

The CIA collaborated closely with South African intelligence, one of the principal focuses being the African National Congress, the leading anti-apartheid organization which had been banned and exiled. The Agency cooperated in suppressing internal dissent, provided specific warnings of planned attacks by the ANC and information about ANC members residing in neighboring countries; on at least one occasion, in Mozambique in 1981, this led to South Africa sending an assassination squad to wipe out the fingered individuals. The CIA was also responsible for the capture of ANC leader Nelson Mandela. Additionally, for a number of years in the 1970s and 80s, the US supported South Africa in the UN, and the CIA violated the UN's arms embargo against South Africa (of which the US was a declared supporter) by covertly providing the country with weapons and supporting its efforts to militarily determine the political makeup of Southern Africa.[26]

Bolivia, 1964–75

An armed popular revolt in 1952 had defeated the military and reduced it to a small, impotent and discredited force. But under US guidance and aid, there was a slow but certain rejuvenation of the armed forces. By 1964, the military, with the indispensable support of the CIA and the Pentagon, was able to overthrow President Victor Paz, whom the United States had designated a marked man because of his refusal to support Washington's Cuba policies. The US continued to dictate who should lead Bolivia long after.

In 1967, a CIA operation, employing some of the Agency's Cuban exile agents, tracked down Che Guevara, resulting in his summary execution.

Australia, 1972–75

The CIA channeled millions of dollars to the Labor Party's opposition, but failed to block Labor's election. When the party took power in December 1972, it immediately rankled Washington by calling home Australian military personnel from Vietnam and denouncing US bombing of Hanoi, among other actions against the war. The government also displayed less than customary reverence for the intelligence and national security games so dear to the heart of the CIA. Edward Gough Whitlam, the new prime minister, was slowly but surely sealing his fate. Through complex supra-legal maneuvering, the US, the British and the Australian opposition were eventually able to induce Governor-General John Kerr—who had a long history of involvement with CIA fronts—to "legally" dismiss Whitlam in 1975.

Iraq, 1972–75

As a favor to a very important ally, the Shah of Iran, President Nixon and National Security Adviser Henry Kissinger provided military aid to the Kurds fighting for their autonomy in Iraq, Iran's perennial foe. Though the military aid was to total some $16 million, the object—unknown to the Kurds—was not to win them their autonomy, but to sap the Iraqi resources and distract them from Iran. Said a CIA memo of 1974: "Iran, like ourselves, has seen benefit in a stalemate situation...in which Iraq is intrinsically weakened by the Kurds' refusal to relinquish semi-autonomy. Neither Iran nor ourselves wish to see the matter resolved one way or the other." The congressional Pike Committee, later investigating the CIA, commented: "This policy was not imparted to [the Kurds], who were encouraged to continue fighting. Even in the context of covert action, ours was a cynical enterprise."

In 1975, oil politics brought Iraq and Iran together, and the latter, along with the United States, abandoned the Kurds to a terrible fate. At a crucial point, the Kurds were begging Kissinger for help, but he completely ignored their pleas. Kurd forces were decimated; several hundred of their leaders were executed. Later, when questioned about this by the Pike Committee, Kissinger responded: "Covert action should not be confused with missionary work."[27]

Portugal, 1974–76

A bloodless military coup in 1974 brought down the US-supported 48-year fascist regime that was the world's only remaining colonial power. This was followed by a program centered on nationalization of major industries, workers' control, a minimum wage, land reform and other progressive measures. Washington and multinational officials who were on the board of directors of the planet were concerned. Destabilization became the order of the day: covert actions; attacks in the US press; subverting trade unions; subsidizing opposition media; economic sabotage through international credit and commerce; heavy financing of selected candidates in elections; a US cut-off of Portugal from certain military and nuclear information commonly available to NATO members; NATO naval and air exercises off the Portuguese coast, with 19 NATO warships moored in Lisbon's harbor, regarded by most Portuguese as an attempt to intimidate the provisional government.[28] The Portuguese revolution was doomed. The CIA-financed candidates took and retained power for years.

East Timor, 1975–99

While East Timor was undergoing a process of decolonization from Portugal in 1975, various political groupings were formed on the island. In August one of the parties, the UDT, attempted a coup against Portuguese rule, which was almost certainly instigated by Indonesia. A brief civil war broke out, in which a movement of the left, Fretilin, gained the upper hand. By September, Fretilin had prevailed and in November declared East Timor's independence from Portugal. Nine days later, Indonesia invaded East Timor. The invasion was launched the day after US President Gerald Ford and Secretary of State Henry Kissinger had left Indonesia after giving President Suharto permission to use American arms, which, under US law, could not be used for aggression. Indonesia was Washington's most valuable ally in Southeast Asia, and, in any event, the United States was not inclined to look kindly on any leftist government.[29]

Indonesia soon achieved complete control over East Timor, with the help of American arms and diplomatic support. Daniel Moynihan, who was US ambassador to the UN at the time, later wrote that the "United States wished things to turn out as they did, and worked to bring this about. The Department of State desired that the United Nations prove utterly ineffective in whatever measures it undertook. This task was given to me, and I carried it forward with no inconsiderable success."[30]

Amnesty International estimated that by 1989, Indonesian troops had killed 200,000 people out of a population of between 600,000 and 700,000. The United States stood virtually alone in the world with its consistent support of Indonesia's claim to East Timor, and downplayed the slaughter to a remarkable degree, at the same time supplying Indonesia with all the military hardware and training it needed to carry out the job. Despite denials to the contrary, Washington continued this military aid up to and including the period of extensive massacres of pro-independence Timorese in 1999 by Indonesian soldiers and their militia allies.[31]

In 1995, a senior official of the Clinton administration, speaking of Suharto, said: "He's our kind of guy."[32]

Angola, 1975–1980s

The United States, China and South Africa supported one side of the civil war, while the Soviet Union and Cuba supported the other side. It dragged on bloodily, horribly and pointlessly for decades, and simmers yet, perhaps half a million lives lost, widespread hunger and what is said to be the highest amputee rate in the world, caused by the innumerable land mines. In the early years Henry Kissinger personally prevented what might well have been a peaceful solution, but the man was wholly obsessed with countering Soviet moves anywhere on the planet—significant or trivial, real or imagined, *fait accompli* or anticipated. In the 1990s, Washington tried to rein in its client, Jonas Savimbi, head of UNITA, to keep him from prolonging the war, but it would have been immensely better for the people of Angola if the US had not intervened at all in Angolan politics beginning in the early 1960s. The Russians would then have had no interest. Nor Henry Kissinger.

Jamaica, 1976

Prime Minister Michael Manley got on Washington's bad side, by supporting the wrong faction in Angola, by establishing diplomatic relations with Cuba, and by going up against the transnational aluminum companies. The United States employed many tactics in an attempt to defeat Manley's bid for reelection in 1976, but failed.[33]

Honduras, 1980s

The US turned Honduras into an instant colony in the early 1980s, a military base with thousands of American troops, to support counter-insurgency operations in El Salvador and Guatemala, and, above all, to serve as a staging area, supply center and refuge for the Contras and their war against the Nicaraguan government. Inasmuch as the unin-terrupted continuance of such operations required a quiescent popula-tion, the US gave the Honduran military and police the training, arms, equipment and funds needed to efficiently suppress dissidents— the anti-American types (who mockingly referred to their country as the U.S.S. Honduras), those involved in solidarity campaigns for the Salvadoran rebels and the Sandinistas of Nicaragua and those striving for social change within Honduras, though still far from becoming a guerrilla threat.[34] "American diplomats," observed the *New York Times* in 1988, "exercise more control over domestic politics in Honduras than in any other country in the hemisphere, and in private that fact is universally acknowledged here."[35]

Nicaragua, 1978–90

When the Sandinistas overthrew the Somoza dictatorship in 1978, it was clear to Washington that they might well be that long-dreaded beast—"another Cuba". Under President Carter, attempts to sabotage the revolution took diplomatic and economic forms. Under Reagan, violence was the method of choice. For eight terribly long years, the people of Nicaragua were under attack by Washington's proxy army, the Contras, formed from Somoza's vicious National Guardsmen and other supporters of the dictator. It was all-out war, aiming to destroy the progressive social and economic programs of the government, burning down schools and medical clinics, raping, torturing, mining harbors, bombing and strafing. These were the charming gentlemen Ronald Reagan liked to call "freedom fighters".

In 1990, the US seriously interfered in national elections, result-ing in the defeat of the Sandinistas.[36]

As with Cuba, we'll never know what kind of progressive society the Sandinistas might have created if allowed to live in peace and not have to spend half their budget on fighting a war. Oxfam, the inter-national development organization, said that from its experience of working in 76 developing countries, Nicaragua under the Sandinistas was "exceptional in the strength of that government's commit-ment...to improving the condition of the people and encouraging their active participation in the development process."[37]

A decade after returning to the rule of the free market, Nicaragua had become one of the poorest nations in the hemisphere, with more than half its people suffering from malnutrition and with illiteracy widespread.

Philippines, 1970s–1990s

Another scenario of poverty, social injustice, death squads, torture, etc. leading to wide-ranging protest and armed resistance...time once again for the US military and CIA to come to the aid of the govern-ment in suppressing such movements. In 1987 it was revealed that the Reagan administration had approved a $10 million, two-year plan for increased CIA involvement in the counter-insurgency campaign.[38] The CIA undertook large-scale psychological warfare operations and US military advisers routinely accompanied Philippine troops during their maneuvers.[39] The Philippines has long been the most strategic location for US war-making in Asia, the site of several large American military bases, which have been the object of numerous protests by the citizens. In 1991, the US embassy informed the media that embassy polls indicated that 68 percent, 72 percent, even 81 percent of the Philippine people favored the bases. The polls, however, never exist-ed. "I made the numbers up," an embassy official conceded.[40]

Seychelles, 1979–81

The country's leader, France Albert René, amongst other shortcom-ings in the eyes of Washington, was a socialist, pursued non-align-ment, wanted to turn the Indian Ocean into a nuclear-free zone and was not happy that his island nation was the home of a US Air Force satellite tracking station. For this he was the object of various US destabilization conspiracies beginning in 1979. In November 1981, the CIA reportedly was behind a mercenary invasion of the island nation, which originated in South Africa and got no further than an armed battle at the Seychelles airport.[41]

South Yemen, 1979–84

Partly to cater to the wishes of next-door Saudi Arabia, and partly as Cold-War reflex, the US supported paramilitary forces in South Yemen to undermine the government, which was perceived as the proverbial "Soviet satellite", as opposed to North Yemen, which was seen to be the proverbial "pro-Western" good guys. North and South had been fighting on and off for years. The US sent North Yemen military aid and trained paramilitary forces to blow up bridges and carry out other acts of sabotage in the South. In March 1982, a 13-man paramilitary team was captured in the South; under torture, they confessed (honestly) to a CIA training connection and 12 were executed; the operation soon came to an end. Reagan's CIA Director, William Casey, a genuine anti-Soviet primitive, had been convinced that the South Yemenis were part of a Soviet-run international terrorist network, along with Cubans, the Italian Red Brigades and the IRA.[42] In reality, since 1979, the Soviet Union had been providing military support and advisers to both North and South, sometimes at the very same time, and even helped North Yemen to put down a leftwing guerrilla movement.[43] In 1990, North and South combined into one country, the Republic of Yemen. The Cold War as vaudeville.

South Korea, 1980

In May, the United States—which had the first and last word on matters military in South Korea—acting on a government request, released some South Korean forces from the combined US-Korean command to be used by military strongman Chun Doo Hwan to suppress an uprising of students and workers in the city of Kwangju.[44] The protestors were pressing for an end to martial law, the arrest of dissidents and their families and friends, fraudulent elections, torture and unmet social needs. A brutal crackdown followed, estimates of the death toll ranging between several hundred and 2,000, with a number of gross atrocities committed by the armed forces.[45] The US support came from the Carter administration, heralded as human-rights advocates. Said a State Department spokesman: "Our situation, for better or worse, is that Korea is a treaty ally, and the US has a very strong security interest in that part of the world."[46]

In February 1981, Chun was honored by being invited to the White House as President Reagan's first state visitor; the US and South Korea engaged in the first joint military exercises of the new administration; the administration asked Congress to delay publication of the annual worldwide report on human rights while the South Korean president was still in Washington, to avoid embarrassing him; and Reagan, in his toast to Chun, was moved to declare: "You've done much to strengthen the tradition of 5,000 years' commitment to freedom."[47] In 1996, a Korean court convicted Chun of treason and murder, and sentenced him to death, for his role in the Kwangju massacre.

Chad, 1981–82

The Reagan administration's obsession with Moammar Qaddafi of Libya knew no limits: geographical, legal or ethical. Libya maintained a military force in neighboring Chad at the request of that government—which was faced with armed insurgents—and to serve Libya's desire for a friendly government on its border. The United States wanted to replace the Chadian government with one not very friendly to Libya, at the same time giving free rein to anti-Qaddafi Libyan exiles in Chad to mount attacks on Libya from across the border.

Thus it was that the US, along with France, the former colonial power in Chad, employed bribes and political pressures to induce the Chad government to ask the Libyans to leave—which Libya reluctantly did—and to replace them with forces of the Organization of African Unity. The OAU was given a vague mandate to maintain security in Chad. This proved to be a sort of Trojan horse. The CIA rebuilt an opposition Chadian force in the Sudan and provided it with money, arms, political support and technical assistance. Then, as the OAU stood by doing nothing, this army, led by Hissen Habré, succeeded in overthrowing the Chadian government in June 1982.[48]

With US support, Habré went on to rule for eight years, during which his secret police reportedly killed tens of thousands, tortured as many as 200,000, and disappeared an undetermined number. In 2000, some of his torture victims succeeded in having him indicted in Senegal, where he resided, calling him "Africa's Pinochet".[49]

Grenada, 1979–83

How impoverished, small, weak or far away must a country be before it is not a threat to the US government? In a 1979 coup, Maurice Bishop and his followers had taken power in this island country of 110 thousand, and though their actual policies were not as revolutionary as Castro's, Washington was again driven by its fear of "another Cuba", particularly when public appearances by the Grenadian leaders in other countries of the region met with great enthusiasm.

Reagan administration destabilization tactics against the Bishop government began soon after the coup, featuring outrageous disinformation and deception. Finally came the invasion in October 1983, which put into power individuals more beholden to US foreign policy objectives. The US suffered 135 killed or wounded; there were also some 400 Grenadian casualties, and 84 Cubans, mainly construction workers. The invasion was attended by yet more transparent lies, created by Washington to justify its gross violations of international law.

Suriname, 1982–84

A plot by the United States to overthrow the government because it allegedly was falling into "the Cuban orbit". It was to be an invasion by some 300 men, half US and South American and half Surinamese. The CIA had actually informed Congress of its plan to use a paramilitary force, which President Reagan had authorized. Congress was not enthused, but William Casey and his CIA cowboys went ahead with their planning anyway, and were induced to call it off only after the scheme was discovered by the internal security agency of the Netherlands, the former colonial power in Suriname, when it was known as Dutch Guiana.

Libya, 1981–89

The official reason for the Reagan administration's intense antipathy toward Moammar Qaddafi was that he supported terrorism. In actuality, the Libyan leader's crime was not his support for terrorist groups per se, but that he was supporting the *wrong* terrorist groups; i.e., Qaddafi was not supporting the same terrorists that Reagan was, such as the Nicaraguan Contras, UNITA in Angola, Cuban exiles in Miami, the governments of El Salvador and Guatemala and the US military in Grenada. The one band of terrorists the two men supported in common was the Moujahedeen in Afghanistan.

On top of this, Washington has a deep-seated antipathy toward Middle East oil-producing countries that it can't exert proper control over. Qaddafi was uppity, and he had overthrown a rich ruling clique and instituted a welfare state. He and his country would have to be put in their place. In 1981, US planes shot down two Libyan planes in Libyan air space. Five years later, the United States bombed one of Qaddafi's residences, killing scores of people. There were other attempts to assassinate the man, operations to overthrow him, economic sanctions, and a major disinformation campaign reporting one piece of nonsense after another, including conspicuous exaggerations of his support for terrorism, and shifting the blame for the 1988 bombing of PanAm 103 to Libya and away from Iran and Syria when the Gulf War campaign required the support of the latter two countries. To Washington, Libya was like magnetic north: the finger always pointed there.

Fiji, 1987

Prime Minister Timoci Bavrada was ousted in a military coup only a month after taking office in April following a democratic election. Bavrada, of the Labour Party, made Washington officials unhappy by identifying himself with the non-aligned movement, and even more so by taking office with a pledge to reinstate Fiji as a nuclear-free zone, meaning that nuclear-powered or nuclear-weapons-carrying ships could not make port calls. When Bavrada's predecessor, R.S.K. Mara, instituted the same policy in 1982, he was put under great US pressure to drop it. Said the former US ambassador to Fiji that year, William Bodde, Jr., "a nuclear free zone would be unacceptable to the US given our strategic needs...the US must do everything possible to counter this movement."[50] The following year, Mara dropped the policy. Bavrada would clearly not be so easily swayed. He had taken office as part of a Nuclear-Free-Pacific Coalition.

Two weeks after Bavrada took office, American UN Ambassador Vernon Walters visited the island. The former Deputy Director of the CIA has had a history of showing up shortly before, during, or shortly after CIA destabilization operations. Walters met with Bavrada, ostensibly to discuss UN matters. He also met with Lt. Col. Sitiveni Rabuka, third-in-command of the Army. Two weeks later, Rabuka led a military coup which ousted Bavrada.

During Bavrada's month in office, a multi-layered "Libyan scare" campaign suddenly and inexplicably broke out in the Pacific area. The Reagan administration had already been exposed for its phoney Libya-scare campaign in the United States. When the Fiji coup took place, Rabuka and his supporters pointed to the Libyan "threat" as justifying the coup.[51]

There are more of such "coincidences" in this drama, including appearances in Fiji before the coup of the National Endowment for Democracy (q.v.) and its funding, some of the CIA's labor mafia, and units of the US military in the Pacific.[52]

The day after the coup, a Pentagon source, while denying US involvement, declared: "We're kinda delighted...All of a sudden our ships couldn't go to Fiji, and now all of a sudden they can."[53]

Panama, 1989

Less than two weeks after the fall of the Berlin Wall, the United States showed its joy that a new era of world peace was now possible by invading Panama, as Washington's mad bombers struck again. On December 20, 1989, a large tenement barrio in Panama City was wiped out; 15,000 people were left homeless. Counting several days of ground fighting between US and Panamanian forces, 500-something natives dead was the official body count—i.e., what the United States and the new US-installed Panamanian government admitted to. Other sources, examining more evidence, concluded that thousands had died. Additionally, some 3,000 Panamanians were wounded, 23 Americans died, 324 were wounded.

Question from reporter: "Was it really worth it to send people to their death for this? To get Noriega?"

George Bush: "Every human life is precious, and yet I have to answer, yes, it has been worth it."

Manuel Noriega had been an American ally and informant for years until he outlived his usefulness. But getting him was hardly a major motive for the attack. Bush wanted to send a clear message to the people of Nicaragua, who had an election scheduled in two months, that this might be their fate if they reelected the Sandinistas. Bush also wanted to flex some military muscle to illustrate to Congress the need for a large combat-ready force despite the very recent dissolution of the "Soviet threat". The official explanation for the American ouster was Noriega's drug trafficking, which Washington had known about for years and had not been at all bothered by. And they could easily have gotten their hands on the man without wreaking such terrible devastation upon the Panamanian people.[54]

Afghanistan, 1979–92

The striking repression of women in Afghanistan carried out by the Taliban Islamic fundamentalists is well known. Much less publicized is that in the late 1970s and most of the 1980s Afghanistan had a government committed to bringing the incredibly underdeveloped country into the 20th century (never mind the 21st), including giving women equal rights. The United States, however, poured billions of dollars into waging a terrible war against this government, simply because it was supported by the Soviet Union. By aiding the fundamentalist opposition, Washington knowingly and deliberately increased the probability of a Soviet intervention.[55] And when that occurred, the CIA became the grand orchestrator: hitting up Middle-Eastern countries for huge financial support, on top of that from Washington; pressuring and bribing neighboring Pakistan to rent out its country as a military staging area and sanctuary; supplying a great arsenal of weaponry and military training.

In the end, the United States and the Taliban "won", and the women, and the rest of Afghanistan, lost. More than a million dead, three million disabled, five million refugees, in total about half the population.

El Salvador, 1980–92

Salvador's dissidents tried to work within the system. But with US support, the government made that impossible, using repeated electoral fraud and murdering hundreds of protestors and strikers. In 1980, the dissidents took to the gun, and civil war. Washington responded immediately.

Officially, the US military presence in El Salvador was limited to an advisory capacity. In actuality, military and CIA personnel played a more active role on a continuous basis. About 20 Americans were killed or wounded in helicopter and plane crashes while flying reconnaissance or other missions over combat areas, and considerable evidence surfaced of a US role in the ground fighting as well. The war came to an official end in 1992 with these results: 75,000 civilian deaths; the US Treasury depleted by six billion dollars; meaningful social change thwarted; a handful of the wealthy still own the country; the poor remain as ever; dissidents still have to fear right-wing death squads; there would be no profound social change in El Salvador.

Haiti, 1987–94

The US supported the Duvalier family dictatorship for 30 years, then opposed the reformist priest, Jean-Bertrand Aristide. Meanwhile, the CIA was working intimately with death squads, torturers and drug traffickers. With this as background, in 1994 the Clinton White House found itself in the awkward position of having to pretend— because of all their rhetoric about "democracy"—that they supported the democratically-elected Aristide's return to power after he had been ousted in a 1991 military coup. After delaying his return for more than two years, Washington finally had its military restore Aristide to office, but only after obliging the priest to guarantee that he would not help the poor at the expense of the rich, literally; and that he would stick closely to free-market economics. This meant that Haiti would continue to be the assembly plant of the Western Hemisphere, with its workers receiving starvation wages, literally. If Aristide had thoughts about breaking the agreement forced upon him, he had only to look out his window—US troops were stationed in Haiti for the remainder of his term.

Bulgaria, 1990–91

In November 1999, President Clinton visited Bulgaria and told a crowd in Sofia that he hailed them for throwing off communism and holding fair elections.[56] What he failed to mention was that after one of their fair elections had been won by the communists, the US government had proceeded to overthrow them.

In 1990, the National Endowment for Democracy (NED) poured more than $1.5 million into Bulgaria in an attempt to defeat the Bulgarian Socialist Party (the former Communist Party) in the June 1990 national election. On the basis of population, this was equivalent to a foreign power injecting some $38 million into an American electoral campaign. The main recipient of NED largesse was the leading opposition party, the Union of Democratic Forces, which received $517,000, in addition to its newspaper receiving $233,000.[57] Much to the shock and dismay of Washington, the BSP won.

This would not do. Washington's ideological bottom line was that the Bulgarian Socialist Party could not, and would not, be given the chance to prove that a democratic, socialist-oriented mixed economy could succeed in Eastern Europe while the capitalist model was already beginning to disillusion people all around it. NED stepped in with generous funding and advice to the specific opposition groups which carried out a campaign of chaos lasting almost five months: very militant and disruptive street demonstrations, paralyzing labor strikes, sit-ins, hunger strikes, arson...parliament was surrounded, the government was under siege...until finally the president was forced to resign, followed by some of his ministers; lastly, the prime minister gave up his office.

In 1991, NED again threw hundreds of thousands of dollars into the election; this time, what NED calls the "democratic forces" won.[58]

Albania, 1991–92

A tale very similar to that of Bulgaria. A Communist government won overwhelming endorsement in the March 1991 elections, followed immediately by two months of widespread unrest, including street demonstrations and a general strike lasting three weeks, which finally led to the collapse of the new government by June.[59] NED had been there also, providing $80,000 to the labor movement and $23,000 "to support party training and civic education programs".[60]

A new election was held in March 1992. During the election campaign, US political strategists and diplomats, including the American ambassador, openly accompanied candidates of the Democratic Party (the Communists' chief opposition) on their stumping tours and got out the message that said—frankly and explicitly—If the Communists win again, there will be no US aid, and "a lot of Western investors and governments are going to direct their aid elsewhere". The NED, once again, was there with all kinds of goodies for "the good guys", including brand new Jeep Cherokees.[61] The Democratic Party won.

Somalia, 1993

It was supposed to be a mission to help feed the starving masses. Before long, the US was trying to rearrange the country's political map by eliminating the dominant warlord, Mohamed Aidid, and his power base. On many occasions, beginning in June, US helicopters strafed groups of Aidid's supporters and fired missiles at them. Scores were killed. Then, in October, a daring attempt by some 120 elite American forces to kidnap two leaders of Aidid's clan resulted in a horrendous bloody battle. The final tally was five US helicopters shot down, 18 Americans dead, 73 wounded, 500 to 1000 Somalians killed, many more injured.

It's questionable that getting food to hungry people was as important as the fact that four American oil giants were holding exploratory rights to large areas of land and were hoping that US troops would put an end to the chaos which threatened their highly expensive investments. There was also the Pentagon's ongoing need to sell itself to those in Congress who were trying to cut the military budget in the post-Cold War world. "Humanitarian" actions and (unnecessary) amphibious landings by US Marines on the beach in the glare of TV cameras were thought to be good selling points. Washington designed the operation in such a way that the show would be run by the US military and not the United Nations, under whose aegis it supposedly fell.

In any event, by the time the Marines landed, the worst of the famine was over. It had peaked months before.[62]

Iraq, 1990s

Mental hospitals and prisons are filled with people who claim to have heard voices telling them to kill certain people, often people they'd never met before, people who'd never done them any harm, or threatened any harm.

American soldiers went to the Middle East to kill the same kind of people after hearing a voice command them: the voice of George Bush.

Relentless bombing for more than 40 days and nights, against one of the most advanced nations in the Middle East, devastating its ancient and modern capital city; 177 million pounds of bombs falling on the people of Iraq, the most concentrated aerial onslaught in the history of the world to that time; depleted uranium weapons incinerating people, causing cancers and sundry congenital problems; blowing up chemical and biological weapon and oil facilities, a terrible poisoning of the atmosphere; burying soldiers alive, deliberately; the infrastructure destroyed, with dreadful effects on health; sanctions continued into the 21st century, multiplying the health problems; more than a million children dead from all of these factors, even more adults. UNICEF, in an August 1999 report, stated that in southern and central Iraq, the death rate for children under five had more than doubled in the years of the sanctions.

Until the present day, the US and Great Britain have continued to launch missiles against the burned-out ash called Iraq, as their planes fly over the country on virtually a daily basis, the authority for which Washington and London derive from each other. In the first eight months of 1999, the two countries flew some 10,000 sorties over Iraq, unleashing more than 1,000 bombs and missiles on more than 400 targets, killing or wounding many hundreds of people. Said US Brig. General William Looney, a director of this operation:

If they turn on their radars we're going to blow up their goddamn SAMs. They know we own their country. We own their airspace...We dictate the way they live and talk. And that's what's great about America right now. It's a good thing, especially when there's a lot of oil out there we need.[63]

It can be said that the United States has inflicted more vindictive punishment and ostracism upon Iraq than upon Germany or Japan after World War II.

Noam Chomsky has written: "It's been a leading, driving doctrine of US foreign policy since the 1940s that the vast and unparalleled energy resources of the Gulf region will be effectively dominated by the United States and its clients, and, crucially, that no independent, indigenous force will be permitted to have a substantial influence on the administration of oil production and price."

This may have been Iraq's crime, not that they invaded Kuwait in 1990, an invasion encouraged by the United States and provoked by Washington's close ally, Kuwait, itself; an invasion that gave the US all the pretext it needed to take action. Iraq's invasion was, after all, no more than Indonesia had done to East Timor, with Washington's blessing.

Peru, 1990s–present

For more than a decade the US has provided Peru with an unending stream of military advisers and trainers, Navy Seals and Green Berets, all manner of arms and equipment, surveillance flights, radar stations in the Andes, whatever—all to one of the most dictatorial and repressive regimes in the Western Hemisphere, condemned by Amnesty International, Human Rights Watch/Americas and State Department Human Rights reports for its medieval prisons, routine torture and other human-rights violations, led by an autocrat named Alberto Fujimori.

For what purpose has this support been rendered? The official Washington explanation is to fight drugs. But whereas four air force officers, including one of Fujimori's personal military pilots, were arrested after 383 pounds of cocaine were found on their military plane; whereas on four separate occasions cocaine was seized from navy ships, totaling 220 pounds;[64] whereas Fujimori's closest adviser, Vladimir Montesino, has a history of being a drug kingpin, and formerly a lawyer for drug traffickers;[65] whereas Montesino, who has long been on the CIA payroll, runs the intelligence service, which also has its hands deep into the drug cookie jar and was publicly condemned by the US Senate in 1999 for its corruption;[66] and whereas the military is known to have tipped off drug traffickers to DEA raids and physically protected the traffickers' cocaine caches from seizure by the police[67]…What can Washington possibly be thinking?

They're thinking of the usual: helping the government suppress guerrilla movements is the main priority. In 1997, Fujimori ordered the summary execution of 14 leftists, most of them very young, who had taken over the Japanese ambassador's home to press for human rights and economic improvements, and tried to surrender peacefully before being shot in cold blood. The commandos who carried out the raid received training and sophisticated technological help from the United States for their operation, including overflights of the RU-38A airplane, which can photograph a building and gauge the thickness of its walls, amongst a host of other details crucial to planning the raid.[68]

The United States did not aid in the execution of these young people because of drug trafficking.

Mexico, 1990s–present

The Mexican government "will need to eliminate the Zapatistas to demonstrate their effective control of the national territory and of security policy…[and] will need to consider carefully whether or not to allow opposition victories if fairly won at the ballot box." Thus reads a 1995 memorandum from Riordan Roett, a consultant on Latin America's emerging markets, working for Chase Manhattan Bank in New York.[69]

He was speaking of the movement of indigenous people in Mexico who were, and still are, demanding their economic and political rights and their autonomy. These desires, however, conflict with the needs of NAFTA and other components of the globalized economy, which want the Zapatistas out of certain areas—or at least not claiming ownership to the land—for various reasons, oil and other natural resources being amongst them, as well as the decidedly bad example being set for other Mexican and Central American peasants. NAFTA's plans call for the "subsistence" agriculture long practiced by the indigenous people to be "modernized"; i.e., to produce "high-profit" export crops, such as rubber and lumber.[70]

In the name of fighting drugs, the United States has poured hundreds of millions of dollars of military aid and training into Mexico, bringing in the usual complement of American police agents, Army advisers, CIA operatives and Special Forces.[71] And all in support of a remarkably corrupt government, military, "paramilitary" and police, many of whom are involved in drug trafficking themselves, carry out massacres and regularly engage in torture and other violations of human rights.[72] The Zapatistas claim that US and Argentine advisers have been providing training to the paramilitaries, the main force behind this newest "dirty war", so terribly familiar to Latin America.[73]

The American military aid has included sophisticated surveillance technology to track the Zapatistas in forests and hills, and hundreds of helicopters, which have been used to attack communities with machine guns, rockets and bombs. Such US aid and training is, still, commonplace in the Third World. In an excellent series on the subject in 1998, the *Washington Post* pointed out that:

> [Even] where armed domestic opposition is negligible or nonexistent, U.S. forces are teaching armies how to track down opponents, surprise them in helicopter attacks, kill them with more proficiency, or, in some cases, how to lead house-to-house raids in "close quarters combat" designed for cities.[74]

Much of the military aid to Mexico has been in violation of congressional laws banning military assistance to foreign security units guilty of human-rights violations.[75]

Oddly enough, no one accuses the Zapatistas of being involved with drug trafficking, so Washington's effective participation in the war being waged against them can only be seen in ideological terms.

Colombia, 1990s–present

By the end of the decade, Colombia—the most violent nation in the world—had become the third largest recipient of US military aid, with hundreds of American military personnel posted there in a growing number of military and radar bases to aid in counter-insurgency actions against leftist guerrillas. The US has aided government bombing raids and other military functions by providing helicopters, intelligence information about guerrilla movements, satellite images and communications intercepts. At times, US planes fly overhead during combat operations. The guerrillas claim that Americans are conducting covert counterinsurgency operations and warned that they will be targeted.[76]

Again, the public rationale given for taking sides in a civil war has been "to fight drugs". To drive home this point, US drug czar Barry McCaffrey routinely refers to the leading guerrilla group, FARC, as "narco-traffickers". But the DEA's Acting Administrator testified in 1999 that the DEA had "not yet really come to the conclusion" that "the FARC and ELN are drug trafficking entities per se",[77] even though the guerrillas do finance themselves in part through protecting and "taxing" drug producers.

However, the main recipient of the American aid, the Colombian military, is involved in drug trafficking, at the same time being intimately linked to paramilitary forces which are also active in drug trafficking and in protecting drug producers.[78] In November 1998, a Colombian Air Force cargo plane that landed at Ft. Lauderdale, Florida was found to contain 1,639 pounds of cocaine. In 1996, Colombian Air Force officers tried to smuggle heroin to the United States aboard the plane used by then-President Ernesto Samper.[79] Samper himself was labeled a "drug trafficker" by a senior Clinton administration official.[80]

As Senator Patrick Leahy (D-Vt.) pointed out in 1999, in speaking of Colombia: "What we are really seeing is a ratcheting up of a counterinsurgency policy masquerading as a counter-drug policy."[81]

In a 1994 report, Amnesty International estimated that more than 20,000 people had been killed in Colombia since 1986, mainly by the military and its paramilitary allies—"not in the 'drug wars' but for political reasons". Many of the victims were "trade unionists, human-rights activists and leaders of legal left-wing movements." Amnesty charged that "U.S.-supplied military equipment, ostensibly delivered for use against narcotics traffickers, was being used by the Colombian military to commit these abuses in the name of 'counter-insurgency'."[82] As with Mexico, much of this aid is in violation of congressional human-rights laws. The Pentagon has barely masked its scorn of these restrictions.[83]

A March 1997 letter by members of the House Foreign Operations Subcommittee to Secretary of State Albright stated that "efforts by the Colombian government to take action to curb the increased abuses committed by paramilitary groups, or to curb extrajudicial executions, disappearances, torture, political killings and other forms of human rights abuses committed by security forces [i.e., the regular military] are not sufficient to warrant the provision of over $100 million in military assistance and the resumption of lethal aid."[84]

The lethal aid, however, has continued. Washington suspects that the Colombian insurgents, if they ever took power, would just not fit in very well in the globalized economy of the New World Order.

Yugoslavia, 1995–99

In April 1996, President Clinton visited Russia during a pause in the brutal military struggle between Moscow and its breakaway province of Chechnya. At a press conference, the president declared:

> You say that there are some who say we should have been more openly critical. I think it depends upon your first premise; do you believe that Chechnya is a part of Russia or not? I would remind you that we once had a Civil War in our country in which we lost on a per-capita basis far more people than we lost in any of the wars of the 20th century over the proposition that Abraham Lincoln gave his life for, that no State had a right to withdraw from our Union.[85]

Three years later Clinton destroyed much of Yugoslavian civilized life and culture in Operation Bomb for Humanity, in effect rejecting the idea that Slobodan Milosevic had the right to try to prevent the province of Kosovo from withdrawing from the Federal Republic of Yugoslavia. The United States, under the cover of NATO, intervened in a civil war less violent than the American civil war; indeed, a lot less violent, and of shorter duration, than several other civil conflicts going on in the world at the same time, such as in Turkey, Sri Lanka, Indonesia/East Timor, Angola and other places in Africa; and it was the supposed extreme (one-sided?) violence of Serbia against the Kosovars that tore at the heartstrings of the kindly American and NATO leaders.

To those who argue that the US couldn't be saving the entire world, it must be pointed out that far from simply not saving certain peoples, Washington had been actively *supporting* Turkey and Indonesia for years in their mailed-fist military suppressions, and helped Croatia carry out, and then cover up, its ethnic cleansing of the Krajina Serbs in 1995.[86] Turkey, in fact, had nearly threatened to veto the NATO decision that it could act on Kosovo unless Ankara was assured that this policy could never be applied to Turkey's treatment of Kurds.[87]

But it was imperative for the United States that certain principles be established: 1)that NATO—in the absence of the Cold War, the Soviet Union and the Warsaw Pact—still had a purpose in life; 2)that NATO had the right to intervene anywhere, even outside of its own geographical boundaries, and without having to seek explicit authority from the UN Security Council; 3)that NATO was to be the military arm of the New World Order (corporate headquarters located in Washington, DC).

Yugoslavia was not inclined to worship these principles; nor, as we have seen, had the Serbs shown proper reverence for joining the club of globalized American allies *cum* obedient junior partners. Most of their industry and financial sector was still state owned. They had not even banned the word "socialism" from polite conversation yet. Veritable dinosaurs they were! All in all, an ideal humanitarian bombing target. The fact that Milosevic is a dictator was of no strategic significance, except for its propaganda value.

So Yugoslavia, which for years had feared an attack from the East (the Soviet Union), instead was devastated by the Western "free world". While the bombing attacks were being carried out, Serbian TV was also targeted, because it was broadcasting things *which the United States did not like*. The bombs took the lives of many of the station's staff, and both legs of one of the survivors, which had to be amputated to free him from the wreckage.[88]

"Once you kill people because you don't like what they say," observed noted British foreign correspondent, Robert Fisk, "you change the rules of war."[89]

Perhaps the strangest aspect of the whole conflict is the collective amnesia that appears to have afflicted countless intelligent, well-meaning people, who are convinced that the US/NATO bombing took place *after* the mass forced deportation of ethnic Albanians from

Kosovo was well underway; which is to say that the bombing was launched to *stop* this "ethnic cleansing". In actuality, the systematic forced deportations of large numbers of people did not begin until a few days after the bombing began, and was clearly a reaction to it, born of extreme anger and powerlessness. This is easily verified by looking at a daily newspaper for the few days before the bombing began the night of March 23/24, and the few days after. Or simply look at the *New York Times* of March 26, page 1, which reads:

> ...with the NATO bombing already begun, a deepening sense of fear took hold in Pristina [the main city of Kosovo] that the Serbs would *now* vent their rage against ethnic Albanian civilians in retaliation [emphasis added].

On March 27, we find the first reference to a "forced march" or anything of that sort.

But the propaganda version may already be set in marble. It's the neatest con-game since the church sprang "papal infallibility" upon a gullible people.

There's a lot more, hay mucho más, il y a beaucoup plus, es gibt noch viel mehr

In addition to the above, there have been literally dozens of other serious American interventions in every corner of the world, against both governments and movements, from the 1950s on. The amount of US government roguery to be uncovered appears to be infinite, while the author's time is finite. The US intervention machine has been, more or less, on automatic pilot...perpetual war for perpetual peace.

Narco-terrorists gonna get your mama

US government officials often seem desirous of identifying leftist guerrillas with drug trafficking, whether the linkage is factual or not. They also like to make use of the expression "narco-terrorists" in speaking of the guerrillas. These linguistic associations may serve a function beyond the purely descriptive. Here is Special Forces commander Col. John Waghelstein, speaking in 1987 about this linkage:

> A melding in the American public's mind and in Congress of this connection would lead to the necessary support to counter the guerril-

la/narcotics terrorists in this hemisphere...Congress would find it difficult to stand in the way of supporting our allies with the training, advice and security assistance necessary to do the job. Those church and academic groups that have slavishly supported insurgency in Latin America would find themselves on the wrong side of the moral issue. Above all, we would have the unassailable moral position from which to launch a concerted effort using Department of Defense (DOD) and non-DOD assets.[90]

Victims Memorial Museums

For several years, Cold-War conservatives have been planning for the opening of "The Victims of Communism Memorial Museum" near the Mall in Washington. This building has been commissioned by an act of Congress and signed by President Clinton. The literature its backers put out in behalf of this project is egregiously inaccurate and propagandistic. But that is not the point I wish to make here so much as to call for the erection of "The Victims of Anti-Communism Memorial Museum"; right next door would be a good spot. Displays dealing with the interventions described above and with the torture and support of terrorism detailed in other chapters would provide more than enough material to fill a goodly-sized edifice.

CHAPTER 18

Perverting Elections

It shall be unlawful for a foreign national directly or through any other person to make any contribution of money or other thing of value, or to promise expressly or impliedly to make any such contribution, in connection with an election to any political office or in connection with any primary election...

Title 2, United States Code Amended (USCA), Section 441e(a)

Thus the legal basis, if not the political, for the indignation expressed by both Republican and Democratic members of Congress at revelations that the Chinese may have tried to use covert campaign donations to influence American policy.

Washington policymakers, however, have long reserved the unrestrained right to pour large amounts of money into elections of other countries (including those which also prohibit foreign contributions) and taint the electoral system in numerous other ways, as we shall see below.

Elections and this thing called democracy

During the Clinton administration, the sentiment has been proclaimed on so many occasions by the president and other political leaders, and dutifully reiterated by the media, that the thesis: "Cuba is the only non-democracy in the Western Hemisphere" is now nothing short of received wisdom in the United States.

Let us examine this thesis carefully for it has a highly interesting implication.

Throughout the period of the Cuban revolution, 1959 to the present, Latin America has witnessed a terrible parade of human rights violations—systematic, routine torture; legions of "disappeared" people; government-supported death squads picking off selected individuals; massacres *en masse* of peasants, students and other groups, shot down in cold blood. The worst perpetrators of these acts during all or part of this period have been the military and associated paramilitary squads of El Salvador, Guatemala, Brazil, Argentina, Chile, Colombia, Peru, Mexico, Uruguay, Haiti and Honduras.

Not even Cuba's worst enemies have charged the Castro government with any of these violations, and if one further considers education and health care—each guaranteed by the United Nations "Universal Declaration of Human Rights" and the "European Convention for the Protection of Human Rights and Fundamental Freedoms"—"both of which," said President Clinton, "work better [in Cuba] than most other countries",[1] then it would appear that during the more-than-40 years of its revolution, Cuba has enjoyed one of the very best human-rights records in all of Latin America.

If, despite this record, the United States can insist that Cuba is the only "non-democracy" in the Western Hemisphere, we are left with the inescapable conclusion that this thing called "democracy", as seen from the White House, may have little or nothing to do with many of our most cherished human rights. Indeed, numerous pronouncements emanating from Washington officialdom over the years make plain that "democracy", at best, or at most, is equated solely with elections and civil liberties. Not even jobs, food and shelter are part of the equation.

Thus, a nation with hordes of hungry, homeless, untended sick, barely literate, unemployed and/or tortured people, whose loved ones are being disappeared and/or murdered with state connivance, can be said to be living in a "democracy"—its literal Greek meaning of "rule of the people" implying that this is the kind of life the people actually *want*—provided that every two years or four years they have the right to go to a designated place and put an X next to the name of one or another individual who promises to relieve their miserable condition, but who will, typically, do virtually nothing of the kind; and provided further that in this society there is at least a certain minimum of freedom—how much being in large measure a function of one's wealth—for one to express one's views about the powers-that-be and the workings of the society, without undue fear of punishment, regardless of whether expressing these views has any influence whatsoever over the way things are.

It is not by chance that the United States has defined democracy in this narrow manner. Throughout the Cold War, the absence of "free and fair" multiparty elections and adequate civil liberties were what marked the Soviet foe and its satellites. These nations, however, provided their citizens with a relatively decent standard of living insofar as employment, food, health care, education, etc., without omnipresent Brazilian torture or Guatemalan death squads. At the same time, many of America's Third World allies in the Cold War— members of what Washington liked to refer to as "The Free World"— were human-rights disaster areas, who could boast of little other than the 60-second democracy of the polling booth and a tolerance for dissenting opinion so long as it didn't cut too close to the bone or threaten to turn into a movement.

Naturally, the only way to win Cold-War propaganda points with team lineups like these, was to extol your team's brand of virtue and damn the enemy's lack of it, designating the former "democracy" and the latter "totalitarianism".

Thus it is, that Americans are raised to fervently believe that no progress can be made in any society in the absence of elections. They are taught to equate elections with democracy, and democracy with elections. And no matter how cynical they've grown about electoral politics at home, few of them harbor any doubt that the promotion of free and fair elections has long been a basic and sincere tenet of American foreign policy.

In light of this, let us examine the actual historical record.

Philippines, 1950s

Flagrant manipulation by the CIA of the nation's political life, featuring stage-managed elections with extensive disinformation campaigns, heavy financing of candidates, writing their speeches, drugging the drinks of one of the opponents of the CIA candidate so he would appear incoherent, plotting the assassination of another candidate. The Agency covertly set up an organization called National

Movement for Free Elections, the better to promote its agenda, and trusting citizens joined up all over the country. The *New York Times* was also trusting. It praised the Philippine's political and electoral development, declaring that "It is not without reason that the Philippines has been called "democracy's showcase in Asia".[2]

Italy, 1948–1970s

See "Interventions" chapter.

Lebanon, 1950s

The CIA provided funds to support the campaigns of President Camille Chamoun and selected parliamentary candidates; other funds were targeted against candidates who had shown less than total enchantment with US interference in Lebanese politics.[3]

Indonesia, 1955

A million dollars were dispensed by the CIA to a centrist coalition's electoral campaign in a bid to cut into the support for President Sukarno's party and the Indonesian Communist Party.[4]

Vietnam, 1955

The US was instrumental in South Vietnam canceling the elections scheduled to unify North and South because of the certainty that the North Vietnamese communist leader, Ho Chi Minh, would easily win.[5]

British Guiana/Guyana, 1953–64

For 11 years, two of the oldest democracies in the world, Great Britain and the United States, went to great lengths to prevent Cheddi Jagan—three times the democratically elected leader—from occupying his office. Using a wide variety of tactics—from general strikes and disinformation to terrorism and British legalisms, the US and Britain forced Jagan out of office twice during the period.[6]

Japan, 1958–1970s

The CIA emptied the US treasury of millions to finance the conservative Liberal Democratic Party in parliamentary elections, "on a seat-by-seat basis", while doing what it could to weaken and undermine its opposition, the Japanese Socialist Party. The result was 38 years in power for the Liberal Democratic Party, comparable to the reign of the Christian Democrats in Italy, also sponsored by the CIA; these tactics kept both Japan and Italy from developing a strong multi-party system.[7]

The 1961–63 edition of the State Department's annual *Foreign Relations of the United States*, published in 1996, includes an unprecedented disclaimer that, because of material left out, a committee of distinguished historians thinks "this published compilation does not constitute a 'thorough, accurate and reliable documentary record of major United States foreign policy decisions'," as required by law. The deleted material involved US actions from 1958–1960 in Japan, according to the State Department's historian.[8]

Nepal, 1959

By the CIA's own admission, it carried out an unspecified "covert action" on behalf of B.P. Koirala to help his Nepali Congress Party win the national parliamentary election. The NCP won a majority of seats in the new legislature and Koirala became prime minister. It was Nepal's first national election ever, and the CIA was there to initiate them into the wonderful workings of democracy.[9]

Laos, 1960

CIA agents stuffed ballot boxes to help a hand-picked strongman, Phoumi Nosavan, set up a pro-American government.[10]

Brazil, 1962

The CIA and the Agency for International Development expended millions of dollars during federal and state elections in support of candidates opposed to President João Goulart. The Agency also dipped into its bag of dirty tricks to torment the campaigns of various candidates.[11]

Dominican Republic, 1962

In October 1962, two months before election day, US Ambassador John Bartlow Martin got together with the candidates of the two major parties and handed them a written notice, in Spanish and English, which he had prepared. It read in part: "The loser in the forthcoming election will, as soon as the election result is known, publicly congratulate the winner, publicly recognize him as the President of all the Dominican people, and publicly call upon his own supporters to so recognize him...Before taking office, the winner will offer Cabinet seats to members of the loser's party. (They may decline)."[12]

The United States also worked with the Dominican government to deport some 125 people—supporters of the former dictator Trujillo as well as "Castro/Communists"—to the US and elsewhere, who were not allowed to return until after the election. This was "to help maintain stability so elections could be held", as Martin put it.[13]

As matters turned out, the winner, Juan Bosch, was ousted in a military coup seven months later, a slap in the face of democracy which neither Martin nor any other American official did anything about.

Guatemala, 1963

The US overthrew the regime of General Miguel Ydigoras because he was planning to step down in 1964, leaving the door open to an election; an election that Washington feared would be won by the former president, liberal reformer and critic of US foreign policy, Juan José Arévalo. Ydigoras's replacement made no mention of elections.[14]

Bolivia, 1966

The CIA bestowed $600,000 upon President René Barrientos and lesser sums to several right-wing parties in a successful effort to influence the outcome of national elections. Gulf Oil contributed two hundred thousand more to Barrientos.[15]

Chile, 1964–70:

There were major US interventions into national elections in 1964 and 1970, and into congressional elections in the intervening years.

Socialist Salvador Allende fell victim in 1964, but won in 1970 despite a multimillion, multifaceted CIA operation against him. The Agency then orchestrated his downfall in a 1973 military coup.[16]

Portugal, 1974–5

In the years following the coup in 1974 by military officers who talked like socialists, the CIA revved up its propaganda machine while funneling many millions of dollars to support "moderate" candidates, in particular Mario Soares and his (so-called) Socialist Party. At the same time, the Agency enlisted social-democratic parties of Western Europe to provide further funds and support to Soares. It worked. The Socialist Party became the dominant power.[17]

Australia, 1974–75

See "Interventions" chapter.

Jamaica, 1976

A CIA campaign to defeat social democrat Michael Manley's bid for reelection, featuring disinformation, arms shipments, labor unrest, economic destabilization, financial support for the opposition and attempts upon Manley's life. Despite it all, he was victorious.[18]

Panama, 1984, 1989

In 1984, the CIA helped finance a highly questionable presidential electoral victory for one of Manuel Noriega's men. The opposition cried "fraud", but the new president was welcomed at the White House. By 1989, Noriega was no longer a Washington favorite, so the CIA provided more than $10 million dollars to those opposing Noriega's candidate as well as providing for clandestine radio and TV broadcasts to influence the vote. When the Noriega man "won", Washington, on this occasion, expressed its moral indignation about the fraudulent election.[19]

Nicaragua, 1984, 1990

In 1984, the United States, trying to discredit the legitimacy of the Sandinista government's scheduled election, covertly persuaded the leading opposition coalition to not take part. A few days before election day, some other rightist parties on the ballot revealed that US diplomats had been pressing them to drop out of the race as well.[20] The CIA also tried to split the Sandinista leadership by placing phoney full-page ads in neighboring countries.[21] But the Sandinistas won handily in a very fair election monitored by hundreds of international observers.

Six years later, the National Endowment for Democracy (NED), Washington's specially created stand-in for the CIA, poured in millions of dollars to defeat the Sandinistas in the February elections. NED helped organize the Nicaraguan opposition, UNO, building up the parties and organizations that formed and supported this coalition. The successful UNO was the only political party to receive US aid, even though eight other opposition parties fielded candidates.[22]

Perhaps most telling of all, the Nicaraguan people were made painfully aware that a victory by the Sandinistas would mean a continuation of the relentlessly devastating war being waged against them by Washington.

Haiti, 1987–1988

After the Duvalier dictatorship came to an end in 1986, the country prepared for its first free elections the following year. However, Haiti's main trade union leader declared that Washington was working to undermine the left. US aid organizations, he said, were encouraging people in the countryside to identify and reject the entire left as "communist". Meanwhile, the CIA was involved in a range of support for selected candidates until the Senate Intelligence Committee ordered the Agency to cease its covert electoral action.[23]

Bulgaria, 1990–1991 and Albania, 1991–1992

With no regard for the fragility of these nascent democracies, the US played a major role in ousting their elected governments. See "Interventions" chapter.

Russia, 1996

For four months (March–June), a group of veteran American political consultants worked secretly in Moscow in support of Boris Yeltsin's presidential campaign. Although the Americans were working independently, President Clinton's political guru, Dick Morris, acted as their middleman to the administration, and Clinton himself told Yeltsin in March that he wanted to "make sure that everything the United States did would have a positive impact" on the Russian's electoral campaign. Boris Yeltsin was being counted on to run with the globalized-free market ball and it was imperative that he cross the goal line. The American consultants in Moscow scripted a Clinton-Yeltsin summit meeting in April to allow the Russian to "stand up to the West", just like the Russian Communist Party—Yeltsin's main opponent—insisted they would do if they won.

The Americans emphasized sophisticated methods of message development, polling, focus groups, crowd staging, direct-mailing, etc., urged more systematic domination of the state-owned media, and advised against public debates with the Communists. Most of all they encouraged the Yeltsin campaign to "go negative" against the Communists, painting frightening pictures of what the Communists would do if they took power, including much civic upheaval and violence, and, of course, a return to the worst of Stalinism. With a virtual media blackout against them, the Communists were extremely hard pressed to respond to the attacks or to shout the Russian equivalent of "It's the economy, stupid."

It is impossible to measure the value of the American consultants' contributions to the Yeltsin campaign, for there's no knowing which of their tactics the Russians would have employed anyhow if left to their own devices, how well they would have applied them, or how things would have turned out. But we do know that before the Americans came on board, Yeltsin was favored by only six percent of the electorate. In the first round of voting, he edged the Communists 35 percent to 32, and was victorious in the second round 54 to 40 percent. "Democracy," declared *Time* magazine, "triumphed."[24]

Mongolia, 1996

The National Endowment for Democracy worked for several years with the opposition to the governing Mongolian People's Revolutionary Party (the former communists, who had won the 1992 election) to achieve a very surprising electoral victory. In the six-year period leading up to the 1996 elections, NED spent close to a million dollars in a country with a population of some 2.5 million, the most significant result of which was to unite the opposition into a new coalition, the National Democratic Union. Borrowing from Newt Gingrich's Contract With America, the NED drafted a "Contract With the Mongolian Voter", which called for private property rights, a free press and the encouragement of foreign investment.[25] The MPRR had already instituted Western-style economic reforms, which had led to widespread poverty and wiped out much of the communist social safety net. But the new government promised to accelerate the reforms, including the privatization of housing.[26] The *Wall Street Journal* was ecstatic that "shock-therapy" was now going to become even more shocking, as with the sale of state enterprises. The newspaper's editorial was entitled "Wisdom of the Steppes".[27] The new government was one that Washington could expect to be more hospitable to American corporations and intelligence agencies than the MPRR. Indeed, by 1998, the National Security Agency had set up electronic listening posts in Outer Mongolia to intercept Chinese army communications, and the Mongolian intelligence service was using nomads to gather intelligence in China itself.[28]

Bosnia, 1998

Bosnia effectively became an American protectorate, with Carlos Westendorp—the Spanish diplomat appointed to enforce Washington's offspring: the 1995 Dayton peace accords—as the colonial Governor-General. Before the September elections for a host of offices, Westendorp removed 14 Croatian candidates from the ballot because of alleged biased coverage aired in Bosnia by neighboring Croatia's state television and politicking by ethnic Croat army soldiers. After the election, Westendorp fired the elected president of the Bosnian Serb Republic, accusing him of creating instability. In this scenario those who appeared to support what the US and other

Western powers wished were called "moderates", and allowed to run for and remain in office. Those who had other thoughts were labeled "hard-liners", and ran the risk of a different fate. When Westendorp was chosen to assume this position of "high representative" in Bosnia in May 1997, *The Guardian* of London wrote that "The US secretary of state, Madeleine Albright, praised the choice. But some critics already fear that Mr. Westendorp will prove too lightweight and end up as a cipher in American hands."[29]

Further evidence of Washington's love affair with elections

There have also been the occasions where the United States, while (perhaps) not interfering in the election process, was, however, involved in overthrowing a democratically-elected government, such as in Iran 1953, Guatemala 1954, the Congo 1960, Ecuador 1961, Bolivia 1964, Greece 1967 and Fiji 1987.

In other countries, US interventions resulted in free, or any, elections being done away with completely for large stretches of time, as in Iran, South Korea, Guatemala, Brazil, Congo, Indonesia, Chile and Greece.

CHAPTER 19

Trojan Horse: The National Endowment for Democracy

How many Americans could identify the National Endowment for Democracy? An organization which often does exactly the opposite of what its name implies. The NED was set up in the early 1980s under President Reagan in the wake of all the negative revelations about the CIA in the second half of the 1970s. The latter was a remarkable period. Spurred by Watergate—the Church Committee of the Senate, the Pike Committee of the House and the Rockefeller Commission, created by the president, were all busy investigating the CIA. Seemingly every other day there was a new headline about the discovery of some awful thing, even criminal conduct, the CIA had been mixed up in for years. The Agency was getting an exceedingly bad name, and it was causing the powers-that-be much embarrassment.

Something had to be done. What was done was not to stop doing these awful things. Of course not. What was done was to shift many of these awful things to a new organization, with a nice sounding name—the National Endowment for Democracy. The idea was that the NED would do somewhat overtly what the CIA had been doing covertly for decades, and thus, hopefully, eliminate the stigma associated with CIA covert activities.

It was a masterpiece. Of politics, of public relations and of cynicism.

Thus it was that in 1983, the National Endowment for Democracy was set up to "support democratic institutions throughout the world through private, nongovernmental efforts". Notice the "nongovern-mental"—part of the image, part of the myth. In actuality, virtually every penny of its funding comes from the federal government, as is clearly indicated in the financial statement in each issue of its annual report. NED likes to refer to itself as an NGO (non-governmental organization) because this helps to maintain a certain credibility abroad that an official US government agency might not have. But NGO is the wrong category. NED is a GO.

Allen Weinstein, who helped draft the legislation establishing NED, was quite candid when he said in 1991: "A lot of what we do today was done covertly 25 years ago by the CIA."[1] In effect, the CIA has been laundering money through NED.

The Endowment has four principal initial recipients of funds: the International Republican Institute; the National Democratic Institute for International Affairs; an affiliate of the AFL-CIO (such as the American Center for International Labor Solidarity); and an affiliate of the Chamber of Commerce (such as the Center for International Private Enterprise). These institutions then disburse funds to other institutions in the US and all over the world, which then often dis-burse funds to yet other organizations.

In a multitude of ways, NED meddles in the internal affairs of for-eign countries by supplying funds, technical know-how, training, edu-cational materials, computers, fax machines, copiers, automobiles and so on, to selected political groups, civic organizations, labor unions, dissident movements, student groups, book publishers, newspapers, other media, etc. NED programs generally impart the basic philosophy that working people and other citizens are best served under a system of free enterprise, class cooperation, collective bargaining, minimal government intervention in the economy and opposition to socialism in any shape or form. A free-market economy is equated with democ-racy, reform and growth, and the merits of foreign investment are emphasized.

From 1994 to 1996, NED awarded 15 grants, totaling more than $2,500,000, to the American Institute for Free Labor Development, an organization used by the CIA for decades to subvert progressive labor unions.[2] AIFLD's work within Third World unions typically involved a considerable educational effort very similar to the basic NED philosophy described above. The description of one of the 1996 NED grants to AIFLD includes as one its objectives: "build union-management cooperation".[3] Like many things that NED says, this sounds innocuous, if not positive, but these in fact are ideological code words meaning "keep the labor agitation down…don't rock the status-quo boat". The relationship between NED and AIFLD very well captures the CIA origins of NED.[4]

The Endowment has funded centrist and rightist labor organizations to help them oppose those unions which were too militantly pro-worker. This has taken place in France, Portugal and Spain amongst many other places. In France, during the 1983–4 period, NED supported a "trade union-like organization for professors and students" to counter "left-wing organizations of professors". To this end it funded a series of seminars and the publication of posters, books and pamphlets such as "Subversion and the Theology of Revolution" and "Neutralism or Liberty".[5] ("Neutralism" here refers to being unaligned in the Cold War.)

NED describes one of its 1997–98 programs thusly: "To identify barriers to private sector development at the local and federal levels in the Federal Republic of Yugoslavia and to push for legislative change…[and] to develop strategies for private sector growth."[6] Critics of Yugoslav President Slobodan Milosevic have been supported by NED grants for years.[7]

In short, NED's programs are in sync with the basic needs and objectives of the New World Order's economic globalization, just as the programs have for years been on the same wavelength as US foreign policy.

Because of a controversy in 1984—when NED funds were used to aid a Panamanian presidential candidate backed by Manuel Noriega and the CIA—Congress enacted a law prohibiting the use of NED funds "to finance the campaigns of candidates for public office." But the ways to circumvent the spirit of such a prohibition are not difficult to come up with; as with American elections, there's "hard money" and there's "soft money".

As described in the "Elections" and "Interventions" chapters, NED successfully manipulated elections in Nicaragua in 1990 and Mongolia in 1996 and helped to overthrow democratically elected governments in Bulgaria in 1990 and Albania in 1991 and 1992. In Haiti in the late 1990s, NED was busy working on behalf of right wing groups who were united in their opposition to former president Jean-Bertrand Aristide and his progressive ideology.[8] NED has made its weight felt in the electoral-political process in numerous other countries.

NED would have the world believe that it's only teaching the ABCs of democracy and elections to people who don't know them, but in all five countries named above there had already been free and fair elections held. The problem, from NED's point of view, is that the elections had been won by political parties not on NED's favorites list.

The Endowment maintains that it's engaged in "opposition building" and "encouraging pluralism". "We support people who otherwise do not have a voice in their political system," said Louisa Coan, a NED program officer.[9] But NED hasn't provided aid to foster progressive or leftist opposition in Mexico, El Salvador, Guatemala, Nicaragua or Eastern Europe—or, for that matter, in the United States—even though these groups are hard pressed for funds and to make themselves heard. Cuban dissident groups and media are heavily supported however.

NED's reports carry on endlessly about "democracy", but at best it's a modest measure of mechanical electoral democracy they have in mind, not economic democracy; nothing that aims to threaten the powers-that-be or the way-things-are, unless of course it's in a place like Cuba.

The Endowment played an important role in the Iran-Contra affair of the 1980s, funding key components of Oliver North's shadowy "Project Democracy" network, which privatized US foreign policy, waged war, ran arms and drugs and engaged in other equally charming activities. At one point in 1987, a White House spokesman stated that those at NED "run Project Democracy".[10] This was an exaggeration; it would have been more correct to say that NED was the public arm of Project Democracy, while North ran the covert end of things. In any event, the statement caused much less of a stir than if—as in an earlier period—it had been revealed that it was the CIA which was behind such an unscrupulous operation.

NED also mounted a multi-level campaign to fight the leftist insurgency in the Philippines in the mid-1980s, funding a host of private organizations, including unions and the media.[11] This was a replica of a typical CIA operation of pre-NED days.

And between 1990 and 1992, the Endowment donated a quarter-million dollars of taxpayers' money to the Cuban-American National Foundations, the ultra-fanatic anti-Castro Miami group. The CANF, in turn, financed Luis Posada Carriles, one of the most prolific and pitiless terrorists of modern times, who was involved in the blowing up of a Cuban airplane in 1976, which killed 73 people. In 1997, he was involved in a series of bomb explosions in Havana hotels.[12]

The NED, like the CIA before it, calls what it does supporting democracy. The governments and movements whom the NED targets call it destabilization.[13]

CHAPTER 20

The United States versus the World at the United Nations

Amerca, we have all been taught for more than half a century, is the leader of "The Free World". If this is so, it's proper to ask: Where are the followers? Where is the evidence that Washington's world view sways the multitude of other governments and leaders by virtue of other than the US being a 10,000-pound gorilla zillionaire? Where is the loyalty and admiration engendered by intellectual or moral leadership? To enlist support for its wars in Korea, Vietnam, Afghanistan, the Persian Gulf and Yugoslavia, the United States had to resort to bribery, threats and chicanery. At the United Nations, with noteworthy regularity, Washington has found itself—often alone, sometimes joined by one or two other countries—standing in opposition to General Assembly resolutions aimed at furthering human rights, peace, nuclear disarmament, economic justice, the struggle against South African apartheid and Israeli lawlessness and other progressive causes.

The table below shows a portion of this pattern. It covers an arbitrarily chosen 10-year period, 1978 through 1987, and is composed of the following sections:

1978–1981: All voting in the General Assembly examined; only those resolutions for which the US cast a solitary "no" vote or was joined by one or two other nations are listed.

1982–1983: All voting in the General Assembly examined; only those resolutions for which the US cast a solitary "no" vote are listed.

1984–1987: Only a sample of General Assembly resolutions are shown, primarily for diversity.

In total, almost 150 examples are given. The number of abstentions is not shown. There were many other resolutions in this period where Israel cast a solitary "no" vote and the US was the sole abstainer.

Voting on resolutions of the Security Council and the Economic and Social Council are not included here, but these votes show a very similar pattern. In the Council, a US solitary "no" vote is of course enough to defeat a measure.

The 1983 US invasion of Grenada was almost universally condemned in Latin America, only the military dictatorships of Chile, Guatemala and Uruguay expressing support. The United Nations voted its disapproval overwhelmingly. To this President Reagan responded: "One hundred nations in the UN have not agreed with us on just about everything that's come before them where we're involved, and it didn't upset my breakfast at all."[1]

One of the evils of communist states, we were always told, was that they were oblivious to world opinion.

...a decent respect to the opinions of mankind...

The Declaration of Independence

Date/Issue   Resolution Number   Yes-No Vote

1978

Dec. 15   33/75   119-2 (US, Israel)
Urges the Security Council, especially its permanent members, to take all necessary measures for insuring UN decisions on the maintenance of international peace and security

Dec. 18   33/110   110-2 (US, Israel)
Living conditions of the Palestinian people

Dec. 18   33/113C   97-3 (US, Israel, Guatemala)
Condemnation of Israeli human rights record in occupied territories

Dec. 19   33/136   119-1 (US)
Calls upon developed countries to increase quantity and quality of
development assistance to underdeveloped countries

1979
Jan. 24   33/183M   114-3 (US, France, UK)
To end all military and nuclear collaboration with apartheid South
Africa

Jan. 29   33/196   111-1 (US)
Protectionism of developing countries' exports

Nov. 23   34/46   136-1 (US)
Alternate approaches within the UN system for improving the
enjoyment of human rights and fundamental freedoms

Nov. 23   34/52E   121-3 (US, Israel, Australia)
Return of inhabitants expelled by Israel

Dec. 11   34/83J   120-3 (US, UK, France)
Negotiations on disarmament and cessation of nuclear arms race

Dec. 12   34/90A   111-2 (US, Israel)
Demand that Israel desist from certain human rights violations

Dec. 12   34/93D   132-3 (US, UK, France)
Strengthening arms embargo against South Africa

Dec. 12   34/93I   134-3 (US, UK, France)
Assistance to the oppressed people of South Africa and their liberation movement

Dec. 14   34/100   104-2 (US, Israel)
Against support for intervention in the internal or external affairs of
states

Dec. 14   34/113   120-2 (US, Israel)
Request for report on the living conditions of Palestinians in occupied
Arab countries

Dec. 14   34/133   112-3 (US, Israel, Canada)
Assistance to Palestinian people

Dec. 14   34/136   118-2 (US, Israel)
Sovereignty over national resources in occupied Arab territories

Dec. 17   34/158   121-2 (US, Israel)
Prepare and carry out the UN Conference on Women

Dec. 17   34/160   122-2 (US, Israel)
Include Palestinian women in agenda of UN Conference on Women

Dec. 19   34/199   112-1 (US)
Safeguarding rights of developing countries in multinational trade negotiations

1980

Nov. 3   35/13E   96-3 (US, Israel, Canada)
Requests Israel to return displaced persons

Dec. 5   35/57   134-1 (US)
Establishment of a New International Economic Order to promote the growth of underdeveloped countries and international economic co-operation

Dec. 5   35/75   118-2 (US, Israel)
Condemns Israeli policy regarding the living conditions of Palestinian people

Dec. 11   35/119   134-3 (US, UK, France)
Implementation of the Declaration on the Granting of Independence to Colonial Countries and Peoples

Dec. 11   35/122C   118-2 (US, Israel)
Israeli human rights practices in occupied territories [Same day, similar resolutions, 35/122E—119-2 vote, and 35/122F—117-2]

Dec. 11   35/136   132-3 (US, Israel, Canada)
Endorse Program of Action for Second Half of UN Decade for Women

Dec. 12   35/145A   111-2 (US, UK)
Cessation of all nuclear test explosions

Dec. 12   35/154   110-2 (US, Albania)
Declaration of non-use of nuclear weapons against non-nuclear states

Dec. 15   35/169C   120-3 (US, Israel, Australia)
Rights of Palestinians

Dec. 15   35/174   120-1 (US)
Emphasizing that the development of nations and individuals is a human right

Dec. 16   35/206J   137-3 (US, UK, France)
Assistance to oppressed people of South Africa and their national liberation movement

1981
Oct. 28   36/12   145-1 (US)
Anti-racism; condemns apartheid in South Africa and Namibia

Oct. 28   36/13   124-1 (US)
Condemns collaboration of certain States and transnational corporations with the South African government

Oct. 28   36/15   114-2 (US, Israel)
Demand that Israel cease excavations of certain sites in E. Jerusalem

Nov. 9   36/18   123-1 (US)
To promote co-operative movements in developing countries (agricultural, savings and credits, housing, consumer protection, social services, etc.)

Nov. 9   36/19   126-1 (US)
The right of every state to choose its economic and social system in accord with the will of its people, without outside interference in whatever form it takes

Nov. 13   36/27   109-2 (US, Israel)
Condemns Israel for its bombing of an Iraqi nuclear installation

Dec. 1   36/68   133-3 (US, UK, Guatemala)
Condemns activities of foreign economic interests in colonial territories

Dec. 4   36/73   109-2 (US, Israel)
Condemns Israeli policy regarding living conditions of the Palestinian people

Dec. 9   36/84   118-2 (US, UK)
Cessation of all test explosions of nuclear weapons

Dec. 9   36/87B   107-2 (US, Israel)
Establishment of a nuclear-weapon free zone in the Middle East

Dec. 9   36/92J   78-3 (US, Canada, Brazil)
World-wide action for collecting signatures in support of measures to
prevent nuclear war, curb the arms race and promote disarmament

Dec. 9   36/96B   109-1(US)
Urges negotiations on prohibition of chemical and biological weapons

Dec. 9   36/98   101-2 (US, Israel)
Demands Israelis renounce possession of nuclear weapons

Dec. 10   36/120A   121-2 (US, Israel)
Rights of the Palestinian people

Dec. 10   36/120B   119-3 (US, Israel, Canada)
Palestinian rights

Dec. 10   36/120E   139-2 (US, Israel)
Status of Jerusalem

Dec. 14   36/133   135-1 (US)
Declares that education, work, health care, proper nourishment,
national development, etc. are human rights

Dec. 16   36/146A   141-2 (US, Israel)
Palestinian refugees in the Gaza Strip

Dec. 16   36/146B   121-3 (US, Israel, Canada)
Rights of displaced Palestinians to return to their homes

Dec. 16   36/146C   117-2 (US, Israel)
Revenues derived from Palestinian refugees' properties

Dec. 16   36/146G   119-2(US, Israel)
Establishment of University of Jerusalem for Palestinian refugees

Dec. 16   36/147C   111-2 (US, Israel)
Israeli violations of human rights in occupied territories

Dec. 16   36/147F   114-2 (US, Israel)
Condemns Israeli closing of universities in occupied territories

Dec. 16   36/149B   147-2 (US, Israel)
Calls for the establishment of a new and more just world information
and communications order

Dec. 16   36/150   139-2 (US, Israel)
Opposes Israel's decision to build a canal linking the Mediterranean
Sea to the Dead Sea

Dec. 17   36/172C   136-1 (US)
Condemns aggression by South Africa against Angola and other
African states

Dec. 17   36/172H   129-2 (US, UK)
To organize an international conference of trade unions on sanctions
against South Africa

Dec. 17   36/172   126-2 (US, UK)
To encourage various international actions against South Africa

Dec. 17   36/172N   139-1(US)
Support of sanctions and other measures against South Africa

Dec. 17   36/172O   138-1 (US)
Cessation of further foreign investments and loans for South Africa

Dec. 17   36/173   115-2 (US, Israel)
Permanent sovereignty over national resources in occupied Palestine
and other Arab territories

Dec. 17   36/226B   121-2 (US, Israel)
Non-applicability of Israeli law over the Golan Heights

Dec. 18   36/234B   127-1 (US)
UN accounting changes for 1980–1

1982 [only solitary US votes]
Oct. 28   37/7   111-1
World Charter for protection of the ecology

Nov. 15   37/11   136-1
Setting up UN conference on succession of states in respect to state property, archives and debts

Dec. 3   37/47   124-1
Appeal for universal ratification of the convention on the suppression and punishment of apartheid

Dec. 9   37/69E   141-1
Promoting international mobilization against apartheid

Dec. 9   37/69G   138-1
Drafting of international convention against apartheid in sports

Dec. 9   37/69H   134-1
Cessation of further foreign investments and loans for South Africa

Dec. 9   37/73   111-1
Need for a comprehensive nuclear-test-ban treaty

Dec. 9   37/78A   114-1
Request to US and USSR to transmit a status report on their nuclear arms negotiations [USSR abstained]

Dec. 9   37/83   138-1
Prevention of arms race in outer space

Dec. 10   37/94B   131-1
Support of UNESCO's efforts to promote a new world information and communications order

Dec. 13   37/98A   95-1
Necessity of a convention on the prohibition of chemical and bacteriological weapons

Dec. 16   37/103   113-1
Development of the principles and norms of international law relating to the new economic order

Dec. 17   37/131   129-1
Measures concerning the UN Joint Staff Pension Board, including prevention of exclusion of certain UN employees

Dec. 17   37/137   146-1
Protection against products harmful to health and the environment

Dec. 18   37/199   131-1
Declares that education, work, health care, proper nourishment, national development, etc. are human rights

Dec. 20   37/204   141-1
Motion for a review of the implementation of the Charter of Economic Rights and Duties of States

Dec. 21   37/237/XI   132-1
Adequacy of the conference facilities of the Economic Commission for Africa at Addis Ababa

Dec. 21   37/251   146-1
Development of the energy resources of developing countries

Dec. 21   37/252   124-1
Restructuring international economic relations toward establishing a new international economic order

1983

Nov. 22   38/19   110-1
International Convention on the Suppression and Punishment of the Crime of Apartheid

Nov. 22   38/25   131-1
The right of every state to choose its economic and social system in accord with the will of its people, without outside interference in whatever form it takes

Dec. 5   38/39E   149-1
Disseminating material and organizing conferences in the campaign against apartheid

Dec. 5   38/39I   140-1
Urges the Security Council to consider sanctions against South Africa as a protest against apartheid

Dec. 5   38/39K   145-1
Authorizes the International Convention against Apartheid in Sports to continue its consultations

Dec. 15   38/70   147-1
Outer space should be used for peaceful purposes; prevention of an arms race in outer space

Dec. 16   38/124   132-1
Declares that education, work, health care, proper nourishment, national development, etc. are human rights

Dec. 19   38/128   110-1
Development of the principles and norms of international law relating to the new world economic order

Dec. 19   38/150   137-1
Transport and Communications Decade in Africa

Dec. 20   38/182   116-1
Prohibition of the development and manufacture of new types and systems of weapons of mass destruction

Dec. 20   38/183M   133-1
Requests nuclear-arms states to submit to General Assembly annual reports on measures taken for prevention of nuclear war and reversing the arms race

Dec. 20   38/187A   98-1
Urges intensification of negotiations to achieve an accord on a prohibition of chemical and bacteriological weapons

Dec. 20   38/188G   113-1
Requests a study on the naval arms race

Dec. 20   38/188H   132-1
Independent Commission on Disarmament and Security Issues

Dec. 20   38/202   126-1
Strengthening the capacity of the UN to respond to natural and other disasters

1984 [selected resolutions]

Nov. 8   39/9   134-2 (US, Israel)
Cooperation between the UN and the League of Arab States

Nov. 16   39/14   106-2 (US, Israel)
Condemns Israeli attack against Iraqi nuclear installation

Nov. 23   39/21   145-1
Report of the Committee on the Elimination of Racial Discrimination

Dec. 5   39/411   119-2 (US, UK)
Reaffirming the right of St. Helena to independence

Dec. 5   39/42   121-2 (US, UK)
Condemns support of South Africa in its Namibian and other policies

Dec. 11   39/49A   127-2 (US, Israel)
Rights of the Palestinian people

Dec. 11   39/49D   121-3 (US, Israel, Canada)
Convening a Middle-East peace conference

Dec. 12   39/62   125-1
Prohibition of development and manufacture of new types of weapons
of mass destruction

Dec. 12   39/65B   84-1
Prohibition of chemical and bacteriological weapons

Dec. 13   39/72G   146-2 (US, UK)
International action to eliminate apartheid

Dec. 13   39/73   138-2 (US, Turkey)
Law of the sea.

Dec. 14   39/95A   120-2 (US, Israel)
Israeli human rights violations in occupied territories

Dec. 14   39/95H   143-2 (US, Israel)
Condemns assassination attempts against Palestinian mayors and calls
for apprehension and prosecution of the perpetrators

Dec. 17   39/147   94-2 (US, Israel)
Condemns Israel's refusal to place its nuclear facilities under
International Atomic Energy Agency safeguards

Dec. 17   39/148N   123-1
Nuclear-test ban, cessation of nuclear-arms race, nuclear disarmament

Dec. 17   39/151F   141-1
Request to continue UN study on military research and development

Dec. 17   39/161B   143-1
Commemorating the 25th anniversary of the Declaration on the
Granting of Independence to Colonial Countries and Peoples

Dec. 18   39/224   146-2 (US, Israel)
Economic and social assistance to the Palestinian people

Dec. 18   39/232   118-2 (US, Israel)
Support of the UN Industrial Development Organization

Dec. 18   39/233   120-1
Industrial Development Decade for Africa

Dec. 18   39/243   123-2 (US, Israel)
Staff and administrative questions regarding the Economic
Commission for Western Asia

1985
Dec. 13   40/114   134-1
Indivisibility and interdependence of economic, social, cultural, civil
and political rights

Dec. 13   40/124   130-1
Alternative approaches within the UN system for improving the
enjoyment of human rights and fundamental freedoms

Dec. 13   40/148   121-2 (US, Israel)
Measures to be taken against Nazi, Fascist and neo-Fascist activities

Dec. 17   40/445   133-1
International cooperation in the interrelated areas of money, finance,
debt, resource flow, trade and development

1986

Oct. 27   41/11   124-1
Zone of peace and co-operation in the South Atlantic

Dec. 3   41/68A   148-1
New world information order, led by UNESCO, to eliminate existing imbalances in the information and communications fields

Dec. 4   41/90   126-1
Review of the Implementation of the Declaration of the Strengthening of International Security

Dec. 4   41/91   117-1
Need for result-oriented political dialogue to improve the international situation

Dec. 4   41/92   102-2 (US, France)
Establishment of a comprehensive system of international peace and security

Dec. 4   41/128   146-1
Declaration on the right to development

Dec. 4   41/151   148-1
Measures to improve the situation and ensure the human rights and dignity of all migrant workers

Dec. 8   41/450   146-1
Protection against products harmful to health and the environment

1987

Oct. 15   42/5   153-2 (US, Israel)
Cooperation between the UN and the League of Arab States

Nov. 12   42/18   94-2 (US, Israel)
Need for compliance in the International Court of Justice concerning military and paramilitary activities against Nicaragua

Dec. 2   42/69J   145-2 (US, Israel)
Calls upon Israel to abandon plans to remove and resettle Palestinian refugees of the West Bank away from their homes and property

Dec. 7   42/101   150-0-1 (US sole abstainer)
A call for a "convention on the rights of the child"

Dec. 7   42/159   153-2 (US, Israel)
Measures to prevent international terrorism, study the underlying
political and economic causes of terrorism, convene a conference to
define terrorism and to differentiate it from the struggle of people for
national liberation

Dec. 8   42/162B   140-1
Financing the training of journalists and strengthening
communication services in the underdeveloped world

Dec. 11   42/176   94-2 (US, Israel)
Ending trade embargo against Nicaragua

Dec. 11   42/198   154-1
Furthering international co-operation regarding the external debt
problems

Dec. 11   42/441   131-1
Preparation of summary records for a UN conference on
Trade and Development

Necessity of ending the US embargo against Cuba

1992   59-2 (US, Israel)*
1993   88-4 (US, Israel, Albania, Paraguay)
1994   101-2 (US, Israel)
1995   117-3 (US, Israel, Uzbekistan)
1996   138-3 (US, Israel, Uzbekistan)**
1997   143-3 (US, Israel, Uzbekistan)
1998   157-2 (US, Israel)
1999   155-2 (US, Israel)

* Romania also voted "no", by mistake.
** For the first time, all 15 European Union countries voted yes.

It should be remembered that for years American political leaders and
media were fond of labeling Cuba an "international pariah".

Food is not a human right

As noted above, in 1982 and 1983, the US was alone in voting against a declaration that education, work, health care, proper nourishment and national development are human rights. It would appear that even 13 years later, official American attitudes had not "softened". In 1996, at a United Nations-sponsored World Food Summit, the US took issue with an affirmation by the summit of the "right of everyone to have access to safe and nutritious food". The United States insisted that it does not recognize a "right to food". Washington instead championed free trade as the key to ending the poverty at the root of hunger, and expressed fears that recognition of a "right to food" could lead to lawsuits from poor nations seeking aid and special trade provisions.[2]

Some other items you may have missed about the US at the UN

In 1949, the United States induced UN Secretary-General Trygve Lie to agree to a written secret agreement with the US State Department whereby, in violation of basic liberties and of the United Nations Charter, applicants for and incumbents in UN secretariat positions would be "screened", without their knowledge, by US agents. Although directed in the first instance against American citizens—who, numbering about 2,000, then constituted approximately half of the UN headquarters personnel—the influence of this clandestine agreement extended to UN employees of other nationalities, and permeated UN specialized agencies abroad. The agreement was an attempt to formalize a policy that had already been well established: a State Department policy aimed at excluding committed internationalists from the international civil service and aligning that service with partisan US attitudes.[3]

In 1952, "on the basis of confidential information supplied by the United States Government", Lie dismissed three American secretariat employees who had invoked the Fifth Amendment before a Senate subcommittee on internal security. Seven other American employees, who had done the same, were placed on compulsory leave with pay.[4]

In 1983, the American Deputy UN Ambassador told other UN members that if they wanted to move UN headquarters out of the United States, the Reagan administration would do nothing to stop them. Said Charles Lichenstein: "We will put no impediments in your way. The members of the US mission will be down at the docks waving you farewell as you sail into the sunset."[5]

CHAPTER 21

Eavesdropping on the Planet

Any sound that Winston made, above the level of a very low whisper, would be picked up by it...There was of course no way of knowing whether you were being watched at any given moment...You had to live—did live, from habit that became instinct—in the assumption that every sound you made was overheard, and, except in darkness, every movement scrutinized.

George Orwell, *1984*

George didn't have it quite right about the darkness. Night-vision technology is becoming more science-fictionish even as you read this. And he wrote of one country, Oceania. A large country to be sure, but certainly not the entire world. Could he have imagined how it would be only sixteen years further into the future?

Can people in the year 2000 imagine a greater invasion of privacy on all of earth, in all of history?

Like a mammoth vacuum cleaner in the sky, the National Security Agency (NSA) sucks it all up: fax, home phone, cellular phone, email, telex...satellite transmissions, fiber-optic communications traffic, microwave links...voice, text, images...if it runs on electromagnetic energy, NSA is there, with high, high tech. Seven days a week. Twenty-four hours a day. Perhaps billions of messages sucked up each day. Who knows how many? No one escapes. Not presidents, prime ministers, the UN Secretary-General, the pope, the Queen of

England, transnational corporation CEOs, friend, foe, your Aunt Lena...if god has a phone, it's being monitored...maybe your dog isn't being tapped. The oceans will not protect you. American submarines have been attaching tapping pods to deep underwater cables for decades.

Under a system codenamed ECHELON—launched in the 1970s to spy on Soviet satellite communications—the NSA and its (very) junior partners in Britain, Australia, New Zealand and Canada operate a network of massive, highly automated interception stations, covering the globe amongst them. In multiple ways, each of the countries involved is breaking its own laws, those of other countries, and international law— the absence of court-issued warrants permitting surveillance of named individuals is but one example. But who is to stop them?

In 1999, the House Intelligence Committee of the US Congress sought internal NSA documents about its compliance with the law that prohibits it from deliberately eavesdropping on Americans, either in the United States or overseas, unless the Agency can establish probable cause to believe that they are agents of a foreign government committing espionage or other crimes. NSA stonewalled the committee.[1]

Apart from specifically-targeted individuals and institutions, the ECHELON system works by indiscriminately intercepting very large quantities of communications and using computers to identify and extract messages of interest from the mass of unwanted ones. Every intercepted message—all the embassy cables, the business deals, the sex talk, the birthday greetings—is searched for keywords, which could be anything the searchers think might be of interest. Computers can "listen" to telephone calls and recognize when keywords are spoken. Those calls are extracted and recorded separately, to be listened to in full by humans.[2] The list of specific targets at any given time is undoubtedly wide ranging, at one point including the likes of Amnesty International and Christian Aid.[3]

However, the people running ECHELON are not actually superhuman: they admit they have serious technical problems; they can't always intercept the Internet as easily as they'd like; fiber-optic transmissions (which transmit a vast volume of digital data as a stream of light) pose even greater difficulties; and the data they collect is growing exponentially, overwhelmingly—sorting and analyzing the random communications in a meaningful way presents a prodigious challenge.

On the other hand, encryption expert Whitfield Diffie of Sun Microsystems suggests that these alarms raised by NSA may be a self-interested ruse. "What the agency wants us to believe—they used to be great, but these days they have trouble reading the newspaper, the Internet is too complicated for them, there is so much traffic and they can't find what they want. It may be true, but it is what they have been 'saying' for years. It's convenient for NSA to have its targets believe it is in trouble. That doesn't mean it isn't in trouble, but it is a reason to view what spooky inside informants say with skepticism."[4] He might have added that raising such alarms also helps greatly at budget time.

ECHELON is carried out without official acknowledgment of its existence, let alone any democratic oversight or public or legislative debate as to whether it serves a human purpose. Which is to say: What gives the United States the right to do this? In Great Britain, when Members of Parliament have raised questions about the activities of the NSA and its ever-expanding base in Menwith Hill, North Yorkshire, the government has consistently refused to supply any information.

The base in England is now the NSA's largest listening post in the world. Sprawling across 560 acres, it has an operations center and on-site town, including houses, shops, a chapel, a sports center and its own uninterruptible electricity supply.[5]

The extensiveness of the ECHELON global network is a product of decades of intense Cold War activity. Yet with the end of the Cold War, its budget—far from being greatly reduced—has been increased, and the network has grown in both power and reach; yet another piece of evidence that the Cold War was not a battle against something called "communism".

The European Parliament in recent years has been waking up to this intrusion into the continent's affairs. The parliament's Civil Liberties Committee commissioned a report, which appeared in 1998 and recommended a variety of measures for dealing with the increasing power of the technologies of surveillance. It bluntly advised: "The European Parliament should reject proposals from the United States for making private messages via the global communications network [Internet] accessible to US intelligence agencies." The report urged a fundamental review of the involvement of the NSA in Europe, suggesting that the agency's activities be either scaled down, or become more open and accountable. It also denounced Britain's role as a double-agent, spying on its own European partners.[6]

"It is profoundly shocking and should provoke a general outcry," Jean-Pierre Millet, a French lawyer specializing in computer crime, told the French newspaper *Le Figaro*. "Britain's European partners have a right to be furious but [the British] won't abandon their pact with the US."[7]

Such concerns have been privately expressed by governments and members of the European Parliament since the end of the Cold War, but the US has continued to expand ECHELON surveillance in Europe, principally because of heightened interest in commercial espionage—to uncover industrial information that would provide American corporations with an advantage over foreign rivals.

German security experts have found that ECHELON is engaged in heavy commercial spying in Europe. Victims have included such German firms as the wind generator manufacturer Enercon. In 1998, Enercon developed what it thought was a secret invention, enabling it to generate electricity from wind power at a far cheaper rate than before. However, when the company tried to market its invention in the United States, it was confronted by its American rival, Kenetech, which announced that it had already patented a near-identical development. Kenetech then brought a court order against Enercon to ban the sale of its equipment in the US. In a rare public disclosure, an NSA employee, who refused to be named, agreed to appear in silhouette on German television to reveal how he had stolen Enercon's secrets. He said he used satellite information to tap the telephone and computer link lines that ran between Enercon's research laboratory and its production unit some 12 miles away. Detailed plans of the company's invention were then passed on to Kenetech.[8]

In 1994, Thomson S.A. and Airbus Industrie, both based in France, also lost lucrative contracts, snatched away by American rivals aided by information covertly collected by the NSA and CIA.[9] The same agencies also eavesdropped on Japanese representatives during negotiations with the United States in 1995 over auto parts trade.[10]

German industry complains that it is in a particularly vulnerable position because the government forbids its security services from conducting similar industrial espionage. "German politicians still support the rather naive idea that political allies should not spy on each other's businesses. The Americans and the British do not have such illusions," said journalist Udo Ulfkotte, a specialist in European industrial espionage.[11]

In 1999, Germany demanded that the United States recall three CIA operatives for their activities in Germany involving economic espionage. The news report stated that the Germans "have long been suspicious of the eavesdropping capabilities of the enormous U.S. radar and communications complex at Bad Aibling, near Munich", which is in fact an NSA intercept station. "The Americans tell us it is used solely to monitor communications by potential enemies, but how can we be entirely sure that they are not picking up pieces of information that we think should remain completely secret?" asked a senior German official.[12] Japanese officials most likely have been told a similar story by Washington about the more than a dozen signals intelligence bases which Japan has allowed to be located on its territory.[13]

The European Union and the FBI

Despite all the above expressed misgivings, the Council (or Council of Ministers) of the European Union has been working closely with the FBI since the early 1990s to develop a system for intercepting telecommunications in its member countries to serve the "law enforcement community" (police, immigration, customs, and internal security). ECHELON, by contrast, is run by and serves the "military-intelligence community."

Known as the EU-FBI telecommunications surveillance system (sometimes referred to as ENFOPOL), it would carry tapping of the Internet to a new level. Specialized software would be installed at Internet Service Providers (ISP) which would be remotely ("virtually") controlled by law enforcement agencies. The effect would be to automate the interception of messages. How feasible this is technically remains to be seen.

Furthermore, if the ISPs provided "encoding, compression or encryption" to one of their customers, they would have to provide it *en clair* (decrypted) to the law enforcement agencies. ISPs and network operators (e.g., satellite communications networks) would not be granted new or extended operating licenses at national level unless they complied.

Like much in the EU-FBI agreement, these requirements are inspired by the FBI. It's something the Bureau couldn't get away with at home. There has been strong resistance from some of the communication companies in Europe as well, but the master plan proceeds unfazed, putting forth recommendations about amendments to national laws to "ensure that surveillance will be possible within the new systems". The plans include extending the system to countries outside the European Union.

As of the end of 1999, the final draft of the agreement was not yet ready to be submitted to EU states for ratification; one reason for the delay was that various security services had been exerting full-court presses to maximize surveillance coverage and minimize control and accountability.[14]

Encryption

In their quest to gain access to more and more private information, the NSA, the FBI and other components of the US national security establishment have been engaged for years in a campaign to require American telecommunications manufacturers and carriers to design their equipment and networks to optimize the authorities' wiretapping ability, and to impose a national civilian cryptography standard designed to allow the government to decode encrypted communications at will. The power to favor or block approval of a company's exports has been one of the carrot-and-stick tools employed by the security establishment. Some industry insiders say they believe that some US machines approved for export contain NSA "back doors" (also called "trap doors").

The United States has been trying to persuade European Union countries as well to allow it "back-door" access to encryption programs, claiming that this was to serve the needs of law-enforcement agencies. However, a report released by the European Parliament in

May 1999 asserts that Washington's plans for controlling encryption software in Europe have nothing to do with law enforcement and everything to do with US industrial espionage.

The NSA has also dispatched FBI agents on break-in missions to snatch code books from foreign facilities in the United States, and CIA officers to recruit foreign communications clerks abroad and buy their code secrets, according to veteran intelligence officials.[15]

And yet more license?

The US Justice Department as well has been pressing Congress to make it easier for law enforcement authorities to obtain search warrants to secretly enter homes or offices and disable security on personal computers by ascertaining passwords and installing devices that override encryption programs, this as a prelude to a wiretap or a further search.[16]

Meanwhile, federal agencies are running "anonymous remailers", the Internet entities which allow people to send email without revealing their true email address. Worldwide users of these particular remailing services have no idea that their partner in privacy protection is an American government spook of some kind. This might in fact cause problems for some of the users, whose number probably includes dissidents and human-rights activists in nations with repressive governments, whistle blowers in companies or government agencies, those wishing to report crimes and war atrocities, and gay Web surfers who anonymously chat in online communities without fear of retribution by neighbors or employers. Moreover, NSA reportedly concluded agreements several years ago with Lotus, Microsoft, and Netscape aimed at preventing other anonymous email; i.e., some of what was beyond NSA's control. These companies have further bent to the pressure of their government by secretly inserting a "back door" in their software sold abroad to defeat cryptographic methods. Lotus has admitted to this.[17]

And the FBI is now enjoying its newest Big-Brother toy: "roving wiretaps", which allows the tapping of any phone physically near the targeted subject, including those of friends, neighbors, business associates and strangers; be it pay phone, cellular phone or borrowed phone; regardless of who's speaking on the phone, as long as the targeted subject might use it.[18]

Cowardly new world

It's as if the national security establishment feels that it has an inalienable *right* to listen in; as if there had been a constitutional amendment, applicable to the entire world, stating that "Congress shall make no law abridging the freedom of the government to intercept the personal communications of citizens." And the Fourth Amendment had been changed to read: "Persons shall be secure in their persons, houses, papers, and effects, against unreasonable searches and seizures, except in cases of national security, real or alleged."

The worst possible scenario

When pressed on moral, legal, privacy or any other grounds to justify their electronic fishing expeditions, which are expanding like the universe after the Big Bang, the anti-privacy police invariably fall back on some version of: "What if terrorists are planning a terrible act and communicating the details to each other over the telephone (email/fax)? Through tapping, we could find out their plans in advance and stop them."

If they can resort to the worst possible scenario—which in all likelihood has never happened and never will unless the terrorists were all born yesterday, on Mars, and the authorities are outrageously lucky in the extreme—then others can paint their own worst scenarios. For example, in the course of the countless eavesdrops, information is bound to be picked up about people cheating on their spouses. Imagine each time this leaks out—great arguments at home, depression, spousal abuse, divorce, murder, suicide…and think of the children. Not to mention the possibility of blackmail or forcing the person to engage in espionage or treason. All it takes to flag a communication is for one of the parties to use a couple or so of the key words in the ECHELON "dictionary"—"He lives in a lovely old **white house** on **Clinton** Street, right near me. I can **shoot** over there in two minutes."

The greatest intelligence scam of the century

For decades, beginning in the 1950s, the Swiss company Crypto AG sold the world's most sophisticated and secure encryption technology. The firm staked its reputation and the security concerns of its clients on its neutrality in the Cold War or any war. The purchasing nations, some 120 of them—including prime US intelligence targets such as Iran, Iraq, Libya and Yugoslavia—confident that their communications were protected, sent messages from their capitals to their embassies, military missions, trade offices and espionage dens around the world, via telex, radio and fax. And all the while, because of a secret agreement between the company and NSA, these governments might as well have been hand delivering the messages to Washington, uncoded. For their Crypto AG machines had been rigged before being sold to them, so that when they used them the random encryption key could be automatically and clandestinely transmitted along with the enciphered message. NSA analysts could read the messages as easily as they could the morning newspaper. German intelligence was in on it as well and may even have been the actual owner of Crypto AG.

In 1986, because of US public statements concerning the La Belle disco bombing in West Berlin, the Libyans began to suspect that something was rotten with Crypto AG's machines and switched to another Swiss firm, Gretag Data Systems AG. But it appears that NSA had that base covered as well. In 1992, after a series of suspicious circumstances over the previous few years, Iran came to a conclusion similar to Libya's, and arrested a Crypto AG employee who was in Iran on a business trip. He was eventually ransomed, but the incident became well known and the scam began to unravel in earnest.[19]

Microsoft Windows

NSA has done something similar with computers. In September 1999, leading European investigative reporter Duncan Campbell revealed that NSA had arranged with Microsoft to insert special "keys" into Windows software, in all versions from 95-OSR2 onwards. An American computer scientist, Andrew Fernandez of Cryptonym in North Carolina, had disassembled parts of the Windows instruction code and found the smoking gun—Microsoft's developers had failed to remove the debugging symbols used to test this software before they released it. Inside the code were the labels for two keys. One was called "KEY". The other was called

"NSAKEY". Fernandez presented his finding at a conference at which some Windows developers were also in attendance. The developers did not deny that the NSA key was built into their software, but they refused to talk about what the key did, or why it had been put there without users' knowledge. Fernandez says that NSA's "back door" in the world's most commonly used operating system makes it "orders of magnitude easier for the US government to access your computer."[20]

In February 2000, it was disclosed that the Strategic Affairs Delegation (DAS), the intelligence arm of the French Defense Ministry, had prepared a report in 1999 which also asserted that NSA had helped to install secret programs in Microsoft software. According to the DAS report, "it would seem that the creation of Microsoft was largely supported, not least financially, by the NSA, and that IBM was made to accept the [Microsoft] MS-DOS operating system by the same administration." The report stated that there had been a "strong suspicion of a lack of security fed by insistent rumours about the existence of spy programmes on Microsoft, and by the presence of NSA personnel in Bill Gates' development teams." The Pentagon, said the report, was Microsoft's biggest client in the world.[21]

CHAPTER 22

Kidnapping and Looting

In 1962, the United States kidnapped about 125 people from the Dominican Republic, and took them to the US and elsewhere.

A suspected drug smuggler was spirited out of Honduras and taken to the US in 1988, although the Honduran constitution prohibits the extradition of Honduran citizens for trial in other countries. Presumably, in this case, it was carried out with the approval of the Honduran government under US pressure.

In December 1989, the American military grabbed Manuel Noriega in Panama and hustled him off to Florida.

The following year, the Drug Enforcement Administration paid bounty hunters to abduct Dr. Humberto Alvarez Machain from his medical office in Guadalajara, Mexico, fly him to El Paso and turn him over to the DEA.

A Cypriot businessman, Hossein Alikhani, accused of violating US sanctions against Libya, was lured on board a plane in the Bahamas in 1992 in a US Customs sting and abducted to Miami.

Increasing numbers of Colombians, charged with drug offenses, are being shipped to the US since Washington succeeded in forcing the government to remove a prohibition against extradition in December 1997.[1]

In 1992, the US Supreme Court, ruling in the Alvarez Machain case, declared that although it may be "shocking" in its violation of basic principles of international law, kidnapping foreign citizens in their own country is a legally acceptable way to get them to face charges in a US court for violating American law. Chief Justice

William H. Rehnquist was willing to record for history his observation that the extradition treaty between the United States and Mexico could be ignored because the treaty didn't explicitly say "no kidnapping allowed".[2]

If memory serves, the United States fought a war in 1812 with Great Britain over this practice.

If people can be taken with impunity, how much easier with papers and other material goods.

Europe

In the dying days of World War II, the fascist leaders of Hungary escaped to the West with a trainload of loot belonging to the Hungarian Jewish bourgeoisie—from furs and stamp collections to artwork and oriental rugs, and at least one crate of wedding rings confiscated from Holocaust victims. The train got as far as Austria, where American Army forces stopped them. US officers, and likely the lower ranks as well, helped themselves to all manner of goodies. After the war, despite repeated pleas from the Hungarian Jewish community, very few of the valuables were returned to their original owners. In 1949, Washington transferred 1,181 paintings of the Hungarian booty to Austria in violation of international treaties stipulating that "cultural property" looted during the Second World War should be returned to "the country of origin". The Truman administration wished to prevent such treasures from falling into the hands of Communist regimes in Eastern Europe; better in the hands of the Austrians, the willing accomplices of Adolf Hitler.[3]

Guatemala

In the wake of the CIA-engineered coup of 1954, the United States confiscated a huge amount of documents from the Guatemalan government, primarily in the hope of uncovering the hand of The International Communist Conspiracy behind the government of Jacobo Arbenz. This, after all, has been Washington's official rationale to this day for overthrowing Arbenz. If this is what was indeed discovered in the documents, it has not been made public.

Grenada

In the midst of its completely illegal and destructive invasion of the island in October 1983, the United States found time to rifle through government files and take a large quantity of documents back home. Washington officials then proceeded to give selected documents to the press to publish—such as those dealing with meetings of Grenadian government leaders and military cooperation agreements with foreign countries—hoping that this would lend credence to the official US government position that Cuba and Russia were planning to take over the island and use it as a springboard for destabilizing the entire Caribbean. The documents, however, evidenced no such thing.[3] Indeed, CIA Director William Casey was later to admit that the documents "were not a real find".[4]

Panama

During their invasion of December 1989, the United States confiscated thousands of boxes of government documents, which they refused to return.[5] The occupying American forces roamed the land free from the restraints of any higher power. Along the way they helped themselves to all manner of other documents, files and archives from the offices of the media, political parties (particularly those of the left), labor unions, etc.[6]

The US also seized more than 52,000 weapons, as well as armored personnel carriers and rocket launchers. Panama later asked for compensation for the material.[7]

There has been no return of anything nor any compensation paid.[8]

Germany

Sometime shortly after the collapse of the East German government in 1990, the CIA managed to spirit away the top-secret archives of the country's intelligence agency, the Stasi. For the next nine years, the United States refused to return the material—with the exception of some bits and pieces now and then—despite the repeated requests of the German government. President Clinton for some time refused to even discuss the matter with German chancellor Gerhard Schroeder. Finally, in October 1999, the CIA announced that they would turn over what appears to be a substantial portion of the files, but the Agency would still retain a large number of selected files. The Stasi files contain information on numerous individuals whose identity the CIA would prefer not be exposed, presumably including their own agents who were spying on West Germany, whom the Stasi knew about; many other files might be valuable to the Agency because the individuals would be highly vulnerable to blackmail, for whatever purpose they could be used by the CIA.[9]

Iraq

In the wake of the Persian Gulf War in 1991, Kurdish groups captured some 18 tons of Iraqi government documents, which the United States later took possession of. The papers now reside at the University of Colorado at Boulder and are open to the public.[10] Iraq has not asked for the return of the documents, perhaps realizing the utter futility and groveling nature of such a request.

Haiti

While returning Jean-Bertrand Aristide to power in 1994, the US military helped themselves to an estimated 160,000 documents, audio and videotapes (some of torture sessions), and "trophy photos" of mutilated victims, belonging to the Haitian military and paramilitary organizations. The United States has refused to hand back its booty unless it can select which ones to return, censoring any it wishes, and unless Haiti agrees to certain detailed restrictions on use of the material. The decades-long CIA involvement with sundry Haitian dictatorships, armed forces, death squads, torturers, drug traffickers and miscellaneous corruption gives Washington more than enough reason to keep the material from wide dissemination. However, Haitian President Rene Preval has stated: "Our position is we want all the documents back, unaltered, period."

The Haitian government has asked for the documents several times since 1995, in public letters, private correspondence, press conferences and international arenas. Among the supporters of its request have been the UN/OAS human rights mission to Haiti, scores of present and former members of the US Congress, religious and solidarity groups in the United States and abroad, three Nobel Peace Prize win-

ners, Amnesty International and Human Rights Watch. The UN
Human Rights Commission has demanded the return of the documents so that the truth of "where the responsibility lies in each case"
of human rights violations could be determined. Even the British
Foreign Office raised the issue with the US State Department.
Advocates for the return of the documents say that the absence of evidence concerning some of those who took part in the 1991 coup that
overthrew the democratically-elected Aristide contributes to the inse-
curity and injustice plaguing Haiti today.

For several years, Haiti and its supporters in the United Nations
Commission on Human Rights and in the General Assembly have
tried to bring to a vote a resolution calling for the United States to
return the documents. But the US delegation has been able to maneu-
ver the proceedings to block such a vote.[11]

CHAPTER 23

How the CIA Sent Nelson Mandela to Prison for 28 Years

When Nelson Mandela was released from prison in February 1990, President George Bush personally telephoned the black South African leader to tell him that all Americans were "rejoicing at his release".[1]

This was the same Nelson Mandela who was imprisoned for almost 28 years because the CIA tipped off South African authorities as to where they could find him.

And this was the same George Bush who was once the head of the CIA and who for eight years was second in power of an administration whose CIA and National Security Agency collaborated closely with the South African intelligence service, providing information about Mandela's African National Congress.[2] The ANC was a progressive nationalist movement whose influence had been felt in other African countries; accordingly it had been perceived by Washington as being part of the legendary International Communist Conspiracy. In addition to ideology, other ingredients in the cooking pot the United States and South Africa both ate from was that the latter served as an important source of uranium for the United States, and the US was South Africa's biggest supporter at the United Nations.

On August 5, 1962, Nelson Mandela had been on the run for 17 months when armed police at a roadblock outside Howick, Natal flagged down a car in which he was pretending to be the chauffeur of a white passenger in the back seat. How the police came to be there was not publicly explained. In late July 1986, however, stories appeared in three South African newspapers (picked up shortly thereafter by the London press and, in part, CBS-TV) which shed considerable light on the question. The stories told of how a CIA officer, Donald C. Rickard by name, under cover as a consular official in Durban, had tipped off the Special Branch that Mandela would be disguised as a chauffeur in a car headed for Durban. This was information Rickard had obtained through an informant in the ANC. One year later, at a farewell party for him in South Africa, at the home of the notorious CIA mercenary, Colonel "Mad Mike" Hoare, Rickard himself, his tongue perhaps loosened by spirits, stated in the hearing of some of those present that he had been due to meet Mandela on the fateful night, but tipped off the police instead. Rickard refused to discuss the affair when approached by CBS-TV.[3]

CBS-TV newsman Allen Pizzey did interview journalist James Tomlins on the air when the story broke in 1986. Tomlins, who was in South Africa in 1962, stated that Rickard had told him of his involvement in Mandela's capture.[4]

On June 10, 1990, *The Atlanta Journal and Constitution* reported that an unidentified, retired US intelligence officer had revealed that within hours of Mandela's arrest, Paul Eckel, then a senior CIA operative, had told him: "We have turned Mandela over to the South African security branch. We gave them every detail, what he would be wearing, the time of day, just where he would be. They have picked him up. It is one of our greatest coups."[5]

After Mandela's release, the White House was asked if Bush would apologize to the South African for the reported US involvement in his arrest at an upcoming meeting between the two men. In this situation, a categorical denial by the White House of any American involvement in the arrest would have been *de rigueur*. However, spokesman Marlin Fitzwater replied: "This happened during the Kennedy administration...don't beat me up for what the Kennedy people did."[6]

The CIA stated: "Our policy is not to comment on such allegations." This is what the Agency says when it feels that it has nothing to gain by issuing a statement. On a number of other occasions, because it thought that it would serve their purpose, the CIA has indeed commented on all kinds of allegations.

While Mandela's youth and health ebbed slowly away behind prison walls, Donald Rickard retired to live in comfort and freedom in Pagosa Springs, Colorado. He resides there still today.

CHAPTER 24

The CIA and Drugs: Just Say "Why Not?"

In my 30-year history in the Drug Enforcement Administration and related agencies, the major targets of my investigations almost invariably turned out to be working for the CIA.

Dennis Dayle, former chief of an elite DEA enforcement unit.[1]

1947 to 1951, France

Corsican and Mafia criminal syndicates in Marseilles, Sicily and Corsica—benefiting from CIA arms, money and psychological warfare—suppressed strikes and wrestled control of labor unions from the Communist Party. In return, the CIA smoothed the way for the gangsters to be left unmolested, and unindicted, and to reestablish the heroin racket that had been restrained during the war—the famous "French Connection" that was to dominate the drug trade for more than two decades and was responsible for most of the heroin entering the United States.[2]

1950s to early 1970s, Southeast Asia

The Nationalist Chinese army, defeated by the communists in 1949 and forced into exile, became part of an army formed by the CIA in Burma to wage war against Communist China. The Agency closed its eyes to the fact that their new clients were becoming the opium barons of The Golden Triangle (parts of Burma, Thailand and Laos), the world's largest source of opium and heroin. Air America, the CIA's principal airline proprietary, flew the drugs all over Southeast Asia, to sites where the opium was processed into heroin, and to trans-shipment points on the route to Western customers.[3]

During the US military involvement in Vietnam and Laos, the CIA worked closely with certain tribal peoples and warlords engaged in opium cultivation. In exchange for tactical or intelligence support from these elements, the Agency protected their drug operations. Air American pilots were again engaged in flying opium and heroin throughout the area to serve the personal and entrepreneurial needs of the CIA's various military and political allies, at times lining their own pockets as well; on occasion, the proceeds also helped finance CIA covert actions off budget; ultimately, the enterprise turned many GIs in Vietnam into heroin addicts.

The operation was not a paragon of discretion. Heroin was refined in a laboratory located on the site of CIA headquarters in northern Laos. After two decades of American military intervention, Southeast Asia had become the source of 70 percent of the world's illicit opium and the major supplier for America's booming heroin market.[4]

1973–80, Australia

The Nugan Hand Bank of Sydney had close, if not to say intimate, ties to the CIA. Among the bank's officers were a network of US generals, admirals and former (or "former") CIA men, including William Colby, recently the Agency's director, who was one of the bank's lawyers. Bank co-founder Michael Hand had been a Green Beret and CIA contract agent in Laos, working with Air America. Many of the depositors whose money first helped the bank get started were Air America employees.

The bank rapidly expanded, with branches in Saudi Arabia, Europe, Southeast Asia, South America and the US. It became one of the banks of choice for international drug traffickers (whom Nugan Hand actively solicited), money launderers, arms dealers and the CIA (which used the bank for its payouts for covert operations). In 1980, amidst several mysterious deaths, the bank collapsed, $50 million in debt.[5]

1970s and 1980s, Panama

For more than a decade, Panamanian strongman, General Manuel Noriega, was a highly paid CIA asset and collaborator, despite knowledge by US drug authorities as early as 1971 that the general was heavily involved in drug trafficking and money laundering. Noriega facilitated "guns-for-drugs" flights for the Nicaraguan Contras, providing protection and pilots; safe havens for drug cartel officials; and discreet banking facilities for all. Yet, US officials, including CIA Director William Webster and several Drug Enforcement Administration (DEA) officers, sent Noriega letters of praise for his efforts to thwart drug trafficking (albeit only against competitors of his Medellin Cartel patrons). William Casey, who became CIA Director in 1981, declared that he didn't denounce Noriega for his relationship with drug traffickers because the Panamanian "was providing valuable support for our policies in Central America, especially Nicaragua".[6]

When a confluence of circumstances led to Noriega falling into political disfavor with Washington, the Bush administration was reluctantly obliged to turn against him. In 1989, the US invaded Panama, kidnapped and imprisoned the general, and falsely ascribed the invasion to the war on drugs whereas several foreign-policy imperatives actually lay behind the operation. Drug trafficking through Panama continued unabated under the new US-installed government.[7] Had Noriega become addicted to communism rather than drug money, the Marines would have landed in Panama City long before.

As further indication of how US officials are in actuality relatively undisturbed about drug trafficking as such—in stark contrast to their public pose—consider the case of the former Panamanian ambassador-at-large in Washington, Ricardo Bilonick. He helped smuggle nearly 40,000 pounds of Colombian cocaine into the US in the early 1980s, but because he could serve a "higher" political purpose by turning state's witness against Noriega, he got off with a three-year sentence, compared to Noriega's 40 years. At his trial, Bilonick received letters of reference from former president Jimmy Carter, former Under-Secretary-of-State William D. Rogers, and a former US ambassador to Panama.[8] There are thousands of men and women languishing in American prisons, charged with cocaine offenses, who—in TOTAL—did not traffic in as much cocaine as Bilonick did.

1980s, Central America

Washington's philosophy was consistent: let 'em traffic in drugs, let 'em murder, rape and torture, let 'em burn down schools and medical clinics...as long as they carry out our wars, they're our boys, our good ol' boys.

Obsessed with overthrowing the leftist Sandinista government in Nicaragua, Reagan administration officials tolerated and abetted drug trafficking as long as the traffickers gave support to the Contras. In 1989, the Senate Subcommittee on Terrorism, Narcotics and International Operations (the Kerry Committee) concluded a three-year investigation by stating:

> There was substantial evidence of drug smuggling through the war zones on the part of individual Contras, Contra suppliers, Contra pilots, mercenaries who worked with the Contras, and Contra supporters throughout the region...U.S. officials involved in Central America failed to address the drug issue for fear of jeopardizing the war efforts against Nicaragua...In each case, one or another agency of the U.S. government had information regarding the involvement either while it was occurring, or immediately thereafter...Senior U.S. policy makers were not immune to the idea that drug money was a perfect solution to the Contras' funding problems.[9]

In Costa Rica, which served as the "Southern Front" for the Contras (Honduras being the Northern Front), there were several different CIA-Contra networks involved in drug trafficking, including that of CIA asset John Hull, an American whose farms along Costa Rica's border with Nicaragua were the main staging area for the Contras. Hull and other CIA-connected Contra supporters and pilots teamed up with George Morales, a major Miami-based Colombian drug trafficker who later admitted to giving more than $4 million in cash to the Contras. Morales' planes were loaded with weapons in Florida, flown to Central America and then brought back with cocaine on board.[10]

In 1989, after the Costa Rica government indicted Hull for drug trafficking, a DEA-hired plane clandestinely and illegally flew him to Miami. The US repeatedly thwarted Costa Rican efforts to extradite Hull back to Costa Rica to stand trial. Another Costa Rican-based drug ring involved anti-Castro Cubans whom the CIA had hired as military trainers for the Contras. Many of the Cubans had long been involved with the CIA and drug trafficking. They used Contra planes and a Costa Rican-based shrimp company, which laundered money for the CIA, to move cocaine to the United States.[11]

In Honduras, in exchange for allowing the US to convert the country into a grand military base, the CIA and DEA turned a virtually blind eye to the extensive drug trafficking of Honduran military officers, government officials and others. The CIA itself enlisted Alan Hyde, a leading Honduran trafficker—the "godfather of all criminal activities", according to US government reports—to use his boats to transport Contra supplies. In exchange, the Agency discouraged counter-narcotics efforts against Hyde. A CIA cable stated that Hyde's "connection to [CIA] is well documented and could prove difficult in the prosecution stage."[12]

There were other way stations along the cocaine highway, such as the Guatemalan military intelligence service, closely associated with the CIA, and which harbored many drug traffickers, and Ilopango Air Force Base in El Salvador, a key component of the US military intervention against the country's guerrillas. Former DEA officer Celerino Castillo, stationed in El Salvador, has written of how Contra planes flew north loaded with cocaine, landed with impunity in various spots in the United States, including an Air Force base in Texas, then returned laden with cash to finance the war. "All under the protective umbrella of the United States Government."

The operation at Ilopango was run by Felix Rodriguez (aka Max Gomez), who reported to Vice President George Bush (President Reagan's "drug czar") and to Oliver North of Reagan's National Security Council staff, where North oversaw Contra operations. (Reagan, after all, had hailed the Contras as the "moral equivalent of our Founding Fathers".) An entry from North's diary, August 9, 1985, reads: "Honduran DC-6 which is being used for runs out of New Orleans is probably being used for drug runs into U.S."

The CIA owned one of Ilopango's airport hangers, and the National Security Council ran another. When Castillo informed DEA headquarters of the details on cocaine flights from El Salvador to the US, his employer effectively ignored the reports; eventually, Castillo was forced out of the agency.[13]

When some authority in the US wasn't clued in about one of the arriving drug flights, and made an arrest, powerful strings were pulled on behalf of dropping the case, acquittal, reduced sentence or deportation. Reportedly, a US Customs Agent was reassigned from his Texas post back to Washington because he was investigating Contra drug deals too vigorously. There is also the case of Honduran general José Bueso Rosa, who was convicted of conspiring to murder the president of Honduras, the plot being financed by a huge cocaine deal. Senior Reagan administration officials intervened with a Federal judge to obtain leniency for Bueso to honor his services to the Contras. He received five years, while other defendants were sentenced to as much as 40 years.[14]

The connections were everywhere: Four companies that distributed "humanitarian" aid to the Contras but were "owned and operated by narcotics traffickers", and under investigation in the United States for drug trafficking, received State Department contracts of more than $800,000.[15] Southern Air Transport, "formerly" CIA-owned, and later under Pentagon contract, was deeply involved in the drug running as well.[16]

A former US Attorney in Miami told the Kerry Committee that Justice Department officials told him that representatives of their department, the DEA and the FBI met in 1986 "to discuss how Senator Kerry's efforts" to push for the hearings "could be undermined".[17]

To make it easier for the CIA to ignore, while benefiting from, the drug trafficking all about them, in 1982 Agency Director William Casey negotiated an extraordinary secret "memo of understanding" with Attorney General William French Smith to spare the CIA from any legal responsibility to report drug trafficking operations of anyone working for it.[18] This agreement was not fully rescinded until 1995.

1990s, South America

Venezuelan General Ramón Guillén Davila was indicted by a federal grand jury in Miami in 1996 for smuggling as much as 22 tons of cocaine into the United States between 1987 and 1991. At the time he was engaged in this activity, Guillén was the head of the Venezuelan National Guard anti-drug bureau and was what the *Miami Herald* called "the CIA's most trusted man in Venezuela". The

CIA, over the objections of the DEA, had approved the "controlled" shipments of cocaine to the United States as some kind of vague operation to gather information about the Colombian drug cartels. It has not been reported what kind of success this operation had, but at least on one occasion, in 1990, a ton of Guillén's cocaine made it to the streets of America. The CIA actually acknowledged this one, categorizing it as "poor judgment and management on the part of several CIA officers".[19]

See the "Interventions" chapter for discussion of how Washington ignored much of the drug trafficking of government and military personnel in Peru, Colombia and Mexico in the 1990s because of the anti-leftist campaigns being waged by these regimes with US support.

1980s to early 1990s, Afghanistan

CIA-supported Moujahedeen rebels engaged heavily in opium cultivation while fighting against the Soviet-supported government. The Agency's political protection and logistical assistance enabled the growers to markedly increase their output. CIA-supplied trucks and mules, which had carried arms into Afghanistan, were used to transport opium to heroin laboratories along the Afghan-Pakistan border. The output is estimated to have provided up to one half of the heroin used annually in the United States and three-quarters of that used in Western Europe. US officials admitted in 1990 that they had failed to investigate or take action against the drug operation because of a desire not to offend their Pakistani and Afghan allies.[20] As in earlier drug-related actions, CIA officers may also have gotten their hands on a portion of the drug money, using it to help finance their operations, or even themselves. In 1993, an official of the DEA called Afghanistan the new Colombia of the drug world.[21]

1986 to 1994, Haiti

While working to keep right-wing Haitian military and political leaders in power, the CIA looked away from their drug trafficking. Joseph Michel Francois, no. 3 man in the military government of 1991–1994, was regularly briefed by the DEA, which shared intelligence with him on suspected drug smuggling operations in Haiti, this, while Francois was himself a leading drug lord, working with the Colombian

Medellin cartel. Francois was part of a new organization, the National Intelligence Service (SIN), created by the CIA in 1986, purportedly to fight the cocaine trade, though SIN officers, Francois and others, themselves engaged in the trafficking.[22]

1980s, the United States and the Cocaine Import Agency

In addition to the cases cited above of drug-laden planes landing in the US unmolested by authorities, there is the striking case of Oscar Danilo Blandón and Juan Norwin Meneses, two Nicaraguans living in California. To support the Contras (particularly during a period in which Congress banned funding for them), as well as enriching themselves, the two men turned to smuggling cocaine into the US under CIA protection. This led to the distribution of large quantities of cocaine into Los Angeles' inner city at a time when drug users and dealers were trying to make the costly white powder more affordable by changing it into powerful little nuggets of "crack". The Nicaraguans funneled a portion of their drug profits to the Contra cause while helping to fuel a disastrous crack explosion in Los Angeles and other cities, and enabling the gangs to buy automatic weapons, sometimes from Blandón himself.

The ties between the two Nicaraguans and the CIA were visible not far beneath the surface, as the following indicate:

When Blandón was finally arrested in October 1986 (after Congress had resumed funding for the Contras and his services were much less needed), and he admitted to crimes that have sent others away for life, the Justice Department turned him loose on unsupervised probation after only 28 months behind bars and subsequently paid him more than $166,000 as an informer.

According to a legal motion filed in a 1990 police corruption trial in Los Angeles: in a 1986 raid on Blandón's money-launderer, the police carted away numerous documents purportedly linking the US government to cocaine trafficking and money-laundering on behalf of the Contras. CIA personnel appeared at the sheriff's department within 48 hours of the raid and removed the seized files from the evidence room. At the request of the Justice Department, a federal judge issued a gag order barring any discussion of the matter.

When Blandón testified in 1996 as a prosecution witness in a drug trial, the federal prosecutors obtained a court order preventing defense lawyers from delving into his ties to the CIA.

Though Meneses was listed in the DEA's computers as a major international drug smuggler and was implicated in 45 separate federal investigations since 1974, he lived openly and conspicuously in California until 1989 and never spent a day in a US prison. The DEA, US Customs, the Los Angeles County Sheriff's Department and the California Bureau of Narcotic Enforcement all complained that a number of the probes of Meneses were stymied by the CIA or unnamed "national security" interests.

Lastly, the CIA-Contra-drugs nexus brings us the case of the US Attorney in San Francisco who gave back $36,800 to an arrested Nicaraguan drug dealer, which had been found in his possession. The money was returned after two Contra leaders sent letters to the court swearing that the drug dealer had been given the cash to buy supplies "for the reinstatement of democracy in Nicaragua". The letters were hurriedly sealed after prosecutors invoked the Classified Information Procedures Act, a law designed to keep national security secrets from leaking out during trials. When a US Senate subcommittee later inquired of the Justice Department the reason for this unusual turn of events, they ran into a wall of secrecy. "The Justice Department flipped out to prevent us from getting access to people, records—finding anything out about it," recalled Jack Blum, former chief counsel to the Kerry Senate subcommittee referred to above, which investigated allegations of Contra cocaine trafficking. "It was one of the most frustrating exercises that I can ever recall."[23]

The more I think about it, it's the difference between manslaughter and murder. It's the intent. The intent was not to poison black America but to raise money for the Contras, and they [the CIA] didn't really care what it came from. If it involved selling drugs in black communities, well, this was the price of admission.

Gary Webb[24]

CHAPTER 25

Being the World's Only Superpower Means Never Having to Say You're Sorry

I will never apologize for the United States of America.
I don't care what the facts are.

George Bush[1]

Cuba

Cuba, said US District Judge James Lawrence King on December 17, 1997, "in outrageous contempt for international law and basic human rights, murdered four human beings in international airspace." He then proceeded to award $187.6 million to the families of the Florida-based Cuban pilots who had been shot down in February 1996 by Cuban jets while on an air mission, destination Cuba.[2] (In actuality, the Cuban government had done no more than any government in the world would have done under the same circumstances. Havana regarded the planes as within Cuban airspace, of serious hostile intent, and gave the pilots explicit warning: "You are taking a risk." Planes from the same organization had gone even further into Cuban territory on earlier occasions and had been warned by Cuba not to return.)

In November 1996, the federal government gave each of the families a down payment of $300,000 on the award, the money coming out of frozen Cuban assets.[3]

Such was justice, anti-communist style.

Totally ignored by the American government, however, was Cuba's lawsuit of May 31, 1999, filed in a Havana court demanding $181.1 billion in US compensation for death and injury suffered by Cuban citizens in four decades of "war" by Washington against Cuba. The document outlined American "aggression", ranging from backing for armed rebel groups within Cuba and the Bay of Pigs invasion in 1961, to subversion attempts from the US naval base of Guantanamo and the planting of epidemics on the island.

Cuba said it was demanding $30 million in direct compensation for each of the 3,478 people it said were killed by US actions and $15 million each for the 2,099 injured. It was also asking $10 million each for the people killed, and $5 million each for the injured, to repay Cuban society for the costs it has had to assume on their behalf. That was "substantially less" than the amount per person fixed by US Judge King in the pilots' case, the document pointed out.

Cuban officials delivered the papers for the suit to the US Interests Section in Havana. The Americans refused to accept them. The Cuban government subsequently announced plans to take the lawsuit to an international forum.[4]

Vietnam

On January 27, 1973, in Paris, the United States signed the "Agreement on Ending the War and Restoring Peace in Vietnam". Among the principles to which the United States agreed was the one stated in Article 21: "In pursuance of its traditional policy [sic], the United States will contribute to healing the wounds of war and to postwar reconstruction of the Democratic Republic of Vietnam [North Vietnam] and throughout Indochina."

Five days later, President Nixon sent a message to the Prime Minister of North Vietnam in which he stipulated the following:

"(1)The Government of the United States of America will contribute to postwar reconstruction in North Vietnam without any political conditions. (2)Preliminary United States studies indicate that the appropriate programs for the United States contribution to postwar reconstruction will fall in the range of $3.25 billion of grant aid over 5 years."[5]

Nothing of the promised reconstruction aid was ever paid. Or ever will be.

However—deep breath here—Vietnam has been compensating the United States. In 1997 it began to pay off about $145 million in debts left by the defeated South Vietnamese government for American food and infrastructure aid. Thus, Hanoi is reimbursing the United States for part of the cost of the war waged against it.[6]

How can this be? The proper legal term is "extortion". The enforcers employed by Washington included the World Bank, the International Monetary Fund, the Export-Import Bank, the Paris Club and the rest of the international financial mafia. The Vietnamese were made an offer they couldn't refuse: Pay up or subject yourself to exquisite forms of economic torture, even worse than the considerable maiming you've already experienced at the hands of our godfathers.[7]

At the Vietnamese embassy in Washington (a small office in an office building), the First Secretary for Press Affairs, Mr. Le Dzung, told the author in 1997 that this matter, as well as Nixon's unpaid billions, are rather emotional issues in Vietnam, but the government is powerless to change the way the world works.

Nicaragua

Under siege by the United States and its Contra proxy army for several years, Nicaragua filed suit in 1984 in the World Court (International Court of Justice), the principal judicial organ of the United Nations, located in The Hague, Netherlands, for relief from the constant onslaught, which included mining its harbors. The Court ruled in 1986 that the US was in violation of international law for a host of reasons, stated that Washington "is under a duty immediately to cease and to refrain from all such acts [of hostility]" and "is under an obligation to make reparation to the Republic of Nicaragua for all injury".

Anticipating the suit, the Reagan administration had done the decent and right thing: It announced, on April 6, 1984, three days before Nicaragua's filing, that the US would not recognize the World

Court's jurisdiction in matters concerning Central America for a two-year period.

Apart from the awesome arbitrariness of this proclamation, the court's ruling of June 27, 1986 actually came after the two-year period had expired, but the United States ignored it anyway. Washington did not slow down its hostile acts against Nicaragua, nor did it ever pay a penny in reparation.[8]

Libya

The April 1986 American bombing of Libya took the lives of scores of people and wounded another hundred or so. The dead included Libyan leader Moammar Qaddafi's young daughter; all of Qaddafi's other seven children as well as his wife were hospitalized, suffering from shock and various injuries. A year later, 65 claims were filed with the White House and the Department of Defense under the Federal Tort Claims Act and the Foreign Claims Act, on behalf of those killed or injured. The claimants, who were asking for up to $5 million for each wrongful death, included Libyans, Greeks, Egyptians, Yugoslavs and Lebanese.[9] Before long, the number of claimants reached to about 340, but none of their claims got anywhere in the American judicial system, with the Supreme Court declining to hear the case.[10]

Panama

For several years following the American invasion of 1989, with its highly destructive bombing and ground combat, many individual Panamanians tried in various ways to receive compensation for the death or injury of themselves or family members, or the wreckage of their homes or businesses. But their legal claims and suits were met by an implacable US government. One American law firm filed claims on behalf of some 200 Panamanians (all non-combatants), first in Panama with US military officials—under provisions of the Panama Canal treaty—who rejected the claims, then in two suits filed in US courts, all the way up to the Supreme Court, with each of the courts declining to hear the cases.[11]

During the years 1990 to 1993, some 300 Panamanians petitioned the Inter-American Commission on Human Rights of the

Organization of American States (OAS) for a finding that the United States had violated many of their rights and was liable for "just compensation". In 1993, the Commission ruled the petition "admissible". But as of fall 1999, it was still pending as to its "merits", which were being "studied".[12] It should be born in mind that over the years, the United States has wielded inordinate influence in the OAS, far more than any other member. Witness Washington's success in getting Cuba suspended from the organization in 1962 and kept out to the present time despite repeated, growing and publicly-expressed support for Cuba's reinstatement by other OAS members.

There was a report some years ago that a few small payments—seemingly somewhat arbitrary—had been made "on the ground" by US officials to Panamanians in Panama. But in December 1999, the State Department Press Office dealing with Panama stated that "the United States has not paid any compensation for combat-related deaths or injuries or property damage due to Operation Just Cause" (this being the not-tongue-in-cheek name given to the American invasion and bombing).[13] Some of the American aid given to Panama since 1989, the State Department added, has been used by Panama for such purposes. The State Department puts the matter thusly, it would appear, to make it clear to the world that they do not feel any guilt or responsibility for what they did to the people of Panama and will not succumb to any kind of coercion to pay any compensation.

On December 20, 1999, the tenth anniversary of the American invasion, hundreds of Panamanians took to the street to demand once again that the US pay damages to civilian victims of the bombing.

Sudan

The El-Shifa pharmaceutical plant had raised Sudanese medicinal self-sufficiency from less than five percent to more than 50 percent, while producing about 90 percent of the drugs used to treat the most deadly illnesses in this desperately poor country. But on August 20, 1998, the United States saw fit to send more than a dozen Tomahawk cruise missiles screaming into the plant, in an instant depriving the people of Sudan of their achievement. Based on a covertly acquired soil sample, Washington claimed that the plant was producing chemical weapons. At the same time the US gave the world the clear impression that the factory's owner, Saleh Idris, was a close associate of terrorists and was involved in money laundering. Washington proceeded to freeze $24 million in Idris's London bank accounts. But the US was never able to prove any of its assertions, while every piece of evidence and every expert testimony that surfaced categorically contradicted the claim about chemical weapons.[14] The case fell apart completely, and in the meantime, Idris sued to recover his money as well as compensation for his pulverized plant.

Finally, in May 1999, the United States unfroze Idris's accounts rather than contest his suit because they knew they had no case. But as of the end of that year, the US had yet to apologize to Sudan or to Idris for the plant's destruction, or for the serious harm done to his reputation, and had yet to compensate him for the loss of the plant and the loss of business, nor the plant's employees for the loss of their jobs and income, or the ten people who were injured. The degree of Washington's arrogance in the whole matter was stunning, from the initial act on. "Never before," observed former CIA official Milt Bearden, "has a single soil sample prompted an act of war against a sovereign state."[15]

Iraq

The American government and media had a lot of fun with an obvious piece of Iraqi propaganda—the claim that a biological warfare facility, bombed during the Gulf War in 1991, had actually been a baby food factory. But it turned out that the government of New Zealand, whose technicians had visited the site repeatedly, and various other business people from New Zealand who had had intimate contact with the factory, categorically confirmed that it had indeed been a baby food factory. The French contractor who had built the place said the same. But Chairman of the Joint Chiefs of Staff, Colin Powell, insisted: "It was a biological weapons facility, of that we are sure."[16] As to American compensation…this stood as much chance as a ground war with Russia in the wintertime.

China

An exception? After the United States bombed the Chinese embassy in Belgrade in May 1999, Washington apologized profusely to Beijing, blaming outdated maps and such. But this, it appears, was just a cover for the fact that the bombing wasn't actually an accident. Two reports in *The Observer* of London in October and November, based on NATO and US military and intelligence sources, revealed that the embassy had been targeted after NATO discovered that it was being used to transmit Yugoslav army communications. The Chinese were doing this after NATO jets had successfully silenced the Yugoslav government's own transmitters.[17]

Over and above the military need, there may have been a political purpose served. China is clearly the principal barrier to US hegemony in Asia. The bombing of the embassy was perhaps Washington's charming way of telling Beijing that this is only a small sample of what can happen to you if you have any ideas of resisting the American juggernaut. Being able to have a much better than usual "plausible denial" for carrying out such a bombing may have been irresistible to American leaders. The chance would never come again.

All of US/NATO's other bombing "mistakes" in Yugoslavia were typically followed by their spokesman telling the world: "We regret the loss of life." These same words were used by the IRA in Northern Ireland on a number of occasions over the years following one of their bombings which appeared to have struck the wrong target. But their actions were invariably called "terrorist".

Guatemala

On March 10, 1999, in a talk delivered in Guatemala City, President Clinton said that US support for repressive forces in Guatemala "was wrong, and the United States must not repeat that mistake." But the word "sorry" did not cross the president's lips, nor did the word "apologize", nor the word "compensation".[18] Forty years of unholy cruelty to a people for which the United States was preeminently responsible was not worth a right word or a penny.

This was the first visit by an American president to Guatemala since Lyndon Johnson went there in 1968, during the height of the oppression by Washington's client-state government. Johnson did not of course say that the current US policy in Guatemala was wrong, when it would have meant a lot more than Clinton saying so 31 years later. LBJ did, however, inform his audience that he had heard that Guatemala was called "the land of eternal spring".[19]

Greece

Clinton's visit to Greece in November 1999 brought out large and fiery anti-American demonstrations, protesting the recent American bombing of Yugoslavia and the indispensable US support for the torturers *par excellence* of the 1967–74 Greek junta. During his one-day stop, the president found time to address a private group—"When the junta took over in 1967 here," he told his audience, "the United States allowed its interests in prosecuting the Cold War to prevail over its interest—I should say its obligation—to support democracy, which was, after all, the cause for which we fought the Cold War. It is important that we acknowledge that." National Security Council spokesman David Leavey was quick to point out that the president's statement about the former junta was "not intended as an apology."[20]

Questions arise. How can it be that the US fought the Cold War to "support democracy" and wound up supporting not only the Greek dictators but dozens of other tyrannies? Were they all simply "wrong" actions, all "mistakes", like in Guatemala? At what point do we conclude that a consistent sequence of "mistakes" demonstrates intended actions and policy? Moreover, if US "interests" in the Cold War "prevailed" over the cause of democracy, we must ask: What are these "interests" that are in conflict, or at least not harmonious, with democracy, these "interests" which are routinely invoked by American statesmen, but never given a proper name? (Hint: follow the money.)

Finally, we have the words of President Clinton spoken in Uganda in March 1998:

> During the Cold War when we were so concerned about being in competition with the Soviet Union, very often we dealt with countries in Africa and in other parts of the world based more on how they stood in the struggle between the United States and the Soviet Union than how they stood in the struggle for their own people's aspirations to live up to the fullest of their God-given abilities.[21]

What is going on here? Guatemala, Greece, Africa, other parts of the world…Is the president disowning a half-century of American foreign policy? Is he saying that the United States brought all that death, destruction, torture and suffering to the world's multitudes for no good reason? That all we were diligently taught about the nobility of the fight against the thing called "communism" was a fraud?

We'll never know what William Clinton really thinks about these things. He probably doesn't know himself. But we do know what he does. As discussed in the "Introduction" and in "Interventions", we know that he has continued the very same kind of policies he now repudiates. And some day a future American president may acknowledge that what Clinton did in Iraq, Colombia, Mexico, Yugoslavia and elsewhere was "wrong" or "mistaken". But that future president, even while the words cross his lips, will be doing the "wrong" thing himself in one corner of the world or another. And for the same "interests".

The United States Invades, Bombs and Kills for It...but Do Americans Really Believe in Free Enterprise?

Since the end of the Cold War, prominent American economists and financial specialists have been advising the governments of Eastern Europe and the former Soviet Union on the creation and virtues of a free-enterprise system.

The US-government-financed National Endowment for Democracy is busy doing the same on a daily basis in numerous corners of the world.

The US-controlled World Bank and International Monetary Fund will not bestow their financial blessings upon any country that does not aggressively pursue a market economy.

The United States refuses to remove its embargo and end all its other punishments of Cuba unless the Cubans terminate their social-ist experiment and jump on the capitalist bandwagon.

Before Washington would sanction and make possible his return to Haiti in 1994, Haitian President Jean-Bertrand Aristide had to guarantee the White House that he would shed his socialist inclinations and embrace the free market.

It would, consequently, come as a shock to the peoples of many countries to realize that, in actuality, most Americans do not believe in the free-enterprise system. It would, as well, come as a shock to most Americans.

To be sure, a poll asking something like: "Do you believe that our capitalist system should become more socialist?" would be met with a resounding "No!"

But, going above and beyond the buzz words, is that how Americans really feel?

Supply and demand

Following the disastrous 1994 earthquake in Los Angeles came the cry from many quarters: Stores should not be raising prices so much for basic necessities like water, batteries and diapers. Stores should not be raising their prices at all at such a time, it was insisted. It's not the California way and it's not the American way, said Senator Dianne Feinstein. More grievances arose because landlords were raising rents on vacant apartments after many dwellings in the city had been rendered uninhabitable. How dare they do that? people wailed. The California Assembly then proceeded to make it a crime for merchants to increase prices for vital goods and services by more than ten percent after a natural disaster.[1]

In the face of all this, one must wonder: Hadn't any of these people taken even a high-school course in economics? Hadn't they learned at all about the Law of Supply and Demand? Did they think the law had been repealed? Did they think it should be?

Even members of congress don't seem to quite trust the workings of the system. They regularly consider measures to contain soaring drug and health-care costs and the possible regulation of the ticket distribution industry because of alleged price abuses.[2] Why don't our legislators simply allow "the magic of the marketplace" to do its magic?

The profit motive

President Calvin Coolidge left Americans these stirring words to ponder: "Civilization and profits go hand in hand." The First Lady, Hillary Clinton, however, has lashed out at the medical and insurance industries for putting their profits ahead of the public's health. "The market," she declared, "knows the price of everything but the value of nothing."[3]

The unions regularly attack companies for skimping on worker health and safety in their pursuit of higher profit.

Environmentalists never sleep in their condemnation of industry putting profits before the environment.

Lawyer bashing has become a veritable American sport.

Judges frequently impose lighter sentences upon lawbreakers if they haven't actually profited monetarily from their acts. And they forbid others from making a profit from their crimes by selling book or film rights, or interviews. The California Senate made this into law in 1994, which directs that any such income of criminals convicted of serious crimes be placed into a trust fund for the benefit of the victims of their crimes.[4]

President George Bush, in pardoning individuals involved in the Iran-Contra scandal, stated: "First, the common denominator of their motivation—whether their actions were right or wrong—was patriotism. Second they did not profit or seek to profit from their conduct."[5]

No less a champion of free enterprise than former senator Robert Dole said, in an attack upon the entertainment industry during his 1996 presidential campaign, that he wanted "to point out to corporate executives there ought to be some limit on profits...We must hold Hollywood accountable for putting profit ahead of common decency."[6]

That same year, the mayor of Philadelphia, Ed Rendell, bemoaning the corporations move to the suburbs—for what he admitted were "perfectly rational" reasons—declared: "If we let the free market operate unconstrained, cities will die."[7]

Finally, we have a congressional debate in May 1998 about imposing sanctions against countries that allow religious persecution. The sanctions were opposed by US business interests, prompting Rep. Tom Coburn (R-Okla.) to declare: "We've got to figure out what we believe in our country. Do we believe in capitalism and money or do we believe in human rights?"[8]

But how can the system conceivably function as it was designed to without the diligent pursuit of profit? Not merely profit, but the *optimization* of profit. Surely an attorney like Mrs. Clinton knows that corporate officers can be sued by stockholders for ignoring this dictum. Yet she and so many others proceed to blast away at one of the pillars of the capitalist temple.

Private entrepreneurship and ownership

Likewise, the American Medical Association has taken aim at another of the temple's honored pillars—patents, that shrine to the quintessential entrepreneur, the inventor. The AMA issued a blistering condemnation of the increasingly popular practice of patenting new surgical and medical procedures, saying it was unethical and would retard medical progress.[9] Is Thomas Edison rolling over in his grave?

A few years ago, the people of Cleveland felt very hurt and betrayed by the owner of the Browns moving his football team to Baltimore. But is it not the very essence of private ownership that the owner has the right to use the thing he owns in a manner conducive to earning greater profit? Nonetheless, Senator John Glenn and Representative Louis Stokes of Ohio announced their plan to introduce legislation to curb such franchise relocation.[10]

Competition and choice

And where is the appreciation for America's supposedly cherished ideal of greater "choice"? How many citizens welcome all the junk mail filling their mailboxes, or having their senses pursued and surrounded by omnipresent advertisements and commercials? People moan the arrival in their neighborhood of the national chain that smothers and drives out their favorite friendly bookstore, pharmacist or coffee shop, squawking about how "unfair" it is that this "predator" has marched in with hobnail boots and the club of "discount prices". But is this not a textbook case of how free, unfettered competition should operate? Why hasn't the public taken to heart what they're all taught—that in the long run competition benefits everyone?

Ironically, the national chains, like other corporate giants supposedly in competition, are sometimes caught in price-fixing and other acts of collusion, bringing to mind John Kenneth Galbraith's observation that no one really likes the market except the economists and the Federal Trade Commission.

The non-profit alternative

The citizenry may have drifted even further away from the system than all this indicates, for American society seems to have more trust and respect for "non-profit" organizations than for the profit-seeking kind. Would the public be so generous with disaster relief if the Red Cross were a regular profit-making business? Would the Internal Revenue Service allow it to be tax-exempt? Why does the Post Office give cheaper rates to non-profits and lower rates for books and magazines which don't contain advertising? For an AIDS test, do people feel more confident going to the Public Health Service or to a commercial laboratory? Why does "educational" or "public" television not have regular commercials? What would Americans think of peace-corps volunteers, elementary-school teachers, clergy, nurses and social workers who demanded in excess of $100 thousand per year? Would the public like to see churches competing with each other, complete with ad campaigns selling a New and Improved God?

Pervading all these attitudes, and frequently voiced, is a strong disapproval of greed and selfishness, in glaring contradiction to the reality that greed and selfishness form the official and ideological basis of our system.

It's almost as if no one remembers how the system is supposed to work any more, or they prefer not to dwell on it. Where is all this leading to? Are the Russian reformers going to wind up as the last true believers in capitalism?

It would appear that, at least on a gut level, Americans have had it up to here with free enterprise—the type of examples given above are repeated in the media each and every day. The great irony of it all is that the mass of the American people are not aware that their sundry attitudes constitute an anti-free enterprise philosophy, and thus tend to go on believing the conventional wisdom that government is the problem, that big government is the biggest problem, and that their salvation cometh from the private sector, thereby feeding directly into pro-free enterprise ideology.

Thus it is that those activists for social change who believe that American society is faced with problems so daunting that no corporation or entrepreneur is ever going to solve them at a profit carry the burden of convincing the American people that they don't really believe what they think they believe; and that the public's complementary mindset—that the government is no match for the private sector in efficiently getting big and important things done—is equally fallacious, for the government has built up an incredible military machine (ignoring for the moment, what it's used for), landed men on the moon, created great dams, marvelous national parks, an interstate highway system, the peace corps, student loans, social security, insurance for bank deposits, protection of pension funds against corporate misuse, the Environmental Protection Agency, the National Institutes of Health, the Smithsonian, the G.I. Bill and much, much more. In short, the government has been quite good at doing what it wanted to do, or what labor and other movements have made it do, like establishing worker health and safety standards and requiring food manufacturers to list detailed information about ingredients.

Activists have to remind the American people of what they've already learned but seem to have forgotten: that they don't want *more* government, or *less* government; they don't want *big* government, or *small* government; they want government *on their side*.

None of the above, of course, will deter The World's Only Superpower from continuing its *jihad* to impose capitalist fundamentalism upon the world.

A couple of more reasons why the *jihad* may have tough going

Nearly half of adult Americans surveyed by the Hearst Corporation in 1987 believed Karl Marx's aphorism: "From each according to his ability, to each according to his need" was to be found in the US Constitution.[11]

Mark Brzezinski, son of Zbigniew, was a post-Cold War Fulbright Scholar in Warsaw: "I asked my students to define *democracy*. Expecting a discussion on individual liberties and authentically elected institutions, I was surprised to hear my students respond that to them, democracy means a government obligation to maintain a certain standard of living and to provide health care, education and housing for all. In other words, socialism."[12]

CHAPTER 27

A Day in the Life of a Free Country

The question is irresistibly upon us.

How do they get away with it?

How does the United States orchestrate economies, subvert democracy, overthrow sovereign nations, torture them, chemicalize them, biologize them, radiate them...all the less-than-nice things detailed in this book, often in the full glare of the international media, with the most stunning contradictions between word and deed...without being mercilessly condemned by the world's masses, by anyone with a social conscience, without being shunned like a leper? Without American leaders being brought before international tribunals, charged with crimes against humanity?

It's no mystery about the silence and collusion, if not the adoration, of other governments and their leaders. It takes buying out only a few men with sleek jet fighters or tons of wheat, canceled debts, the World Bank, the IMF; they've been intimidated, threatened, extorted, bribed, had their egos massaged, their nationalism patronized and had membership in the exclusive private clubs of NATO, the World Trade Organization and the European Union dangled before them. Only the occasional oddball Fidel Castro-type does not shy away from being shunned by respectable international high society.

But what keeps the vast majority of humanity, including the countless victims, from rising up in protest, spewing gross scorn and skepticism, if not bullets?

Being enamored of the United States—a former colony that made good, with its wondrous New World promise of a new life—goes well back into the nineteenth century, and reached new heights with the victory over fascism in the Second World War, then higher yet with America's science-fiction technical wizardry, epitomized by walking on the moon. Soviet Cold-War propaganda made scarcely a dent. Nor did Cold-War truths. Or any truths.

For decades after the close of the Second World War, Western visitors to the Soviet Union and Eastern Europe regularly brought back tales from their professional counterparts as well as the man in the street—the citizens refused to believe that there was homelessness in America or that there was no national health insurance; they were convinced that that was simply communist propaganda. They believed that in the US and Britain, government decisions were never made secretly, and that if a politician told a single lie he would be removed from office, citing Nixon as an example…"We sometimes get copies of the Daily Mail [the London tabloid] from your embassy—it is good to read unbiased world news."[1]…After the close of the Cold War, the chief of the Soviet general staff told the US chairman of the Joint Chiefs of Staff how impressed he was that enlisted people in the US military were not afraid to speak out and were not intimidated by their officers…[2]

Over the years, a number of Third-World leaders, under imminent military and/or political threat by the United States, have made appeals to Washington officials, even to the president in person, under the apparently hopeful belief that it was all a misunderstanding, that America was not really intent upon crushing them and their movements for social change. Amongst others, the Guatemalan foreign minister in 1954, Cheddi Jagan of British Guiana in 1961 and Maurice Bishop of Grenada in 1983 all made their appeals.[3] All were crushed. As recently as 1994, we have the case of the leader of the Zapatista rebels in Mexico, Subcommander Marcos. "Marcos said," it was reported, "he expects the United States to support the Zapatistas once US intelligence agencies are convinced the movement is not influenced by Cubans or Russians." "Finally," Marcos said, "they are going to conclude that this is a Mexican problem, with just and true causes…"[4]

With all due respect to the considerable courage of Señor Marcos, one must seriously question his degree of contact with history, reality and gringos. For many years, the United States has been providing the Mexican military with all the training and tools needed to kill Marcos' followers and, most likely, before long, Marcos himself.

When US bombs fell on Serbia in the spring of 1999, many Serbians expressed their shock and amazement that America— beloved, admired America—could do such a thing. The *Washington Post* interviewed a family in Belgrade: "They regard themselves as pro-American," said the paper. "It is very difficult for us to hate America," the husband declared. "We have always aspired to an American way of life, not a Russian way of life." Added the *Post*: "The fact that the United States is bombing their country shocks and bewilders them."[5] A Serbian poet from the Kosovo capital of Pristina, one Alexander Simovich, was deeply upset by the US bombing which was devastating the city and his life. Yet, we were told that he "loves Bob Dylan and jazz and lyrical poets. In the moments when he still allows himself to dream, he is living in another country, like the United States."[6]

In Russia, most people strongly opposed the bombing and were shocked that it was the United States that was mainly responsible. The US media informed us repeatedly that the level of anti-American sentiment in Russia was easily the greatest in memory. It was as if the Russians were discovering for the first time that the United States had a violent side to it. Such innocence, it must be said, is virtually a form of insanity.

When the Chinese embassy in Belgrade was torn apart by American missiles, the reaction amongst Chinese was disbelief, as they marched in protest. A graduate student at Beijing University said his first thought was that the Americans couldn't have done it. A terrorist must have been to blame. "I feel very sad. I have watched so many American movies and other things. I believe America has so much that is so humane, and so just."

"You were the ideal for so many of us," added a senior Chinese official. "And now your stupid bombs have killed our people."

This attitude was not confined to Chinese who have not set foot in the United States. A Chinese graduate of Stanford University declared that "We used to think the United States was a model. But now you've killed our people. This is the end of our honeymoon with America."[7]

This naiveté, this love affair with the mystique of "America", while certainly touching in a way in this tired old world, is not of immaculate conception. The United States, the inventor and perfecter of modern advertising and public relations, the world's leading producer and distributor of films, TV programs, books, magazines and music, with US Information Service libraries in more than 100 countries, and Voice of America with nearly 90 million listeners...the United States, the world's only information superpower, has flooded the media and the hearts and minds of the earth's multitude with this mystique, playing it for all it's worth, for generations.

Historian Christopher Simpson, in his study, *Science of Coercion*, observed:

> Military, intelligence and propaganda agencies such as the Department of Defense and the Central Intelligence Agency helped bankroll substantially all of the post-World War II generation's research into techniques of persuasion, opinion measurement, interrogation, political and military mobilization, propagation of ideology and related questions."[8]

Little is left to chance in The Selling of America. The Clinton administration announced in 1999 that it was forming a new International Public Information group to "influence foreign audiences" in support of US foreign policy and to counteract propaganda by enemies of the United States. IPI's charter says that control over "international military information" is intended to "influence the emotions, motives, objective reasoning and ultimately the behavior of foreign governments, organizations, groups and individuals."[9]

"It's a free country."

The thought comes with mother's milk.

"It's a free country."

How many times does someone growing up in the United States have to hear those words before it settles comfortably, deep in the "received truth" lobe of the brain?

"It's a free country."

How many in the world have made this adage a basic element of their love affair with America?

"It's a free country."

In the minds of many Americans and foreigners, whether consciously or not, this gives the United States the moral right to do what it does in and to the rest of the world.

"It's a free country."

The following is offered as a corrective.

Overtly and covertly, legally and illegally, the military-industrial complex has joined forces with the prison-industrial complex, linked further to the omnipresent national security-police complex, all clasping hands tightly with the War on Drugs, in a declaration of War on the American People and the Bill of Rights. This Authority Juggernaut—enamored with its own perpetuation, glorification and enrichment—has convinced the American public that without its storm troopers all hell would break loose and the safety and security of the citizenry would be on a life-support machine. In this undertaking, it has had the indispensable assistance of intimidated legislatures, an uniconoclastic judiciary, compliant media, and a president, Bill Clinton, who—in the words of civil-liberties columnist Nat Hentoff—"in this century…has inflicted the most harm on our constitutional rights and liberties".[10]

On any given day, a day like today in fact, or one during last month, or last year, much of the following—*all of it derived directly from actual happenings or disclosures of the past few years*—is taking place somewhere in the United States. Time and again we have been assured that certain practices have been terminated, only to discover that—perhaps with slight modifications—they are still being carried out.

It should be noted that what is presented herein deals essentially with violations of civil liberties and human rights, and does not include the numerous forms of corporate abuse which are economic in nature or which adversely affect people's health.

Many of the violations reflect foreign policy considerations given a domestic twist to bring the "threat" home to US citizens and win support for those policies.

None are more hopelessly enslaved than those who falsely believe they are free.

Johann Wolfgang von Goethe

- In every state, the police or the National Guard and, at times, active-duty army troops, are conducting relentless helicopter drug-surveillance over people's homes and property, setting up roadblocks, interrogating, detaining, harassing and terrifying residents with displays of excessive power.

- In hundreds of American cities, young people are being subjected to a nighttime curfew law; many have a daytime curfew as well.

- The CIA, FBI and other federal agencies are refusing to respond to subpoenas for documents issued by attorneys who need them for the defense of their clients in national security cases in state courts.

- US residents are undergoing assorted harassments and penalties from the federal government for having traveled to, spent money in and/or shipped various goods to Cuba, Libya, Iraq, North Korea, Iran, Yugoslavia or other nations of that ilk. Those who visit the United Nations Mission in New York or the Interests Section in Washington of some of these countries risk being photographed and receiving visits or phone calls from the FBI.

- The CIA is opening and reading mail to and from selected countries. The FBI is peeking at our correspondence, domestic and international, for a host of its own priorities.

- In Western states, police and federal Border Patrol agents are stopping pedestrians and motorists purely because they look Hispanic, and asking them to prove that they're lawful residents of the United States.

- Motorists are being stopped on highways for drug checks, blacks and Hispanics being the most likely to be stopped because of the race-based drug-courier profile being employed. Blacks are being strip searched on streets by police, who then shine a flashlight at their genital and anal areas.

- The INS is holding children (under age 18), mainly from Latin America and China, for months at a time in prison-like conditions, not informing them of their rights, interfering with their attempts to obtain lawyers and failing to facilitate contact with relatives, detaining them perhaps to force their illegal alien parents to come for them, so they can be taken into custody.

- Private corporations are recording employees' phone calls and voice mail, reading their computer files and email, getting logs of what websites they've looked at, videotaping them as they work, observing them in bathrooms and locker rooms with two-way mirrors or hidden cameras, tracking their whereabouts by having them use electronic pass keys, bugging their offices, subjecting them to airport-style electronic searches, testing their urine for drugs, doing extensive security checks on their backgrounds—all this whether or not they have ever behaved poorly on the job, or whether their work involves any danger to anyone.

- At the Naval Academy in Annapolis, a random group of about 300 students is having to undergo urinalysis each week. At other schools, students are obliged to take a urine test in order to join the track team, join the chess club, go to the prom, go on a field trip or drive to and from school; some of these school policies have been approved by courts.

- New Jersey state troopers are enlisting hotel workers along the New Jersey Turnpike to tip them off about suspicious guests who, among other things, pay for their rooms in cash or receive a flurry of phone calls; hotel managers are allowing troopers, without a warrant, to leaf through the credit card receipts and registration forms of guests; the troopers are giving surveillance seminars to train employees to scrutinize guests who fit the profile of drug traffickers, the profile including race and speaking Spanish.

- The Federal Emergency Management Agency (FEMA) is keeping up to date its list of aliens, radicals and other undesirables who will be rounded up and detained in times of "national emergency".

- Juveniles imprisoned at one of the nation's more than 50 so-called "boot camps" are forced to go on endurance runs until blood has soaked their shoes; one has already died from it; at other times, the youngsters are subjected to shackles or handcuffs.

- Women are being arrested for using crack cocaine while pregnant, even if their baby is perfectly normal at birth. Indeed the idea of the "crack baby" may well be a myth.

- Government agencies and private corporations are not giving gay couples or unmarried heterosexual couples the same benefits they offer married heterosexual couples. Homosexuals are being discharged from the military because of their sexual orientation, even if not charged with any misbehavior.

- Task forces of international, federal, military, state and local law enforcement and intelligence agencies, as well as private entities, are employing increased interaction, abundant funds, new laws, new technologies and new octopus-like data bases to spy on and harass activists of many stripes: Irish and Middle-East support groups, human rights, immigrants' rights, civil liberties, prison reform, minorities, labor, environmental, animal rights, nuclear power and anti-imperialism, even if there is no evidence of violence or illegal activities.

  The FBI and police are noting license plate numbers of people attending meetings and demonstrations, photographing people, paying informers to infiltrate groups, breaking into offices to steal mailing and contributor lists, rifling through files and carrying out "harassment arrests" (i.e., charges later dropped). Individual members of these groups are receiving FBI visits at their homes and workplaces, or the Bureau is sending anonymous letters to the person's colleagues implying that s/he is actually an informer, as well as sending assorted poison-pen letters to employers, landlords and spouses designed to produce optimal distress.

- Airport passengers are being detained for hours, even days, and missing flights because they fit a "terrorist profile" based on their nationality, ethnicity, appearance, airport behavior, travel itinerary or other criteria. They are being strip searched, including body cavity searches, X-rayed, forced to take laxatives, their bowel movements monitored.

- The FBI is urging librarians to report on the books taken out by patrons with foreign-sounding names, particularly scientific and technical books. (When this program was first revealed and criticized, the FBI proceeded to do checks on the critics.)

- The Drug Enforcement Administration (DEA) is demanding that a publisher provide it with the names of people who bought a marijuana cultivation book.

- The police are confiscating the cars of customers of prostitutes, sometimes after a female police officer has lured the man into offering her money for sex. It matters not if the car does not belong to the man.

  Other police officers somewhere are forcing prostitutes to perform sex acts by threatening to arrest them if they don't comply.

- Women desiring an abortion are finding various daunting obstacles placed in their path by state and federal authorities.

- The FBI or the police are carrying out a sting operation in order to arrest a black elected official regarded as too charismatic or "uppity". (The *repeated* case of former Washington, DC mayor, Marion Barry, is highly instructive.)

- People are being rejected for housing and employment because of their race.

- Numerous foreign academics and activists are being refused entry to the US to attend a conference due to their ideology and/or the ideology of the conference not being to the liking of the US State Department.

- Language minorities are facing discrimination and hostility from the "English Only" movement.

- US government *agents provocateurs* are encouraging some people, as in the World Trade Center bombing or within militia groups, to carry out a bombing or other terrorist act.

- *The judge sentences you to prison. Then the prison officials sentence you to hell...*Prisoners are being handcuffed or hogtied and forced to lap their food like dogs from plates shoved under their faces...non-violent drug offenders thrown in with dangerous murderers, rapists and robbers, despite court orders to segregate them...guards kicking inmates in the groin, siccing dogs on them...female prisoners being beaten and raped by guards, sold for sex to male prisoners, taken off the grounds to work as prostitutes, forced to perform stripteases for corrections officers (14 states do not outlaw sexual contact between correctional staff and prisoners), women's sex acts photographed by guards, prisoners of both genders kept naked or in their underwear, and monitored by the opposite sex...male prisoners slain, with impunity...guards using tear gas, Mace and pepper spray against prisoners in handcuffs or locked in their cells...prisoners not protected from assaults, physical and sexual, by other prisoners...guards instigating fights between prisoners...inmates kept in shackles, belly chains and handcuffs at all times when outside their cells, even in the shower...chain gangs resurrected...guards who report abuses risk reprisals from prison officials...the California Correction Officers union makes large political contributions to public officials and prosecutors so that the guards can continue to act with impunity.

- Increasingly, those incarcerated in the US, now approaching two million in number, are seeing their rights and privileges taken away or seriously curtailed in regard to academic classes, vocational training, reading materials, sports, exercise, prison law libraries, access to free legal advice, ease of appealing their cases, access to media. They are being charged for room and board, for doctor visits, forbidden to receive packages, forced to shave off beards and long hair and remove earrings; their phone use is limited to a few minutes a week, visits to one hour a month, visiting family members treated rudely and subjected to humiliating searches and disrobings, prisoners being transferred to other prisons very far from their families; HIV-positive and terminally ill prisoners are denied special care, asthmatics not monitored, those on anti-psychotic medications miss their doses, hypertensives cannot get proper diets; prisoners are confined to cells for all but a few hours a week; lights are on in cells 24 hours a day.

- In a new prison being built 3,000 feet up in Big Stone Gap, Virginia, windows in each cell command spectacular views of the valley below. Prison officials are planning to smoke the windows so inmates can't see out.

- Various levels of government agencies are seizing bank accounts of men who supposedly are deadbeat dads, but it's later determined that they aren't.

- Educational institutions are being forced to allow military recruiters on campus to avoid losing government grants for student aid and other purposes.

- The US military is carrying out one of its many urban exercises, such as this one described in Massachusetts: "Last week Navy Seals landed from helicopters on top of some buildings, rappelled down the buildings and had fun and games shooting and throwing dummy explosives around. They woke half the city of Lowell. Early that evening our house shook and the windows rattled violently as several helicopters flew over at no more that 200 feet."
  In some of their exercises in the US, the military uses live ammunition.

- A driver, stopped by the police, tapes the encounter. When he goes to the local police station to complain about his treatment, he is asked to hand the tape over. He's then charged with illegal wiretapping.

- Intercity busses and trains are being boarded by DEA agents to conduct searches of passengers' belongings. Passengers are assured that it's all "voluntary".

- Law enforcement authorities of various stripes are routinely confiscating a computer from the home of someone charged with drug something or other…or whatever…They take the computer back to the office where the good ol' boys can have a thigh-slappin' time reading the personal mail. There's no telling when they'll get around to returning the computer.

- In the Miami area and sections of New Jersey, those who don't toe the anti-Castro party line are being subjected to a wide range of abuses. Suggesting a rapprochement with Cuba, calling for an end to the US embargo, arranging for travel to the island, shipping medicines there, etc., has on hundreds of occasions led to bombings, shootings, death threats, murder, beatings, being driven out of business, fired from a job, forced off the air. Perpetrators of these acts have enjoyed a virtual immunity from prosecution.

- In contrast to Washington's hands-off treatment for anti-Castro terrorists, under the Antiterrorism and Effective Death Penalty Act of 1996, there are 30 foreign "terrorist" organizations which are held in official disdain. The law prohibits persons from "knowingly providing material support or resources to a designated foreign terrorist organization". Thus it is that donating toys to an orphanage operated by Hamas in Jordan, or books to a school run by a Kurdish independence organization, or collecting money for the families of Irish prisoners can be regarded as "association with a known terrorist organization", and be subject to federal prosecution.

Under this legislation, tens of thousands of legal US residents, many here for a decade or more, with families and children born in the US, are being deported or being refused re-entry into the country because of such associations, or because they were once convicted of a crime, even though they've served their sentence, and regardless of how long ago it was; many were convicted of misdemeanors for which no sentence was imposed other than probation of one year, but that is sufficient for expulsion. The INS formerly could look at individual cases and keep out only people judged potentially dangerous. Now, regardless of all other circumstances, the person must be deported. Sometimes they are apprehended and deported when they apply for citizenship.

- The INS is bursting into the homes of Palestinians, legally resident in the US, and dragging them out for distributing the magazine of a Palestinian organization or raising funds for various Palestinian causes which are not involved with violence. They will be incarcerated for an indefinite term, with an indefinite fate, without criminal charges being filed against them. (Aliens, the Justice Department has long believed, and the Supreme Court has now confirmed, do not have the full protection of the Bill of Rights.)

- Various kinds of government agents or private investigators are covertly checking through your garbage, either behind your house or at the dump.

- A Federal judge is sentencing an American citizen to six months in a "halfway house" and 300 hours of community service because he drove a Libyan official, who had been denied a visa, from Mexico to Texas, or in some equally innocuous way, treated a citizen from an Officially-Designated Enemy (ODE) country with simple human dignity.

- The police are beating up and arresting strikers and escorting scab workers into plants, thus taking the side of the employer, as the police have done virtually without exception during 150 years of industrial conflict in the United States.

  Corporations are using many of the more than 10,000 private security firms, which employ some 1.5 million guards, to suppress strike action and intimidate union organizers.

- Law enforcement officers in northern California, taking the side of logging interests once again, are pressing cotton swabs saturated with pepper spray (600 times hotter than cayenne pepper) into the eyes of non-violent people chained to each other, who are protesting the felling of ancient redwoods; protestors are shrieking and writhing in pain as the solution takes effect.

  People are dying in police custody in cases where pepper spray is a contributing factor.

- Banks, telephone companies, utility companies, credit card companies, airlines, bus companies, rental car outlets, storage facilities, hotels and motels and all manner of other private institutions are providing various local, state and federal authorities with all the information about their customers they desire under the ever-expanding legal authorities being granted to law enforcement bodies with scarcely any public hearings or debate.

  The War on Drugs is requiring banks, brokers, casinos and other financial institutions to monitor their customers' financial transactions and report any "unusual" or "suspicious" activity. The information is all fed into the Treasury Department's Financial

Crimes Enforcement Network whose computers spend their days making linkages between individuals and bank accounts, businesses, real estate and other assets.

- States are selling confidential wage, driving and other information about their residents to private information companies and other enterprises.

- Scenarios along the lines of the following from Savannah, Ga. are probably taking place elsewhere: Without warning, a team of armed county and school system officers periodically entered the schools, ordered everyone into the hallways, used dogs to sniff the students' belongings, and scanned the students' bodies with metal detectors. One of the high-school teachers was very upset by this—"Because I teach the Constitution", she explained—and made her feelings known to the authorities. A police officer told her principal that because of her "attitude" problem, she might have to be detained or restrained during future surprise raids. During a subsequent raid, the teacher's son was the only student out of 1,500 to be individually searched. Later, cars in the parking lot were searched, and the police claimed to have found a marijuana cigarette in the teacher's car. The Board of Education suspended her and she was later fired.

- In various schools students are being suspended for: bringing a bottle of the nonprescription painkiller Advil to school; dying their hair an "unacceptable" color; giving a classmate a Midol tablet for relief of menstrual cramps; bringing "drugs" to school—lemon drops; bringing a gift-wrapped bottle of wine as a Christmas gift for a teacher; another punished for carrying a small paring knife to cut her lunch fruit; yet another, a 9-year-old boy, punished for waving his drawing of a gun in class; a six-year-old boy sent home for planting a kiss on a girl's cheek; eight-year-old girls strip searched in school, looking for stolen money (not found); pre-schoolers to 6th grade students given genital exams as part of their physicals; high schools employing random Breathalyser testing to ferret out students who have imbibed alcohol; a 14-year-old girl strip-searched and suspended for two weeks because she told her classmates she could understand how the Columbine shooters felt; and high school students questioned by police who wanted to know if a chemistry textbook was for bomb-making.

This while an eleven-year-old boy is being arrested and accused of incest because a neighbor saw him touching his younger sister "sexually" in their yard. He was held six weeks in a juvenile detention center and shackled in court on at least one occasion. The boy and his parents said he had pulled down his five-year-old sister's underwear to help her urinate.

And two 10-year-old boys who put some soap in their teacher's water bottle are being charged with a felony.

- A high-school teacher is being suspended without pay for teaching mathematics using real-life problems, such as: "Jerome wants to cut his half-pound of heroin to make 20 percent more profit. How many ounces of cut will be needed?"

- Juveniles in reform schools are being hogtied and thrown into isolation cells for weeks at a time; placed in straightjackets; standing with noses pressed against a wall for as long as 16 hours a day; handcuffed naked to beds. Juveniles are being jailed with adult criminals even for just being runaways.

- Prisoners in a state correctional facility who staged a peaceful demonstration against the transfer of other inmates to out-of-state gulags against their will, are being punished with up to a year of solitary, and their time in solitary will not count toward their sentences, according to the Department of Corrections.

- A federal court, created by the Foreign Intelligence Surveillance Act of 1978, is receiving applications for authorization of electronic surveillance within the United States and is rubber-stamping them. In its first 20 years, the court received some 10,000 applications from the Justice Department on behalf of the FBI and the National Security Agency. By all accounts, only one was rejected, on a technicality.

There exists no public record of any kind about the individual cases, nor any oversight. The Clinton administration has expanded the court's mandate to allow it to approve physical break-ins, enabling the Justice Department to bypass the usual warrant procedure in an open court, which would necessitate some accounting of the items to be seized, and an explanation of probable cause that a crime had been committed.

The targets of these wiretaps and burglaries can be under surveillance merely because of belonging to or supporting an organization whose politics are looked upon with disfavor by the US government. Federal agents can now obtain the phone numbers of all incoming and outgoing calls on any lines used or called by suspected foreign agents.

(The FISA court is only the proverbial tip of the iceberg when it comes to the US government listening in on the citizenry. See the "Eavesdropping" chapter for further details.)

- Drunk driving, generally defined in the 1980s as a blood alcohol concentration of .15, was later defined as .10, and then, in some states, as .08. If .08 doesn't do, will Congress and the states go for .06, and then .04? In any event, the scientific validity of these cut-off points has been questioned by the federal government itself.

  Cars of those arrested for drunken driving are being seized by the police, sometimes immediately. At times the police try to keep the car even if the person is acquitted.

- People are being harassed, arrested and/or having their property confiscated for engaging in certain forms of gambling, even in their own homes. Other forms of gambling, which are legitimized by the local or state government, proceed happily unmolested.

- Hundreds of political prisoners are rotting away in American prisons. As US-based human rights groups have testified before the Human Rights Commission of the United Nations in Geneva, these people are being held "as a direct result of actions undertaken in furtherance of a political or social vision". They go back to the black liberation struggles of the 1960s and 70s, particularly members of the Black Panthers; others are native American activists, anti-nuclear activists, opponents of US interventionist policies in Puerto Rico, Central America and elsewhere. A number of these prisoners were set up by FBI dirty tricks under the notorious COINTELPRO (counter-intelligence program), aimed at "neutralizing" Black Panthers and white radicals.

Many have used violence against property, and a few toward police, but persons who commit politically motivated offenses in furtherance of leftist causes receive substantially, often shockingly, harsher treatment than those who commit similar acts for monetary or right-wing reasons. Many were sentenced to more than 50 years for actions, such as possession of explosives, without there being any victims. If the usual sentence for such an act in a particular court or state is 10 years, at the beginning of year 11—certainly by year 15—these people are political prisoners.

It is often not the "worst" prisoners who are thrown into solitary confinement, but rather these political prisoners, as well as the jailhouse lawyers and prisoner activists.

The Congressional Black Caucus, in October 1997, issued a declaration to remind the world of the existence of these political prisoners.

- Aliens who have come to the US from oppressive countries, seeking political asylum, are winding up in Kafkaesque nightmares, wasting away in prison under intolerable conditions, without criminal charges being filed against them, some dying because of unattended health problems, forgotten about until perhaps Amnesty International or some other human rights organization takes up their case. The FBI and the INS are using secret evidence—which neither the accused nor their attorneys have a right to examine—to detain these people and ultimately deport them, even if they are married to American citizens. The aliens are often those who decried human rights abuses in their home country and fled torture and other retribution from their government, which may be putting pressure on Washington to silence and return them by providing the evidence in question.

Many are refused entry to the US because they lack proper documents, when in fact many escape their homeland with false papers. As of 1999, the INS was holding more than 10,000 asylum seekers. In February of that year, the Washington representative of the U.N. High Commissioner for Refugees called upon the United

States to stop detaining such people. Many may be regarded as political prisoners.

- The Boy Scouts are rejecting some young man as a member because he is an atheist, or rejecting an adult as a troop leader because the person is homosexual.

- Some of the more than 10,000 FBI agents are spending their time enticing people on the internet to purchase child porno, or the G-men are pretending online to be a 13-year-old girl in order to lure a man to a meeting. When the man shows up, he's arrested.

- Many foreigners, in the US legally, are sitting in prisons, charged with a crime, without their country's consulate having been informed, without the prisoner being told that he has the right to contact his consulate. Some of them are sitting on death row.

- The IRS, acting as judge, jury and executioner, is subjecting tax-payers to nightmarish collection processes, ordering them to pay taxes they don't owe, failing to credit them for payments made, seizing their cars and bank accounts, boosting tax penalties to meet office quotas and generally wreaking havoc in peoples' lives; an audit is being carried out upon an individual because he or she has upset someone in a very high position in the government.

- Monetary rewards are being paid out to students who report other students for smoking, drinking alcohol, using drugs or violating other school rules.
  DARE and other school-based drug programs are teaching children to turn in their parents for marijuana or other drug violations.
  The mayor of New York has urged citizens to take pictures of people going into sex-video stores and topless bars.
  Other informant schemes call for people to turn in others for not wearing seatbelts, for telling ethnic or racist jokes and for failing to recycle their garbage properly.

- First-time drug offenders, carrying no weapons, including many who were simply couriers or played peripheral roles in drug trafficking, and others with no record of violence or involvement in sophisticated criminal activity, are being sentenced to very long prison terms, with no chance of parole.

- Under "three-strikes" laws, people are being sentenced to 25-to-life terms for petty theft, despite that fact that the three-strikes laws were designed for violent crimes.

- The grand jury system is running amok. Virtually all federal cases use it to obtain indictments. Neither the accused nor his or her lawyer is there, so they can't confront accusers. The system is used as an instrument of terror—relatives testifying against one another with no confidentiality privilege with respect to family members other than husbands and wives: parents called to testify against their children, children against their parents, brother against sister. It lacks due process. It's another secret tool of an expanding executive branch.

- Those wishing to experiment with their mind in the privacy of their home, those seeking transcendence and nirvana, are being punished by the state for their sin. Young men are being sentenced to up to 20 years in prison for possession of less than a gram of LSD, with no evidence presented of them having done any harm to any other person.

- Human Rights Watch is charging state governments, as it did in New York, of violating international law by sentencing drug dealers to prison terms similar to those given to violent offenders. A person convicted in New York of selling two ounces of cocaine receives a mandatory sentence of 15 years to life, the same penalty meted out to a murderer.

- More states are joining the frenzy to make publicly available the names, addresses, biographies (often with detrimental erroneous information) and photos of convicted sex offenders for the rest of their lives, driving these people from their neighborhoods and jobs; this is being done regardless of whether the popular *a priori* view of sex offenders being untreatable is true or not, or whether they're undergoing therapy or not.

- Many hundreds of school books are being dropped from curriculums because of complaints by parents, religious groups and others. Books in public libraries are under attack as well, books which no one is obliged to read—*Catcher in the Rye*, *Huckleberry Finn*, *Oliver Twist*, *The Grapes of Wrath*, *The Diary of Anne Frank*, *I Know Why the Caged Bird Sings* and numerous other lesser-known novels, as well as countless books of history, social studies, geography, even home economics. School newspapers, other curriculum materials, music and art, are also being targeted.

- Individuals who wish to end their lives with dignity and with a minimum of suffering are being denied the assistance of a doctor by state legislatures, the Catholic Church and citizens' groups. In Oregon, after passage by 60 percent of a referendum allowing doctor-assisted suicide, the DEA warned that physicians who help someone commit suicide will risk their licenses to write prescriptions; whether this is ever enforced or not, the threat will have its effect.

- Numerous people who could get exceedingly welcome relief from dreadful symptoms by the use of marijuana are denied the legal right to do so. In states where voters have passed initiatives legalizing the medical use of marijuana, the authorities are throwing up obstacles to make its practice as difficult as they can make it. In Washington, DC, Congress has in effect nullified the passage of such a referendum.

  Cancer patients in great pain are being denied sufficient morphine to relieve their suffering because the War on Drugs has inhibited doctors from prescribing as much as is needed.

- Many people are being placed on death row. Some of them, if they're lucky, will join the 75 men and women released from death row between 1976 and 1998, their cases reversed because they had been found to be innocent after all.

- Hundreds of cities are employing highly armed and trained Special Weapons and Tactics Teams (SWAT), based on military special operations models, and told they're part of a "war" on crime; ready to terrorize the enemy (the citizens) with automatic assault rifles, tanks and grenade launchers, called out even in non-crisis situations; choosing a neighborhood and swooping onto street corners, forcing pedestrians to the ground, searching them, running warrant checks, taking photos and entering all the new "intelligence" into a state database from computer terminals in each patrol car. As they carry out this exercise, they do not trip over many members of the Fortune 500.

- A known militant, but non-violent, opponent of the president is being removed by the Secret Service from a site where the president is going to speak, then released after the speech.

- Defendants and prisoners appearing in court, who don't know their place, are being given 50,000 volt shocks with a torture device known as an electronic security belt.

- Young men are registering with Selective Service, making themselves subject to be drafted for a future war of "national security"— as defined solely by the government, no opposing arguments accepted. Failure to register is punishable by a large fine, imprisonment and/or permanent loss of all federal financial aid and employment.

  Those already in the service are being subjected by the military to a process aimed at breaking down their deep-seated reluctance to kill people they don't know and don't hate, so as to make them willing to risk their lives fighting in one of these "national security" wars, the purpose of which they don't understand at all (or, perhaps, they understand it only too well). They are being forced, under threat of court martial, discharge, deportation if not a citizen and in violation of international human rights standards, to take experimental drugs and vaccines, whose effects on health are unknown.

- Aliens are being denied citizenship for refusing to agree to bear arms in defense of the United States because of their pacifist beliefs, a reason not acceptable to the INS, which insists on a religious basis.

  For a citizen to qualify as a conscientious objector, it means being opposed to participation in all wars, not a selective objection to a particular war, no matter how repulsive it may appear to the individual. (A female Kansas doctor, who was an Army Reserve captain, and refused to serve in the Gulf War, insisting that it was a "public health catastrophe", was kept in military prison for eight months, and Kansas medical authorities moved to revoke her medical license.)

- DEA, ATF, INS, FBI, DIA, Secret Service, US Forest Service, National Park Service, Sheriff's Departments, National Guard and/or other official cowboys, wearing black suits, ski masks and the like, forming massively armed mobs of screaming, swearing agents, helicopters chopping above, battering down doors, raiding people's homes, smashing up furniture, beating up residents, handcuffing them, manhandling pregnant women, terrifying children, separating them from their parents, shooting people dead, looking for drugs or individuals which often are not there—this *jihad* being the outcome of no more than a tip from an informant.

  Heavily-armed bounty hunters, with the force of law behind them, are carrying on in a similar manner to kidnap a person, sometimes killing someone, sometimes the "wrong" person.

  Operators of "pirate" radio stations are also being invaded, with FCC agents, federal marshals, a SWAT team, customs agents and local police comprising the attacking force.

- Forced labor is thriving: people compelled to work off their welfare grants, with no prospect of real employment, sometimes at subminimum wages, or no wages at all; convicted defendants sentenced to "community service"; conscientious objectors obliged to do alternative service, for a period longer than military service, thus being punished for exercising their conscience; inmates denied vital privileges if they refuse to work in prison, many producing for private companies, who get away with paltry wages, no benefits, no unions. (Some prison-made products are being exported, exactly what the US has condemned China for.)

- US embassies abroad are surveilling selected American travelers, fingered by a joint effort of the FBI and the State Department Passport Office.

- The INS and the US Border Patrol at the Mexican border are killing or physically mistreating large numbers of would-be immigrants. In INS centers around the country, thousands of immigrants are being held under inhumane conditions, including heads pushed into toilets, forced drugging and being made to kneel naked and chant "America is Number One."

  Immigrants in prison are also being forced to recite "America is Number One", as they walk by guards who punch and kick them.

- The INS is illegally seizing files of social agency employees working with undocumented immigrants. Lawyers and others working on behalf of victims of abuse are finding it almost impossible to file a complaint and receive a response from the INS or the Border Patrol. Media and human rights groups are virtually excluded.

- Demonstrations against detention centers and other INS practices are being brutally squashed in Los Angeles by a phalanx of local and federal armed forces—riot squads, mounted units, ATF agents, INS commando units, water cannons, tear gas…many protestors are being injured and arrested; some of those not carrying proper documents are being deported directly from a police station.

- Indigent defendants are waiting in jail for many months before the court appoints a lawyer, and then a further wait before they have a chance to speak with the lawyer.

- The notion of bail is rapidly eroding. We're raised to believe that for other than a capital offense, reasonable bail must be offered. We have a long history of not holding people in custody until their guilt has been determined. That's not true anymore. We call the new concept "preventive detention".

- Citizens are being sentenced to inordinately long prison terms, often for life, for providing information, or merely *attempting* to do so, to a country not named the United States of America. The disclosure of the information—in some cases already publicly available, or declassified before the arrest—would typically cause no actual harm at all to the United States, nor to anyone else on earth, except that the act of passing it to an alien nation grates on the sensibilities of those who professionally play the secrets game,

the patriots game and the enemies game. These professional play-
ers are fond of announcing that the "betrayal" has caused "irrepara-
ble harm" or "incalculable damage" to US national security. In
some cases, the information has been passed only to the FBI, in a
sting operation, yet the duped person is put away for decades.

- The federal government is busily creating new documents, at the
  rate of some five million a year, which are unavailable to the ordinary citizens of the republic because they are stamped with words
  like "Secret", "Top Secret", or "Eyes Only".

- Workers in the Defense Department's "Area 51", in the Nevada
  desert, are suffering and dying from inhaling toxic chemicals that
  spew from the burning of hazardous wastes in huge open pits.
  Severe, persistent respiratory distress, cancers, aching guts, ugly
  crusty scales, cracked and bleeding skin, "tissues filled with industrial toxins rarely seen in humans"…But because of the ultra secrecy surrounding Area 51, they can't obtain information about what
  chemicals they've been exposed to in order to get appropriate medical treatment, and they can't claim worker's compensation
  because Area 51 can't be investigated. The place is subject to no
  law of the land save national security.

- Black-uniformed officers in laced-up black boots, wearing black
  berets, with name tags missing, are descending without warning on
  a prison, hauling prisoners, some without clothes, from their beds,
  shackling them and beating them, jumping on their backs; an
  inmate's head is driven into a wall, a sickening cracking sound, the
  prisoner screams, blood splatters the wall and the ground. All to
  demonstrate that the Correction Commissioner doesn't "coddle"
  prisoners.

- Human Rights Watch and the ACLU are finding once again that
  the United States is violating Article 10 of the International
  Covenant on Civil and Political Rights, ratified by the US in
  1992, which requires that all prisoners and detainees "be treated
  with humanity and with respect to the inherent dignity of the
  human person". (In fiscal year 1999, there were 2,324 brutality
  claims against the NYPD, which kills someone every ten days on

average, often unarmed, at times in handcuffs, or in jail; police officers guilty of such actions are not being disciplined; some are later promoted.)

- You're exercising your precious freedom to vote and the only candidates presented to you with more than a snowball-in-hell's chance of winning are those whose ideologies enable them to raise about a half million dollars to contest a seat in the House, about five million for the Senate, and about a hundred million for the White House. Or, increasingly, the candidates themselves are multi-millionaires.

- In California, teenagers are being stopped, harassed, photographed and questioned by police purely because their clothing is thought to be gang attire, or of gang colors.

  In the early morn, sheriff's deputies are descending upon the homes of parents of suspected gang members, warning them that if they don't take responsibility for their children, they could face criminal charges, even jail.

- As in Detroit, New York, Philadelphia, Los Angeles and Indianapolis in recent years, police in large cities are exhibiting a remarkable level of disdain for the laws of the land: giving false information to courts to secure search warrants, or acting without warrants, committing perjury on the stand, allowing the results of botched tests of drugs to be used in criminal cases, staging drug raids in order to steal drugs, money, guns and other valuables, taking money and drugs from dealers in exchange for immunity, robbing and beating people on the streets of their precinct.

  And exhibiting the same disdain for individual rights in numerous search-and-destroy missions against private homes: using special "shock-lock" shotgun rounds to blow apartment doors off their hinges, or shooting off the door locks, tossing in "flash-bang grenades," which produce explosions that terrify and disorient people, illegally searching the inhabitants, menacing them with their guns, firing shots at people without cause, killing people, planting drugs or other false evidence on innocent people and arresting them, tampering with evidence, forcing people outside almost naked, filing false arrest reports, or sometimes filing no charges at all after all this, assaulting or threatening people who make charges against them.

- New cases are being added to the more than 60,000 people suing the city of New York for being illegally strip-searched after being arrested for minor offenses.

- Public relations firms, hired by large corporations and business associations, are utilizing hefty fees, lawyers, detectives, spies and phony "grassroots" campaigns to influence the media and public opinion against food, environmental and other activists and authors who pose a threat to one of their special-interest clients, trying to make the activists look foolish, if not criminal, as they exercise their political rights.

- NBC is canceling an appearance by a nuclear activist because she has criticized General Electric, which owns the network. Another nuclear activist or author, or opponent of military spending, is unwelcome at CBS because it belongs to Westinghouse; while yet another finds doors closed at ABC because of having treated the Disney conglomerate with less than reverence; ditto at CNN, owned by the AOL-Time-Warner octopus; while the advertisers are increasingly influencing the content of the news stories.

  (As A. J. Liebling famously wrote: "If you want freedom of the press, you have to own one.")

- During a new US invasion abroad, the media is being severely restricted as to what it can report to the American people about the war; reporters are required to submit their copy to the Pentagon censor, and are told where they can go, what they can film, who they can interview; those who don't toe the line are transferred by their employer under heavy Pentagon pressure.

- The FBI is placing ads in Vietnamese-language and Russian-language newspapers in the US asking immigrants to report on suspected spies amongst their numbers.

- A prison inmate's sacramental confession to a Catholic priest is surreptitiously being taped by prison officials. The personal mail of inmates, including those awaiting trial, is being read.

- The FBI is staging photos used in a trial, and its crime laboratory is producing scientifically flawed, misleading or altered evidence benefitting the prosecutor's case against a defendant, even allowing a judge to be impeached on false charges. A Bureau official is destroying an internal report critical of an FBI action in a particular case and not disclosing its existence to prosecutors or defense attorneys, or the Bureau is allowing inaccurate and/or incomplete "expert" testimony during court proceedings, tilting it in such a way as to incriminate the accused. A veteran FBI agent who blows the whistle on such goings-on is being harassed and suspended.

- Medical records containing people's most intimate personal information are being gathered and stored in commercial data banks maintained by hospital networks, HMOs, drug companies and insurance companies. These organizations are exerting increasing pressure on doctors and therapists to reveal information about their patients. Corporations are requiring employment applicants to give them full rights to their medical records. Law enforcement and national security agencies are increasingly gaining access to this information. Personal prescription drug information is being marketed.

- Police are setting up more and more cameras to observe the citizenry on public streets.

- Police sting operations are ensnaring gay men and charging them with "soliciting lewdness", under a state anti-sodomy law, which prohibits homosexual couples, but not heterosexual couples, from having consensual oral sex in private. Married men leaving gay sex clubs are being photographed by police, who then extort money from them by threatening to inform their wives or bosses.

- Students are being suspended by their schools for refusing to stand up for the American flag or recite the Pledge of Allegiance, or for something they wrote in the school newspaper or on their own personal home webpage.

- The INS is sending letters to immigrants who have been applying to legalize their status. The letters tell the immigrants to come to the federal building, bring some ID, and the INS will give them a work permit good for a year. When the immigrants eagerly arrive at the INS office, they are promptly arrested and deported.

• Police are stopping cars on the road, stealing money and other goods from the passengers, or taking bribes to refrain from making (false) arrests.

Police officers, now armed with a Supreme Court ruling, are searching the belongings of a passenger in a car simply because they suspect the driver has done something wrong.

• Undercover vice squads in Arizona, wearing black ski masks, are seizing hundreds of copies of an adult newspaper from vending machines.

• Copies of the Cuban newspaper *Gramma* are being seized by customs officials in one American city or another. Videos taken in Iraq are being seized by Customs from returning American citizens.

• Mentally ill people are languishing in prisons all over the country, receiving no treatment and often suffering physical and sexual abuse from other inmates and guards.

• Some persons judged to be mentally ill, retarded or in other ways regarded as "misfits" are being sterilized without their knowledge in secluded corners of various state institutions.

• The DEA, other federal and state agents and police are seizing houses, boats, cars, airplanes, real estate, furnishings, bank accounts and other assets belonging to people suspected of involvement in drug trafficking, or belonging to their spouses, often without a conviction, and whether or not the assets seized were tied to the alleged crime. In one state, a man is losing his home and his business for selling two grams of cocaine. In another, numerous cars are being confiscated from new car dealerships for failing to report all cash transactions involving more than $10,000. Elsewhere, a 75-year-old grandmother is being dispossessed of her home for the sins of her fugitive, drug-dealing son.

The government agencies are selling these assets and using the proceeds for anything from patrol cars to parties. The expected value of forfeitures is at times a determining factor in the question of who to raid. Police are routinely planting drugs and falsifying police reports to establish probable cause for cash seizures. Plea bargains are struck that commonly favor drug kingpins willing to surrender their assets and penalize "mules" with nothing to trade. As of early 1999, there was $2.7 billion in the federal government's "Asset Forfeiture Fund" alone.

- The concept of equal access to legal remedy and justice is being invalidated every day after a decade of deep government cutbacks to the legal aid program, thus robbing the poor of what is often their sole defense against unscrupulous landlords, scam artists, battering spouses, home foreclosure, consumer fraud and many other legal predicaments.

- People going to police stations to lodge complaints against officers are being unceremoniously ushered out.

- Police in Los Angeles are carrying out a pre-dawn commando raid of more than 100 homes in a fishing expedition for individuals and contraband, yielding very little but many frightened and upset residents.

- In many cities, the homeless are being rounded up in parks and other sites supposedly open to the public and taken to places where respectable citizens, particularly tourists, will not be forced to cast eyes upon them.

- People who bring food to the homeless in public parks are being arrested, charged with giving out food without a permit, trespassing or whatever else the authorities can think of; cooking equipment and vehicles are being confiscated.

- An FBI sting operation is entrapping police officers in Washington, DC and elsewhere by offering them bribes to escort supposed drug couriers, resulting in the officers being sentenced to as much as 55 years in prison without the possibility of parole—a veritable life sentence.

- In many states, thousands of people are having their driver's licenses suspended for six months for any drug conviction, whether or not their offenses were related to operation of a motor vehicle.

In some localities, students are being denied a driver's license because their grades and/or attendance records are not good enough.

• Numerous individuals are being harassed and/or arrested because of a "positive alert" from a drug-sniffing dog even though law enforcement and scientific circles have known for many years that most US currency has some amount of cocaine or other drug stuck to it—in Los Angeles it was found that more than 75 percent of all the paper money in circulation was so tainted.

• Several other extreme police brutality cases like Rodney King in Los Angeles and Abner Louima in Brooklyn are taking place, but there are no video cameras or witnesses observing, or the victim dies and his death is ruled accidental or a heart attack.

• A public official who questions the War On Drugs is paying an awful price, like former Surgeon General Jocelyn Elders whose son was sentenced to 10 years in prison for selling one-eighth of an ounce of cocaine to an undercover police officer. His arrest took place five months after the sale, on a warrant issued a week after his mother suggested that the government study the legalization of drugs.

• Then there's the thing called Waco.

And these are the good new days

The Authorities can no longer claim as an excuse for their behavior a threat from anti-Vietnam War radicals or a civil rights movement. The Black Panther Party is history, as is the alleged International Communist Conspiracy. The Central American struggles are over. And J. Edgar Hoover, proving, after all, that he actually had something in common with the rest of humanity, has died.

Yet, from 1991 to 1999, the number of people in US prisons rose by more than 50 percent.

In place of finding a commie under every bed, they now find a drug possessor, user, dealer, shipper or courier. Instead of the Soviet Evil Empire, they now see Rogue Nations out there, Outlaw Nations, Pariah States—enemies need catchy names—with their regiments of terrorists, supporters of terrorists, acquaintances of terrorists, nuclear smugglers, questionable asylum seekers and other anti-American and un-American types. In place of civil rights agitators, the Authority Juggernaut now zooms in on youth gangs, immigrants, environmentalists, welfare recipients, prisoners and a host of other folks with a glaring deficit of political power.

What keeps most Americans from being shocked by the shredding of the Bill of Rights is that they have yet to feel the consequences, either personally or through someone close to them. It would appear, however, that they only have to wait. America's foreign groupies, in the meantime, remain blissfully ignorant of the above and in need of a reality transplant.

Notes

OPENING QUOTES

1. September 1, 1997, cover story, p.160 ff.
2. *Washington Post*, October 23, 1999, p.17
3. *New York Times*, January 29, 1992, p.16
4. *Washington Post*, November 4, 1997, p.13
5. *Public Papers of the Presidents of the United States* (GPO), 1996, Vol. I, p.654, April 28
6. Washington Office of Amnesty International, *Human Rights & US Security Assistance*, 1996, p.1

INTRODUCTION

1   Senate Committee on Veterans' Affairs, *Is Military Research Hazardous to Veterans' Health? Lessons Spanning Half a Century*, December 8, 1994, p.5
2   *Washington Post*, October 2 and 23, 1996 and July 31, 1997 for the estimated numbers of affected soldiers.
3   *Journal of the American Medical Association*, September 1, 1999, p.822
4   *Washington Post*, October 19, 1999, p.3
5   *Is Military Research Hazardous to Veterans' Health?* op. cit., passim
6   John Kenneth Knaus, *Orphans of the Cold War* (New York, 1999), p.312. Knaus was the CIA officer who spoke to the Dalai Lama.
7   *Le Nouvel Observateur* (France), January 15–21, 1998, p.76. There are at least two editions of this magazine; with the perhaps sole exception of the Library of Congress, the version sent to the United States is shorter than the French version, and the Brzezinski interview was not included in the shorter version.
8   *Washington Post*, January 13, 1985, p.30
9   *New York Times*, March 25, 1977, p.10
10 "60 Minutes", May 12, 1996
11 For the full text of the relevant part of his memo, see *The Economist* (London), February 8, 1992, p.66 (US edition)
12 *Washington Post*, April 25, 1999, p.28

13 John Judis, "K Street Gore", *The American Prospect*, July–August 1999, p.18–21

14 Ibid.

15 *Washington Post*, June 18, 1999. After protestors repeatedly disrupted Gore's campaign appearances, the US removed South Africa from the sanction watch list (Ibid., December 4, 1999, p.18)

16 Interview with Reagan at the White House, October 29, 1985, broadcast October 30 on "The World at One", Radio 4, Great Britain.

17 *New York Times*, June 13, 1999

18 Ibid., February 14, 1991, p.16

19 "An Oriana Fallaci Interview: Otis Pike and the CIA", *New Republic* (Washington, DC), April 3, 1976, p.10

20 Borrowed from former CIA analyst David MacMichael

21 Speaking at the National Press Club, Washington, DC, June 25, 1999.

22 Phrase borrowed from media critic Norman Solomon

23 NPR *Morning Edition*, Mara Liasson, June 11, 1999

24 *Washington Post*, March 27, 1999

25 Adolf Hitler, *Mein Kampf* (Houghton Mifflin Co., Boston, 1971; original version 1925) Vol. 1, chapter 10, p.231

26 William Blum, "Hiroshima: Needless Slaughter, Useful Terror", *Covert Action Quarterly* (Washington, DC), #53, Summer 1995, p.22–25

27 William Blum, *Killing Hope: U.S. Military and CIA Interventions Since World War II* (Common Courage Press, Monroe, Maine, 1995), chapter 27

28 *New York Times*, March 9, 1982, p.1; March 23, 1982, p.1 and 14; *The Guardian* (London) November 3, 1983, March 29, 1984; *Washington Post*, May 30, 1986

29 *Los Angeles Times*, September 2, 1991, p.1

30 *Vital Speeches of the Day*, May 1, 1990, p.421, speech delivered March 23, 1990

31 For excellent and concise summaries of how and why the United States planned and achieved world domination, see Noam Chomsky, *What Uncle Sam Really Wants* (Odonian Press, Berkeley, 1992) and Michael Parenti, *Against Empire* (City Lights Books, San Francisco, 1995)

32 Thomas Hauser, *The Execution of Charles Horman* (New York, 1978), p.191. (Horman was an American killed by the Chilean junta in the wake of the coup.)

33 *New York Times*, February 3, 1992, p.8

34 Ibid., January 7, 1983, p.4; *The Guardian* (London), December 6, 1986 (first quote); *Los Angeles Times*, October 25, 1989, p.7 (second quote), and October 26.

35 *AIR FORCE Magazine* (Arlington, VA), March 1991, p.81

36 *New York Times*, March 21, 1999, p.34

37 *Public Papers of the Presidents of the United States* (GPO), 1993, Vol. I, p.1060–1, July 11

38 *The Economist* (London), June 4–10, 1994, p.40

39 *Washington Times*, August 24, 1999, p.1; the words are those of the newspaper and may be a paraphrase of the original

40 *Washington Post*, August 28, 1999, p.3

41 Donald Henderson, "Dangerous Fictions about Bioterrorism", *Washington Post*, November 8, 1999, p.21; see also Roni Kruzman, "Koppel's 'Biowar of the Worlds'", *Extra!* (Fairness and Accuracy in Reporting, NY), January/February 2000, p.21

42 *Washington Post*, October 29, 1999, p.14

43 *Atlanta Journal*, August 4, 1999, p.1

44 *Washington Post*, August 27, 1999

45 State Department, "Patterns of Global Terrorism, 1998", released April 1999, can be read on their website.

46 See, e.g., Tim Weiner, "Military Accused of Lies Over Arms", *New York Times*, June 28, 1993, p.10; Tim Weiner, *Blank Check* (New York, 1990), p.42–43, for CIA's inflated figures regarding Soviets; Anne H. Cahn, "How We Got Oversold on Overkill", *Los Angeles Times*, July 23, 1993, about a GAO study; Douglas Jehl & Michael Ross, "CIA Nominee Faces Charges He Slanted Data", *Los Angeles Times*, September 15, 1991, p.1; Arthur Macy Cox, "Why the U.S., Since 1977, Has Been Misperceiving Soviet Military Strength", *New York Times*, October 20, 1980, p. 19 (Cox was formerly an official with the State Department and the CIA)

47 *The Guardian* (London), January 1, 1999

48 *Washington Post*, October 2, 1998

49 Ibid., September 9, 1998, p.17

50 Mencken: *In Defense of Women* (1920); MacArthur: William Manchester, *American Caesar: Douglas MacArthur, 1880–1964* (Dell, New York, 1978), p.827

51 Jonathan Vankin, *Conspiracies, Cover-ups and Crimes: Political Manipulation and Mind Control in America* (New York, 1991), p.120

52 Parenti, op. cit., p.49

53 "Pentagon's Planning Guidance for the Fiscal Years 1994–1999", *New York Times*, March 8, 1992, p.14

54 *United States Space Command: Vision for 2020*, excerpts are in same sequence as found in the publication; put out by U.S. Space Command, Director of Plans, Peterson AFB, Colorado, August 1997

55 Keith R. Hall, Assistant Secretary of the Air Force for Space and Director of the National Reconnaissance Office, speaking to the National Space Club, September 15, 1997

56 General Joseph Ashy, at the time Commander-in-Chief of the U.S. Space Command, cited in *Aviation Week and Space Technology* (New York), August 5, 1996, p.51

57 October 17, 1963, UN Resolution number 1884

58 From the study's Introduction, p.8. The *Boston Globe*, March 2, 1998, p.5 contains almost the entire passage.

59 Parenti, op. cit., p.80

CHAPTER 1

1 *Washington Post*, August 22, 1998

2 NBC, "Today" show, August 22, 1998

3 *New York Times*, August 22, 1998, p. 15

4 *Washington Post*, August 9, 1998

5 *The Nation*, April 4, 1998

6 *Washington Post*, November 6, 1997

7 Ibid., November 16, 1997

8 *Public Papers of the Presidents of the United States* (GPO), 1996, Vol. I, p.437

9 *The Independent* (London), March 26, 1996, p.8

10 *Washington Post*, January 23, 1997, p.1

11 Inter Press Service (headquartered in Rome) report from the United Nations, February 21, 2000

12 FBI press release, "FBI Policy and Guidelines", Feb. 16, 1999

CHAPTER 2

1 *Washington Post*, March 14, 1996

2 *Los Angeles Times*, August 4, 1996

3 *Washington Post*, August 15, 1996, p.32

4 *Covert Action Information Bulletin* (Washington, DC), #64, Spring 1998, p.29–30

5 Mary Anne Weaver, *The New Yorker*, November 13, 1995, p.62 and 64

6 *Los Angeles Times*, August 2, 1993, p.12

7 Mary Anne Weaver, "Blowback", *The Atlantic Monthly*, May 1996, p.28

8 *Washington Post*, September 6, 1996

9 *Los Angeles Times*, August 6, 1996, p.12

10 *New York Times*, March 8, 1995, p.12; March 9, p.6

11 *Los Angeles Times*, August 4, 1996, p.1

12 Ibid., p.17

13 *Slovo* (Russian newspaper), August 27, 1999, as reported by CDI Russia (Center for Defense Information, Washington, DC internet list on Russia); *Los Angeles Times*, August 4, 1996, p.1; *New York Times*, September 20, 1999, p.9

14 *Los Angeles Times*, August 4, 1996, p.1

15 *New York Times Magazine*, March 13, 1994, p.54

16 Ibid.

17 Ibid.; *Los Angeles Times*, August 2, 1993, p.12

18 *Los Angeles Times*, August 4, 1996

19 Ibid., March 7, 1992, p.14 and August 5, 1996

20 Ibid., August 5, 1996, p.11

21 Weaver, *Atlantic Monthly*, op. cit.; *Los Angeles Times*, August 6, 1996, p.11

22 *Washington Post*, May 26, 1996

23 Ibid., August 28, 1999, p.14

24 *Los Angeles Times*, August 4, 1996, p.2

CHAPTER 3

1   Amnesty International, in a report of January 17, 1994, entitled "KUWAIT: Three years of unfair trials" (AI Index: MDE 17/01/94), states that it "expressed its concern on 1 July 1993 that the trial of 14 defendants, 12 of whom face the possibility of death sentences, accused of participation in an alleged assassination attempt on former United States President George Bush, failed to satisfy international minimum standards." The report makes repeated references to the use of torture by the Kuwaiti government of people accused of collaboration with the occupying Iraqis in 1990. The subsequent convictions and "confession" of one of the defendants may be seen in this context.
    See also *The Guardian* (London), June 29, 1993, p.9 and June 7, 1994, p.9 for further discussion of the questions surrounding the arrests and trial.

2   *Washington Post*, June 27, 1993

3   *Sunday Times* (London), July 6, 1975, p.1. Narut at the time was working at a US naval hospital in Naples, Italy, and made his remarks at a NATO-sponsored conference held in Oslo, Norway the week before.

4   The Select Committee to Study Governmental Operations with Respect to Intelligence Activities (US Senate), *Interim Report: Alleged Assassination Plots Involving Foreign Leaders*, November 20, 1975, p.285

5   *Washington Post*, October 5, 1988, summarizes some of Reagan's executive orders

6   *Los Angeles Times*, October 14, 1989, p.16

7   William Corson, *The Armies of Ignorance* (New York, 1977), p.347

CHAPTER 4

1 Part of a May 23, 1997 release by the CIA of 1,400 pages of classified documents concerning the 1954 coup in Guatemala. It is 20 pages long.

2 One of seven manuals from the Army's Foreign Intelligence Assistance Program, entitled "Project X"; written originally in English in the mid-1960s, later translated into Spanish; provided to Latin American and other Third World countries' military intelligence trainees; also used at School of the Americas; in use until at least 1991; various paragraphs in the original texts were revised by the Pentagon during the 1970s and 80s; released to the public by the Pentagon, September 20, 1996

3 Another of the seven manuals referred to in note 2.

4 Inter Press Service (a well-known and respected Third World news agency headquartered in Rome), March 10, 1997, on the internet

5 KUBARK was a code name used by the CIA, with no particular significance. This is a Vietnam-era training manual, written for use by Americans against the enemy, not for training foreign military services. Also see *New York Times*, February 9, 1997.

6 Much of the material in this manual derives from the KUBARK manual, discussed above. Both HRETM and KUBARK were declassified January 24, 1997. They deal exclusively with interrogation. The Pentagon has stated that HRETM was altered in 1984–85 to discourage torture. This was after a furor was raised in Congress and the press about CIA training techniques used in Central America. For further excerpts see *Baltimore Sun*, January 27, 1997 and the website of School of the Americas Watch—http://www.soaw.org

7 For a complete list of the methods of sabotage, see Holly Sklar, *Washington's War on Nicaragua* (Boston, 1988), p.183–4. For some of the illustrations and Spanish text, see *Covert Action Information Bulletin* (Washington, DC), #22, Fall 1984, p.28

8 *New York Times*, October 17, 1984, p.1 and 12; Sklar, p.177–87

9 Sklar, 186

CHAPTER 5

1 *Baltimore Sun*, June 11, 1995, p.10A

2 *Washington Post*, August 3, 1999, p.10

3 James Becket, *Barbarism in Greece* (New York, 1970), p.xi

4 Proposed 1984, in force 1987, ratified by US 1994

5 *Baltimore Sun*, op. cit.

6 Amnesty International, *Report on Torture* (London, 1973), p.77

7   Becket, p. 15

8   Becket, p.16, see also p.127

9   Kermit Roosevelt, *Countercoup: The Struggle for the Control of Iran* (McGraw-Hill paperback, 1981), p.9. Roosevelt was a CIA officer operating in Iran in the 1950s.

10 Leaf was chief CIA analyst on Iran for five years before resigning in 1973, interviewed by Seymour Hersh in the *New York Times*, January 7, 1979.

11 Robert Fisk, article in *The Independent* (London), August 9, 1998, p.19

12 Thomas Powers, *The Man Who Kept the Secrets: Richard Helms and the CIA* (Pocket Books, New York, 1979) p.155, 157

13 Donald Duncan, *The New Legions* (London, 1967) p.156–9; Duncan describes the Green Beret "interrogation" class he was in.

14 David Wise, "Colby of CIA—CIA of Colby", *New York Times Magazine*, July 1, 1973, p.33–4

15 Telford Taylor, *Nuremberg and Vietnam: an American Tragedy* (New York Times, 1970), p.148–53

16 Richard Harris, *Death of a Revolutionary: Che Guevara's Last Mission* (New York, 1970) p.185–6

17 A.J. Langguth, *Hidden Terrors* (New York, 1978) p.285–7; (Langguth was Saigon Bureau Chief for the *New York Times* in 1965); also see *New York Times*, August 15, 1970

18 Langguth, p.289

19 Manuel Hevia Cosculluela, *Pasaporte 11333: Ocho Años con la CIA* (Havana, 1978), p.284–7. Hevia was a Cuban agent who worked under cover with Mitrione in Uruguay. 1981: *San Francisco Chronicle*, November 2, 1981.

20 Langguth, passim; see index under "torture".

21 Allan Nairn, "C.I.A. Death Squad", *The Nation*, April 17, 1995, p.511–13

22 *Washington Post*, May 12, 1996, p.C1; *Los Angeles Times*, March 31, 1995, p.4

23 From "Statement of Sister Dianne Ortiz, May 6, 1996", distributed by her supporters in Lafayette Park opposite the White House while she was conducting a silent vigil there.

24 *New York Times*, January 11, 1982, p.2.

25 The National Guardsman, identified only as "Manuel", was interviewed in the television documentary "Torture", produced and directed by Rex Bloomstein for Thames Television Ltd. (Great Britain) in 1986 with the cooperation of Amnesty International. Video copy in author's possession.

26 *Baltimore Sun*, lengthy series of articles on US support for Battalion 316, June 11–20, 1995; and January 27, 1997, "Torture Was Taught By CIA";

also see *New York Times*, October 24, 1998 and *The Nation*, November 10, 1997, p.20–22 (David Corn)

27 Philip Wheaton, *Panama Invaded* (New Jersey, 1992), p.14–15; this is from testimony recorded by the staff of the Central American Human Rights Center of San José, Costa Rica, taken in Panama on Jan. 29, 1990 from a Red Cross contact.

28 *Newsweek*, March 22, 1976, p.28 and 31

29 "Chicago Police Used Torture, Report Alleges", *Los Angeles Times*, February 8, 1992, p.1 and 14

30 Holly Burkhalter, "Torture in U.S. Prisons", *The Nation*, July 3, 1995, p.17–18. Burkhalter at the time was the Washington director of Human Rights Watch.

31 See also "Torture in the United States" a report by The Coalition Against Torture and Racial Discrimination, chaired by the World Organization Against Torture, USA (Washington, DC)—www.woatusa.org

Other examples of torture practiced in the US can be found in the present book in "A Day in the Life of a Free Country".

32 *Washington Post*, October 28, 1996. The provision is part of the Antiterrorism and Effective Death Penalty Act of 1996.

33 *Los Angeles Times*, May 13, 1992; *Washington Post*, July 3, 1995

CHAPTER 6

1 See Interventions and other sections of this book. Also see Christopher Simpson, *Blowback* (New York, 1988), John Loftus, *The Belarus Secret* (New York, 1982), Martin Lee, *The Beast Reawakens* (Boston, 1997)

2 *Washington Post*, November 21, 1971, p.13

3 *Los Angeles Times*, September 13, 1988, p.19. For further discussion of this issue, see Russ Bellant, "Old Nazis and the New Right: The Republican Party and Fascists", *Covert Action Information Bulletin* (Washington, DC), #33, Winter 1990, p.27–31

CHAPTER 7

1 *New York Times*, September 20, 1999, p.6

2 Course O-47, taught at SOA while it was still in the Panama Canal Zone, Document 5489, p.5, February 3, 1977, as cited in Penny Lernoux, *Cry of the People: The Struggle for Human Rights in Latin America—The Catholic Church in Conflict With U.S. Policy*, (Penguin Books, NY, 1982), p.167n; for other course descriptions, see p.180–1, 471–3

3 *New York Times*, September 28, 1996, p.22

4 *Washington Post*, February 5, 1968

5 Mark Danner, *The Massacre at El Mozote* (Vintage Books, 1994)

6 *Washington Post*, November 16, 1999, p.31, op-ed column by Leo J. O'Donovan, S.J.

7 See the website of School of the Americas Watch—http://www.soaw.org— Also see *Covert Action Quarterly* (Washington, DC), #46, Fall 1993, p.15–19

8 February 8, 1990, before the Senate Committee on Armed Services

9 For further discussion, see Latin America Working Group (Washington, DC), *Just the Facts: A civilian's guide to U.S. defense and security assistance to Latin America and the Caribbean*, which tells everything one would want to know about training Latin militaries in the US and abroad — bases, military exercises, human-rights restrictions and much more; can be read in full at http://www.ciponline.org/facts

Also see the excellent series in the *Washington Post*, July 12–14, as well as December 13 and 14, 1998

10 *New York Times*, November 18, 1999

11 Michael Klare and Nancy Stein, "Police Terrorism in Latin America", *NACLA's Latin America and Empire Report* (North American Congress on Latin America, NY), January 1974, p.19–23, based on State Department documents obtained by Senator James Abourezk in 1973; ibid., July–August 1976, p.31; also see Jack Anderson, *Washington Post*, October 8, 1973, p.C33; A.J. Langguth, *Hidden Terrors* (New York, 1978), p.242–3

12 *New York Times*, January 23, 1975, p.38; January 26, 1975, p. 42; *NACLA*, op. cit., July–August 1976, p.31–2; Langguth, p.301

13 See Lawrence Rockwood & Amelia Simpson, "Training the world's police", *Foreign Policy in Focus* report, Institute for Policy Studies (Washington, DC), forthcoming July 2000.

14 Thomas E. Skidmore, *Politics in Brazil, 1930–1964* (Oxford University Press, New York, 1967), p.330; also see James Kohl and John Litt, *Urban Guerrilla Warfare in Latin America* (The MIT Press, Cambridge, Mass., 1974), p.39, for further discussion of the strong pro-US, anti-leftist bias of the college's curriculum.

15 Phyllis R. Parker, *Brazil and the Quiet Intervention, 1964* (University of Texas Press, Austin, 1979) p.98, cable to State Department, March 4, 1964

CHAPTER 8

1 *Washington Post*, December 4, 1996, p.1

2 Leonard A. Cole, *Clouds of Secrecy: The Army's Germ Warfare Tests over Populated Areas* (Maryland, 1990), p.12–14

3 *Washington Post*, September 21, 1999, p.1

4 United Nations General Assembly Resolution: "Establishment of a nuclear-weapon-free zone in the region of the Middle East", December 4, 1990, Resolution No. 45/52.

5 *New York Times*, January 24, 1991, p.11

6 Ibid., March 23, 1991

7 Michael Bilton and Kevin Sim, *Four Hours in May Lai* (Viking, New York, 1992), p.175, 209–13

8 *LA Weekly* (Los Angeles), March 9–15, 1990, p.12

9 *New York Times*, January 9, 1971, p.3

10 Telford Taylor, *Nuremberg and Vietnam: an American Tragedy* (New York, 1970), p.140–43

11 *Far Eastern Economic Review* (Hong Kong), October 30, 1997, p.15, 20

12 *Washington Post*, May 25, 1998, p.B4

13 I am indebted to Professor Joan Roelofs of Keene State College, New Hampshire for bringing this concept to my attention.

14 This and most of the other material concerning the complaint to the Tribunal mentioned here were transmitted to the author by Mandel and other complainants.

15 Press Release from Chief Prosecutor Louise Arbour, The Hague, May 13, 1999.

16 *The Observer* (London), December 26, 1999; *Washington Times*, December 30 and 31, 1999; *New York Times*, December 30, 1999

17 *Washington Post*, May 24, 1999, p.1

18 *New York Times*, May 13, 1999, p.1

19 NATO press conference, Brussels, May 25, 1999

20 *Washington Post*, April 22, 1999, p.18

21 Ibid., September 20, 1999, p.1

22 *New York Times*, December 2, 1998, p.1; January 3, 2000

23 *Washington Post*, November 18, 1999, p.1

CHAPTER 9

1 *The Miami Herald*, November 16, 1997. See remarks about leading Cuban exile terrorist, Luis Posada Carriles, in "National Endowment for Democracy" chapter.

2 Associated Press, Tampa, Fla., July 16, 1997

3 Unless otherwise indicated, information about the individual cases can be found in the following: *Miami Herald*, October 21, 1998, p.11A; *Boston Globe*, May 2,3 &4, 1999; press releases of The Center for Justice and Accountability (San Francisco) and the Center for Constitutional Rights (New York), which

have been involved in lawsuits against several of the individuals named; *Covert Action Quarterly* (Washington, DC), #65, Fall 1998, p.45

4 Guatemalan Human Rights Commission (Washington, DC), *Human Rights Update*, April 21, 1995

5 Noam Chomsky, *Z Magazine*, March 1992, p.9, based on an interview given by Gramajo to the *Harvard International Review*

6 EFE (Spanish news agency), dispatch from Miami, November 20, 1999

7 Adam Fifield, "The Apologist in Suburbia", *Village Voice* (New York), May 5, 1998, p.55

8 According to the Center for Justice and Accountability (San Francisco). These men have claimed that they themselves were victims of torture, by the North Vietnamese and/or the National Liberation Front. It was during their treatment in the US for this experience that they recounted their own culpability. The CJA does not wish to reveal their names because this information was obtained in a clinical setting.

9 Asia Resource Center (Washington, DC), *Asia Insights*, Summer 1986, passim; *Los Angeles Times*, many articles throughout the 1980s and later; e.g., August 4, 1985, II, p.1; May 8, 1986, II, p.1; October 17, 1987, II, p.8 (editorial); March 24, 1990, p.33

10 *New York Times*, September 22, 1998, p.12

11 This discussion is derived from "Torture in the United States", a paper produced by the World Organization Against Torture, USA (Washington, DC), October 1998, part 7, "Extraditions", written by Neil Tow.

12 *Washington Post*, February 5, 1997, p.28

13 Associated Press, February 7, 1999

CHAPTER 10

1 For an overview, see John Pilger, "The Long Secret Alliance: Uncle Sam and Pol Pot", *Covert Action Quarterly* (Washington, DC), #62, Fall 1997, p.5–9, plus other sources listed below.

2 Elizabeth Becker, *When the War Was Over: Cambodia and the Khmer Rouge Revolution* (Public Affairs, NY, 1998), p.435

3 *Los Angeles Times*, December 5, 1980, I-B, p.1

4 Linda Mason and Roger Brown, *Rice, Rivalry and Politics: Managing Cambodian Relief* (Univ. of Notre Dame Press, 1983), p.135–6

5 William Shawcross, *The Quality of Mercy: Cambodia, Holocaust and Modern Conscience* (London, 1984), p.289, 395

6 *New York Times*, November 16, 1989, p.16

7 *Washington Post*, July 8, 1985, p.18

8 *Newsweek*, October 10, 1983, p.41

9   *Los Angeles Times*, February 27, 1991

10 *San Francisco Examiner*, August 12, 1990, p.18

11 *Los Angeles Times*, February 27, 1991

12 Adam Fifield, "The Apologist in Suburbia", *The Village Voice* (New York), May 5, 1998, p.55

13 Jack Colhoun, "U.S. Supports Khmer Rouge", *Covert Action Information Bulletin* (Washington, DC), #34, Summer 1990, p.37–40; *Washington Post*, January 10, 1999, op-ed by Peter Goodman; *New York Times*, October 18, 1989, p.29

14 *Weekly Compilation of Presidential Documents* (GPO), April 16, 1998, p.663

CHAPTER 11

1   *The Nation*, September 26, 1994, p.304

2   U.S. Commission on National Security/21st Century, *New World Coming* (Phase I report), September 15, 1999, p.3

3   *Washington Post*, November 16, 1998

4   *Journal of the American Medical Association*, August 25, 1999, p.761

CHAPTER 12

1   International Action Center (New York), *Metal of Dishonor: Depleted Uranium*, p.3–40, 134–149 and elsewhere for a detailed discussion of the properties of DU, its health dangers and the circumstances under which US military personnel and Iraqis may have been exposed to it; p.140–44 for a discussion of the airborne transport of uranium particles.

    See also *The Bulletin of the Atomic Scientists*, November/December 1999, p.42–5, and *Radioactive Battlefields of the 1990s: The United States Army's Use of Depleted Uranium and Its Consequences for Human Health and the Environment*, by the Depleted Uranium Citizens' Network (of the Military Toxics Project), Lewiston, ME, January 16, 1996; www.antenna.nl/wise/uranium/dmtp.html

2   Bill Mesler, "The Pentagon's Radioactive Bullet", *The Nation*, October 21, 1996, p.12–13.

3   *The Independent* (London), November 10, 1991, p.2, two articles.

4   *The Washington Report on Middle East Affairs* (established by retired US foreign service officers), July/August 1995, p.105

5   *Sunday Herald* (Glasgow, Scotland), April 4, 1999

6   *Washington Post*, May 29 and August 19, 1999

7   "Recent Military Accidents In Vieques, Puerto Rico", paper prepared by the office of Puerto Rico's Congressional representative, Carlo Romero-

Barceló, May 1999; *Orlando Sentinel* (Orlando, Florida), May 1, 1999, p.18; Pacifica Radio, "Democracy Now", July 21, 1999

8   *Austin American-Statesman* (Austin, Texas), May 1, 1999, p.8

9   *Washington Post*, December 4, 1999, p.4 and February 1, 2000

10   *The Albuquerque Tribune*, January 26, 1994, p.A1; *Uranium Battlefields Home & Abroad: Depleted Uranium Use by the U.S. Department of Defense*, March 1993, a joint publication of various environmental and community organizations in New Mexico, such as The New Mexico Progressive Alliance for Community Empowerment (pace@nmpace.org); U.S. Army Environmental Policy Institute, *Health and Environmental Consequences of Depleted Uranium Use in the U.S. Army: Technical Report*, June 1995, Appendix B

11   *Radioactive Battlefields*, op. cit., p.3

12   Mesler, p.12

CHAPTER 13

1   Rachel Stohl, "Cluster Bombs Leave Lasting Legacy", report of the Center for Defense Information (Washington, DC), August 5, 1999. There are both anti-personnel and anti-material cluster bombs, or they can be combined in one weapon.

2   *Washington Post*, August 3, 1999

3   *Christian Science Monitor*, June 9, 1999, p.11

4   Ibid.

5   *The Guardian* (London), June 23, 1999, p.12

6   Paul Watson, "Unexploded Weapons Pose Deadly Threat on the Ground", *Los Angeles Times*, April 28, 1999, p.5

7   Handicap International report, 1997, "Living with UXO [Unexploded Ordnance]", funded by United Nations Development Program and the government of Sweden, reported in *Earth Times*, January 15, 1998

8   Center for Defense Information report, op. cit.

9   Ibid.

CHAPTER 14

1   Robert Harris and Jeremy Paxman, *A Higher Form of Killing: The Secret Story of Gas and Germ Warfare* (London, 1982), p.xi

2   Leonard A. Cole, *Clouds of Secrecy: The Army's Germ Warfare Tests over Populated Areas* (Maryland, 1990), p.18

3   *Baltimore Sun*, August 15, 1980, p.7

4   Stephen Endicott and Edward Hagerman, *The United States and Biological Warfare: Secrets from the Early Cold War and Korea* (Indiana University Press, 1998), p.166–7

In January 1998, a Japanese newspaper claimed to have a dozen documents from a Moscow archive that suggested that the Chinese claims about biological warfare were no more than a hoax initiated by the Soviets (Ibid., p.248–9). But this counter-claim raises more questions than it answers, not the least of which is why has the mammoth US publicity machine not said a word about this incredibly advantageous "find"? Nor has Washington apparently asked the Russians to open the archives so the documents can be authenticated. For a discussion of this issue, see the review of the Endicott and Hagerman book by Peter Pringle in *The Nation*, May 3, 1999, p.29–32.

5   *San Francisco Chronicle*, October 8, 1979, p.13; *Washington Post*, October 9, 1979, p.6

6   Endicott and Hagerman, op. cit., p.xi, 49–50, 218

7   Ibid., p.63

8   *San Francisco Chronicle*, April 24, 1980. Oddly enough, it was only in 1999 that the South Korean government ordered an inquiry into a report that in the late 1960s the US military had used Agent Orange and other toxic defoliants along the North Korean border. The report was based on declassified US documents (*Washington Post*, November 17, 1999).

9   The Michigan Agent Orange Commission, *Physician's Information for Care of Vietnam Veterans Exposed to Agent Orange and Other Chemicals*, June 1991, p.4–8; Harris and Paxman, p.192–3.

10 According to Dr. Barry Commoner, director of the Center for Biology of Natural Systems at Washington University, St. Louis, *The Guardian* (London), February 17, 1984.

11 Robert Dreyfuss, "Apocalypse Still", *Mother Jones* (San Francisco), February 2000, p.42ff

12 James Ridgeway, *Village Voice*, Feb. 5, 1991, p.30; *New York Times*, September 9, 1965

13 John Cookson and Judith Nottingham, *A Survey of Chemical and Biological Warfare* (London, 1969), p.15–17

14 Ibid., p.30

15 April Oliver and Peter Arnett, "Did the U.S. Drop Nerve Gas?", *Time*, June 15, 1998, p.37–9

16 *The Washington Post Magazine*, November 29, 1998, p.20 ff.

17 "Tailwind: Rebuttal to the Abrams/Kohler Report", July 22, 1998, can be found on the Internet

18 John Lindsay-Poland, "Toxic Aftertaste", *The Progressive*, (Madison, WI), December 1998, p. 24–27; see also *Washington Post*, January 10, 2000, p.14–5

19 *The Dallas Morning News*, August 20, 1999

20 Philip Wheaton, *Panama Invaded* (New Jersey, 1992), p.16–17, citing the monthly magazine *El Periódico* (Panama City), February 1990, p.8, "Bombardean Pacora con substancias quimicas".

21 *New York Times*, April 28, 1966, p.1.

22 Taylor Branch and George Crile III, "The Kennedy Vendetta", *Harper's* (New York), August 1975, p.52

23 *Washington Post*, March 21, 1977, p.A18

24 Warren Hinckle and William Turner, *The Fish is Red: The Story of the Secret War Against Castro* (Harper & Row, NY, 1981), p.293, based on their interview with the participant in Ridgecrest, California, September 27, 1975.

25 *San Francisco Chronicle*, January 10, 1977

26 Bill Schaap, "The 1981 Cuba Dengue Epidemic", *Covert Action Information Bulletin* (Washington, DC), No. 17, Summer 1982, p.28–31

27 Reported on their website: http://www.cdc.gov/ncidod/dvbid/dengue.htm

28 Jane Franklin, *Cuba and the United States: A Chronological History* (Ocean Press, Melbourne and New York, 1997), p.170. This book states that 188 people died from the dengue epidemic (p.174)

29 *San Francisco Chronicle*, October 29, 1980, p.15

30 *Science* (American Association for the Advancement of Science, Washington, DC), January 13, 1967, p.176

31 *Covert Action Information Bulletin* (Washington, DC), No. 22, Fall 1984, p.35; the trial of Eduardo Victor Arocena Perez, Federal District Court for the Southern District of New York, transcript of September 10, 1984, p.2187–89.

32 For further details of the State Department's side of the issue, see *New York Times*, May 7, 1997, p.9

33 Response to author's query, July 29, 1997, by FAA spokesperson Hank Price

34 UN General Assembly document A/52/128, April 29, 1997

35 As reported to the author by the Cuban UN Mission in New York

36 See, e.g., *San Francisco Chronicle*, July 27, 1981

37 *Washington Post*, September 16, 1977, p.2

38 *Los Angeles Times*, June 18, 1990, p.1

39 There's an abundance of documentation of this. See, e.g., Seth Shulman, *The Threat at Home: Confronting the Toxic Legacy of the U.S. Military* (Beacon Press, Boston, 1992), passim.

CHAPTER 15

1   *New York Times*, January 22, 1999, p.12

2   *Biological Testing Involving Human Subjects by the Department of Defense, 1977*, Hearings before the Subcommittee on Health and Scientific Research of the Committee on Human Resources, US Senate, March 8 and May 23, 1977, p.270

3   Leonard A. Cole, *Clouds of Secrecy: The Army's Germ Warfare Tests over Populated Areas* (Maryland, 1990), chapter 1

4   *San Francisco Chronicle*, October 8, 1979, p.13; *Washington Post*, October 9, 1979, p.6; *Scientific American*, June 1999, p.70–75

5   Cole, chapters 7 and 8; *San Francisco Examiner*, December 22, 1976, p.1; December 23, 1976, p.1; September 17, 1979, p.3; October 19, 1980

6   Cole, Appendix 3, for this and another expert testimony on the potential danger of the same bacteria, submitted to the US Senate, 1977 (see note 2)

7   *San Francisco Chronicle*, December 22, 1976, p.1; April 3, 1981, p.12

8   Ibid., April 3, 1981; *Baltimore Sun*, August 15, 1980, p.7; Cole, p.60–64

9   Cole, p.63–65

10 *Washington Post*, June 9, 1980, p.11

11 *San Francisco Chronicle*, October 14, 1980, p.12

12 Airport and White House: *Washington Post*, December 5, 1984, p.B1

13 *New York Times*, September 19, 1975, p. 14

14 *San Francisco Chronicle*, December 17, 1979, p.5, October 29, 1980, p.15

15 For details of this experiment and the scientists' objections, see Leonard Cole, *The Eleventh Plague* (New York, 1997) p.28–31, based on US Army Chemical Corps, *Summary of Major Events and Problems*, fiscal year 1959, p.101–3

16 *San Francisco Chronicle*, December 4, 1979, p.12

17 Cole, *Clouds of Secrecy*, p.65–9

18 *New York Times*, September 19, 1975, p.14

19 *Washington Post*, December 5, 1984, p.B1

20 *Biological Testing...*, op. cit., p.134. A lengthy list of the open-air CBW testing locations (but without details) can be found on pages 124–140, although for some reason the list doesn't include the occasions where zinc cadmium sulfide was used.

21 US General Accounting Office (GAO), *Nuclear Health and Safety: Examples of Post World War II Radiation Releases at U.S. Nuclear Sites*, November 1993, passim

22 Senate Committee on Veterans' Affairs, *Is Military Research Hazardous to Veterans' Health? Lessons Spanning Half a Century*, December 8, 1994, passim; US General Accounting Office (GAO), *Human Experimentation: An*

Overview on Cold War Era Programs, September 28, 1994, passim; Final Report of the Senate Select Committee to Study Governmental Operations with Respect to Intelligence Activities (The Church Committee), Book 1, *Foreign and Military Intelligence*, April, 1976, p.385–422; Eileen Welsome, *The Plutonium Files: America's Secret Medical Experiments in the Cold War*, (New York, 1999) passim; Jonathan Moreno, *Undue Risk: Secret State Experiments on Humans* (W.H. Freeman & Co., 1999), passim; John Marks, *The Search for the 'Manchurian Candidate': The CIA and Mind Control* (Dell, New York, 1979), passim; Martin Cannon, "Mind Control and the American Government", *Lobster* magazine (Hull, England), #23, 1992, p.2–10; and Aaron Epstein, "At Holmesburg Prison, 320 human guinea pigs", *Philadelphia Inquirer*, November 25, 1979, p.1 ff.

23   From a review of *The Plutonium Files*, op. cit., by Deborah Nelson, *Bookworld* (*Washington Post*), November 21, 1999, based on chapter 22 of the book

24   *Washington Post*, June 9, 1999

25   Hearings before a House Subcommittee of the Committee on Appropriations, "Department of Defense Appropriations for 1970"

CHAPTER 16

1   Jack Anderson, *Washington Post*, October 25, 1969, p.F11; *Washington Post*, April 14, 1998

2   *Los Angeles Times*, August 1, 1998

3   *Covert Action Quarterly* (Washington, DC), #63, Winter 1998, p. 29

4   *U.S. Chemical and Biological Warfare-Related Dual Use Exports to Iraq and their Possible Impact on the Health Consequences of the Persian Gulf War*, Senate Committee on Banking, Housing and Urban Affairs with Respect to Export Administration, reports of May 25, 1994 and October 7, 1994

5   Amy E. Smithson, "Rudderless: The Chemical Weapons Convention at 1 1/2", published September 1998 by the Henry L. Stimson Center (Washington, DC), as part of their Chemical and Biological Weapons Nonproliferation Project; an Executive Summary of the report can be read at: http://www.stimson.org/pubs/cwc/execsum.htm

CHAPTER 17

1   *Imperialism and Social Classes*, (1955, first published in 1919), p.51

2   *America and the World Revolution and Other Lectures* (Oxford University Press, New York, 1962), p.92–3

3   Alfred W. McCoy, *The Politics of Heroin: CIA Complicity in the Global Drug Trade* (Lawrence Hill Books, NY, 1991), p.54–63; Sallie Pisani, *The CIA and the Marshall Plan* (University Press of Kansas, 1991), p.99–105 and elsewhere

4   *New York Times*, May 5, 1947, p.1; May 11, IV, p.5; May 14, p.14 and 24;
    May 17, p.8; May 18, IV, p.4; May 20, p.2; Howard K. Smith, *The State of
    Europe* (London, 1950), p.151 (includes Ramadier quote; similar quote in
    New York Times, May 20)

5   *The Guardian* (London), November 29, 1983

6   *Washington Post*, September 30, 1999, p.1; October 14, p.14; December 29,
    p.19

7   Stewart Steven, *Operation Splinter Factor* (London 1974), passim. For those
    familiar with the story, it will be of interest that I have found a document
    in the National Archives which reveals that the State Department knew
    about Noel Field's imprisonment in Hungary for almost the entire five
    years it was publicly claiming it had no knowledge of his fate.

8   Operation Gladio: *The Observer* (London), June 7, 1992; *Washington Post*,
    November 14, 1990, p.19; *Die Welt* (Germany), November 14, 1990, p.7;
    Los Angeles Times, November 15, 1990, p.6; Philip Willan, *Puppetmasters:
    The Political Use of Terrorism in Italy* (London, 1991), chapter 8

9   *Washington Post*, November 14, 1999, for some aspects of the situation at
    that time; also see *Amnesty International Annual Report* for Guatemala
    1997, 1998, 1999 on AI's website

10 *New York Times*, April 29, 1959, p.1

11 See John Gerassi, *The Coming of the New International* (New York, 1971),
    p.245–56, for an overview of the situation, including a long "self-criticism"
    by the Iraqi Communist Party.

12 Claudia Wright, *New Statesman* magazine (London), July 15, 1983, p.20.
    She doesn't say how the Soviets found out about the plan.

13 *Los Angeles Times*, April 14, 1991, p.M1

14 *Le Monde* (France), February 5, 1963, p.5

15 State Department statement: *Christian Science Monitor*, February 13, 1963,
    p.3

16 *The Guardian* (London), January 1, 1994, p.5

17 Ralph McGehee, *Deadly Deceits: My 25 years in the CIA* (New York, 1983),
    passim. McGehee spent much of his CIA career in Thailand; The
    Committee of Concerned Asian Scholars, *The Indochina Story* (Random
    House, NY, 1970), p.64–69; *New York Times*, November 27, 1966, p.4;
    Washington Post, November 20, 1966, p.22; December 7, 1966

18 *Washington Post*, August 23, 1966

19 Bush quote: *Washington Post*, May 21, 1997, column by Nora Boustany

20 *Washington Post*, January 23, 2000

21 Based on a Dave Barry line

22 CIA internal memorandum of February 25, 1966, declassified March 7, 1977, received by author as a result of an FOIA request.

23 Cable News Network en Español, July 23, 1998; *El Diario-La Prensa* (New York) July 24, 1998; *Clarin* (Buenos Aires) July 22, 1998, p.45

24 Numbers of victims: *New York Times*, January 3, 2000

25 FBI: *New York Times*, February 10, 1999, p.6; Kissinger: US government document declassified in 1999, *The Observer* (London), February 28, 1999, p.3

26 *New York Times*, July 23 1986, p.1; *Baltimore Sun*, November 12, 1995, p.1D; *Covert Action Information Bulletin* (Washington, DC), #12, April 1981, p.24–27; William Minter, *Apartheid's Contras* (London, 1994), chapter 6 and passim. See also "Mandela" and "United Nations" chapters herein.

27 Staff Report of the Select Committee on Intelligence, US House of Representatives, 1975, "the Pike Report". This report can be read in book form: *CIA—The Pike Report* (Spokesman Books, Nottingham, England, 1977), p.56, 195–8, 211–17

28 *Washington Post*, October 9, 1974, p.36; *New York Times*, September 25, 1975, p.1; Evans and Novak in *Washington Post*, October 26, 1974, p.19 (NATO information); *Facts on File*, March 1, 1975, p.131 (NATO exercises). Also see the "Elections" chapter under Portugal.

29 For a detailed history of the East Timor question, 1975–78, see Noam Chomsky and Edward S. Herman, *The Washington Connection and Third World Fascism, Volume I* (Boston, 1979), p.129–204

30 Daniel Moynihan with Suzanne Weaver, *A Dangerous Place* (Boston, 1978), p.247

31 Allan Nairn, "US Complicity in Timor", *The Nation*, September 27, 1999, p.5–6; "U.S. trained butchers of Timor", *The Observer* (London), September 19, 1999

32 *New York Times*, October 31, 1995, p.3. The official was described as someone who deals often on Asia policy. He apparently was referring to Suharto in terms of economic policy, but to make such a remark about a man with the blood of a million or more people on his hands does take a special kind of insensitivity.

33 See "Elections" chapter, Jamaica

34 Holly Sklar, *Washington's War on Nicaragua* (South End Press, Boston, 1988), see "Honduras" in index; Philip Wheaton, *Inside Honduras: Regional Counterinsurgency Base* (Ecumenical Program in Central America and the Caribbean [EPICA], Washington, DC, 1982), passim

35 *New York Times*, May 25, 1988, p.8

36 See "Elections" chapter under Nicaragua

37 Dianna Melrose, *Nicaragua: The Threat of a Good Example?* (Oxfam, Oxford, UK, 1985), p.14

38 *San Francisco Examiner*, March 22, 1987, p.1

39 *New York Times*, December 2, 1989, p.1

40 *Los Angeles Times*, September 28, 1991

41 *Sunday Tribune* (Durban, South Africa), November 29, 1981, p.1 and 52

42 Bob Woodward, *VEIL: The Secret Wars of the CIA 1981–1987* (New York, 1987), p.78–9, 124–5, 215; *New York Times*, April 8, 1982, p.3

43 Fred Halliday, "Russians help to beat leftwing guerrillas", *The Guardian* (London), May 3, 1984, p.7; *New York Times*, March 19, 1980, p.1

44 *New York Times*, May 23, 1980, p.1

45 *The Milwaukee Journal*, August 12, 1980, based on the observations of three American Peace Corps workers in South Korea. Two of the three wrote an article on the events in Korea for *Covert Action Information Bulletin* (Washington, DC), #11, December 1980, p.9–15

46 State Department quote: *The Milwaukee Journal*, op. cit. For an overall discussion of the US relationship to South Korea and the 1980 uprising, see Tim Shorrock, "Debacle in Kwangju", *The Nation*, December 9,1996, p.19–22; *Washington Post*, March 5, 1996, p.5; Bill Mesler, "Korea and the US: Partners in Repression", *Covert Action Quarterly* (Washington, DC), #56, Spring 1996, p.53–57

47 *New York Times*, February 2, 1981, p.8, February 3, p.6

48 Woodward, p.96–7, 157–58, 215; Jonathan Bearman, *Qadhafi's Libya* (Zed Books, London, 1986), p.216–225

49 *New York Times*, February 11, 2000, p.30, editorial

50 Speech at the Pacific Islands Luncheon, Kahala Hilton Hotel, Hawaii, February 10, 1982, cited in a September 1989 paper, "Possible Foreign Involvement in the Fiji Military Coup", p.2, by Owen Wilkes, editor of *Peacelink* and *Wellington Pacific Report*, both of New Zealand.

51 Ibid, p.6–7

52 *The Nation*, August 15/22, 1987, p.117–20; *San Francisco Chronicle*, June 17, 1987; *The National Reporter* (Washington, DC), Fall 1987, p.33–38; *Covert Action Information Bulletin* (Washington, DC), #29, Fall 1987, p.7–10

53 *The Sydney Morning Herald* (Australia), May 16, 1987, p.1

54 The Independent Commission of Inquiry on the U.S. Invasion of Panama, *The U.S. Invasion of Panama: The Truth Behind Operation 'Just Cause'* (South End Press, Boston, 1991), passim; Philip Wheaton, ed., *Panama Invaded* (The Red Sea Press, New Jersey, 1992), passim

55 Inducing the Soviet intervention: See Brzezinski's remarks in the Introduction; also, Robert Gates (former CIA Director), *From the Shadows* (New York, 1996), p.178 — "[President] Carter began numerous covert actions to counter Soviet advances...Well before the invasion of Afghanistan, he approved intelligence findings aimed at countering the Soviets...[in] Afghanistan."

56 *Washington Post*, November 23, 1999

57 National Endowment for Democracy, Washington, DC, *Annual Report, 1990* (October 1, 1989–September 30, 1990), p.23–4.

58 Ibid., 1991, p.41–43

59 *Los Angeles Times*, June 13, 1991, p.14

60 National Endowment for Democracy, Washington, DC, *Annual Report, 1991* (October 1, 1990–September 30, 1991), p.42

61 *Los Angeles Times*, March 9, 1992, p.14

62 Mark Bowden, *Black Hawk Down* (1999), passim; Stephen Shalom, "Gravy Train: Feeding the Pentagon by Feeding Somalia", November 1993, at www.zmag.org/zmag/articles/shalomsomalia.html; oil companies: *Los Angeles Times*, January 18, 1993, p.1

63 Post-war bombing: *Washington Post*, August 30, 1999, p.3, September 18; Looney: Ibid., June 24, 1996

64 Pilot and navy ships: *New York Times*, July 29, 1996, p.6

65 *New York Times*, editorial, November 25, 1996, p.14

66 June 30, 1999, the Senate passed the Foreign Operations, Export Financing, and Related Programs Appropriations Bill, 2000, which contained the condemnation of the intelligence service, SIN.

67 *Washington Post*, November 25, 1990, p.18, December 19, 1990, p.25

68 iF *Magazine* (Arlington, VA), July–August 1997, p.24–25, article by William Blum on this incident; *Washington Post*, April 27, 1997, p.29 (RU-38A plane)

69 *National Catholic Reporter*, March 24, 1995

70 *Viva Chiapas!*, Winter 1995/6, p.1–2, and other issues (a publication of the ecumenical organization, Conversion for Reclaiming Earth in the Americas, Takoma Park, MD)

71 See the series in the *Washington Post*, July 12–14, 1998

72 Drugs: In August 1999, Mexico's former top drug prosecutor, Mario Ruiz Massieu, was charged with laundering $9.9 million in suspected drug payoffs through a Houston bank: *Washington Post*, August 28, 1999, p.7; also see September 9, 1998 regarding Mexican military aiding drug traffickers

Human rights: Amnesty International, *Mexico: The persistence of torture and impunity*, (New York, June 1993), passim; also see later Amnesty reports on Mexico

73 *Viva Chiapas!* op. cit.

74 *Washington Post* series, op. cit.

75 Senator Patrick Leahy (D.-VT) has been the leading sponsor of such legislation, with various versions becoming law since the late 1990s. A discussion of this can be read online at http;//www.ciponline.org/facts. Also see various editions of Amnesty International's *Human Rights & US Security Assistance*.

76 *The Dallas Morning News*, March 18, 1998

77 Testimony of Donnie Marshall before the House Judiciary Committee, Subcommittee on Crime, July 29, 1999, from not-yet-published transcript read in the committee's office

78 *Miami Herald*, October 7, 1997, p.8a; *Washington Post*, February 24, 2000, p.1

79 *New York Times*, November 11, 1998, p.24

80 *Washington Post*, October 4, 1997

81 Ibid., February 18, 1999

82 *Amnesty Action* (AIUSA, NY), Winter 1997, p.1 and 8, reiterating the details of the 1994 report

83 *Washington Post*, December 31, 1998

84 *Colombia Bulletin: A Human Rights Quarterly* (Colombia Support Network, Madison WI), Spring 1997, p.29, article by Carlos Salinas of Amnesty International. For much greater discussion of this intervention, see other issues of this magazine or their website: http://www.igc.org/csn/index.html

85 *Public Papers of the Presidents of the United States* (GPO), 1996, Vol. I, p.614, April 21

86 *New York Times*, March 21, 1999, p.1. "Ethnic cleansing" is what it was labeled by the International Criminal Tribunal for the Former Yugoslavia.

87 *Washington Post*, November 8, 1998, p.3

88 *The Independent* (London), April 24, 1999, p.1

89 Ibid.

90 *Military Review* (Fort Leavenworth, Kansas), "The Professional Journal of the U.S. Army", February 1987, p.46–47

CHAPTER 18

1   *Miami Herald*, October 17, 1997, p.22A

2   Joseph Burkholder Smith (former CIA officer), *Portrait of a Cold Warrior* (New York, 1976), chapters 7, 15, 16, 17; Raymond Bonner, *Waltzing With*

    a Dictator: The Marcoses and the Making of American Policy (New York, 1987), p.39–42; *New York Times* editorial, October 16, 1953, p.26

3   David Wise and Thomas Ross, *The Invisible Government* (New York, 1965,) p.337; Wilbur Crane Eveland, *Ropes of Sand: America's Failure in the Middle East* (NY, 1980), p. 249-50; New York Times, March 31, 1997, p.11

4   Smith, p.210–11

5   Dwight Eisenhower, *The White House Years: Mandate for Change, 1953–1956* (New York, 1963), p.372

6   *The Guardian* (London), December 28, 1984, for a detailed description of the raw cynicism behind the policy to oust Jagan, based on British government documents released in 1984; *The Times* (London), October 7 and 10, 1953; *The Sunday Times* (London), April 16 and 23, 1967

7   *New York Times*, October 9, 1994, p.1, March 31, 1997, p.11; *Los Angeles Times*, March 20, 1995, p.5

8   *Washington Post*, January 24, 1997

9   Duane Clarridge with Digby Diehl, *A Spy For All Seasons: My Life in the CIA* (New York, 1997), p.64–6. Clarridge went on to become a high official in the CIA.

10 *New York Times*, April 25, 1966, p.20

11 Philip Agee, *Inside the Company: CIA Diary* (New York, 1975), p.321; A.J. Langguth, *Hidden Terrors* (New York, 1978) p.92

12 John Bartlow Martin, *Overtaken by Events: The Dominican Crisis From the Fall of Trujillo to the Civil War* (Doubleday, NY, 1966) p.226–8

13 Ibid., p.347–8

14 Georgie Anne Geyer, *Miami Herald*, December 24, 1966; Stephen Schlesinger and Stephen Kinzer, *Bitter Fruit: The Untold Story of the American Coup in Guatemala* (New York, 1982), p.236–44; *New York Herald Tribune*, April 7, 1963, article by Bert Quint, section 2, p.1

15 *Washington Post*, May 17, 1975; *New York Times*, May 17–18, 1975

16 *Covert Action in Chile, 1963–1973*, a Staff Report of The Select Committee to Study Governmental Operations with Respect to Intelligence Activities (US Senate), December 18, 1975, passim

17 *New York Times*, September 25, 1975, p.1, January 7, 1976, p.1; *The Guardian* (London), February 7, 1996 (review of book about Soares' links to CIA)

18 Ernest Volkman and John Cummings, "Murder as Usual", *Penthouse* (New York), December 1977, p.112 ff.; David Corn, *Blond Ghost: Ted Shackley and the CIA's Crusades* (Simon & Schuster, NY, 1994), p.330; Robert Gates (former CIA Director), *From the Shadows* (New York, 1996), p.175

19 1984: *Los Angeles Times*, March 21, 1992, p.2;

1989: *U.S. News & World Report*, May 1, 1989, p.40; *Los Angeles Times*, April 23, 1989, p.1

20 *New York Times*, October 21, 1984, p.12, October 31, p.1

21 *Covert Action Information Bulletin* (Washington, DC) No. 22, Fall 1984, p.27, contains a reproduction of the advertisement

22 William I. Robinson, *A Faustian Bargain: U.S. Intervention in the Nicaraguan Elections and American Foreign Policy in the Post-Cold War Era* (Westview Press, Colorado, 1992) passim; Jacqueline Sharkey, "Anatomy of an Election: How U.S. Money Affected the Outcome in Nicaragua," *Common Cause Magazine* (Washington, DC) May/June 1990

23 *The Guardian* (London), September 22, 1986; *Los Angeles Times*, October 31, 1993, p.1; *New York Times*, November 1, 1993, p.8

24 *Time* , July 15, 1996, p.29–37; Fred Weir, veteran American correspondent in Moscow, analysis dated July 17, 1996, prepared for the Institute for Policy Studies (Washington, DC). Weir at the time was at fweir.ncade@rex.iasnet.ru

   Clinton quote: *Washington Star*, March 27, 1996, p.1, from a State Department cable that paraphrased the Clinton-Yeltsin talk

25 *Washington Post*, April 6, 1997. The dollar amount is derived from the NED Annual Reports, 1991–1996.

26 *New York Times*, July 3, 1996, p.6

27 *Wall Street Journal*, July 3, 1996, p.10

28 *Intelligence Newsletter* (Paris), June 18, 1998. (Though scarcely known amongst non-specialists, this is a well-established and respected source of international intelligence information.)

29 *Los Angeles Times*, September 12, 1998, p.6; March 6, 1999, p.6; *The Guardian* (London), May 31, 1997, p.16

CHAPTER 19

1 *Washington Post*, September 22, 1991

2 NED Annual Reports, 1994–96

3 NED Annual Report, 1996, p.39

4 For further information on AIFLD, see: Tom Barry, et al., *The Other Side of Paradise: Foreign Control in the Caribbean* (Grove Press, NY, 1984), see AIFLD in index; Jan Knippers Black, *United States Penetration of Brazil* (Univ. of Pennsylvania Press, 1977), chapter 6; Fred Hirsch, *An Analysis of Our AFL-CIO Role in Latin America* (monograph, San Jose, California, 1974) passim; *The Sunday Times* (London), October 27, 1974, p.15–16

5 NED Annual Report, November 18, 1983 to September 30, 1984, p.21

6 NED Annual Report, 1998, p.35

7   See NED annual reports of the 1990s.

8   Haiti: *Haiti Progres* (Port-au-Prince, Haiti), May 13–19, 1998

9   *New York Times*, March 31, 1997, p.11

10 *Washington Post*, February 16, 1987; also see *New York Times*, February 15, 1987, p.1

11 *San Francisco Examiner*, July 21, 1985, p.1

12 *New York Times*, July 13, 1998

13 For a detailed discussion of NED, in addition to the sources named above, see: William I. Robinson, *A Faustian Bargain: U.S. Intervention in the Nicaraguan Elections and American Foreign Policy in the Post-Cold War Era* (Westview Press, Colorado, 1992), passim

CHAPTER 20

1   *New York Times*, November 4, 1983, p.16

2   *Washington Post*, November 18, 1996

3   Shirley Hazzard, *Countenance of Truth: The United Nations and the Waldheim Case* (Viking, New York, 1990), p.7. Hazzard worked at the UN from 1952 to 1962.

4   *New York Times*, November 1, 1952, p.1

5   *The Guardian* (London), September 20, 1983. The next day the White House disowned Lichenstein's remark.

CHAPTER 21

1   *Washington Post*, November 13, 1999

2   Overall discussions of ECHELON and related topics:

a) Nicky Hager, *Secret Power: New Zealand's Role in the International Spy Network* (Craig Potton Publishing, Nelson, NZ, 1996), passim;

b) European Union report, "An Appraisal of the Technologies of Political Control", September 1998, in particular Section 7.4, can be read at http://cryptome.org/stoa-atpc.htm;

c) European Parliament report, "Interception Capabilities 2000", April 1999, by Duncan Campbell, can be read at http://www.iptvreports. mcmail.com/interception_capabilities_2000.htm—Campbell (Summary, paragraph 7) writes that this "word spotting" is not yet possible with telephone calls, but that speaker-recognition systems—in effect, "voiceprints"—have been developed and are deployed to recognize the speech of targeted individuals making international telephone calls. However, Wayne Madsen, who was a communications security analyst with the NSA and is currently a senior fellow at Electronic Privacy Information Center,

Washington, DC, has informed the author that word spotting for telephone calls has been used by NSA for many years.

3   *The Observer* (London), June 28, 1992, p.4

4   Seymour M. Hersh, "How the digital age left our spies out in the cold," *The New Yorker*, December 6, 1999, p.58–76.

5   *Sunday Times* (London), May 31, 1998, p.11

6   *The Telegraph* (London), Dec. 16, 1997

7   *The Independent* (London), Aprril 11, 1998

8   *Electronic Telegraph* (London), April 11, 1999

9   *Washington Post*, February 26, 1995, p.1

10 Ibid., October 17, 1995

11 *Electronic Telegraph* (London), April 11, 1999

12 *Washington Post*, September 30, 1999, p.20

13 Hager, op. cit., p.94

14 EU-FBI: *Statewatch* magazine (London), Vol. 7, numbers 1, 4, and 5 (1997); Vol. 8, numbers 5 and 6 (1998); Vol. 9, numbers 2, 3 and 6 (1999). Some of the material can be read online at: http://www.statewatch.org

15 "The working document for the Scientific and Technological Options Assessment (STOA) panel", May 14, 1999, reported by The Technology News Site, May 18, 1999; STOA is an agency of the European Parliament; *Baltimore Sun*, December 10, 1995, article begining on p.1.

16 *Washington Post*, August 20, 1999, p.1

17 Symposium at Harvard Law School, January 28–30, 1996: Speakers Paul Strassman of the National Defense University and William Marlowe of Science Application International Corporation both declared that a number of anonymous internet remailers in the US are run by government agencies, including the CIA. Marlowe said that government agencies in Germany, France and elsewhere did likewise. For some notes made of Marlowe's talk, see: http://ksgwww.harvard.edu/iip/GIIconf/gii2note.html (site visited December 1999); see also *New York Times*, April 19, 1999, p.C4; Lotus, *et al*: Wayne Madsen, *Computer Fraud & Security Bulletin* (Oxford, UK), June 1995; "Interceptions Capabilities 2000" (see note 2), Technical annexe, sections 42 to 44.

18 *USA Today*, October 9, 1998, p.10; *Washington Post*, January 29, 1999, p.23, February 13, 1999, p.27 (Nat Hentoff)

19 *Baltimore Sun*, December 10 and 15, 1995, part of six-part series on the NSA; Wayne Madsen, "Crypto AG: The NSA's Trojan Whore?" *Covert Action Quarterly* (Washington, DC), #63, winter 1998, p.36–42; *Der Spiegel* (Hamburg, Germany), September 2, 1996, p.206–11

20 Duncan Campbell's article of September 3, 1999 can be found on the website of TechWeb: http://www.techweb.com/wire/story/TWB19990903S0014

21 Agence France Presse, February 18 and 21, 2000. Microsoft categorically denied all the charges and the French Defense Ministry said that it did not necessarily stand by the report, which was written by "outside experts".

Chapter 22

1 Dominican Republic: See Elections chapter for further information; Honduras: *New York Times*, May 25, 1988, p.8; Mexico: Ibid., April 20, 1990, p.1; Cypriot: *Washington Post*, April 18, 1999; Colombia: Ibid., October 14, 1999, p.1

2 *Los Angeles Times*, June 21, 1992, p.M1

3 *Washington Post*, October 15, 1999, p.23

4 *New York Times*, November 6, 1983, p.1,18,19; Casey: Bob Woodward, *VEIL: The Secret Wars of the CIA 1981–1987* (New York, 1987), p.294

5 *Los Angeles Times*, June 23, 1990

6 Philip Wheaton, *Panama Invaded* (New Jersey, 1992), p.45, 50–1; plus interview of Wheaton by author

7 *New York Times*, March 20, 1990, p.8

8 As told to the author in November 1999 by the Panamanian embassy in Washington.

9 *Washington Post*, November 22, 1998, p.2; March 3, 1999; October 27, 1999, p.27

10 Ibid., September 4, 1999, p.26

11 Haiti: *The Nation*, February 26, 1996, p.5; *Washington Post*, August 3, 1996; Agence France Press, February 9, 1996, as reported by Haitian Information Bureau, Port-au-Prince, Haiti, February 10, 1996; *New York Times*, November 28, 1995.

   For the most detail, see the announcements of Haiti Advocacy (Washington, DC) and The Campaign for the Return of the FRAPH/FADH Documents at: http://members.bellatlantic.net/~advocacy

Chapter 23

1 *Los Angeles Times*, February 12, 1990

2 *New York Times*, July 23, 1986, p.1

3 *The Guardian* (London), August 15, 1986; *The Times* (London), August 4, 1986

4 CBS-TV interview with Tomlins, August 5, 1986; interview of Pizzey by author, April 25, 1999.

5 *The Atlanta Journal and Constitution*, June 11, 1990, p.1

6 *Los Angeles Times*, June 13, 1990, p.12

CHAPTER 24

1   Peter Dale Scott & Jonathan Marshall, *Cocaine Politics: Drugs, Armies, and the CIA in Central America,* (University of California Press, Berkeley, 1991), p.x–xi. Dayle was speaking in 1991 at Fordham University in NY, as part of a panel concerning drugs, organized by the Christic Institute and other groups.

2   Alfred W. McCoy, *The Politics of Heroin: CIA Complicity in the Global Drug Trade* (New York, 1991), p.43–47, 53–62; Alexander Cockburn and Jeffrey St. Clair, *Whiteout: The CIA, Drugs and the Press* (Verso, NY/London, 1998), p.137–41

3   Christopher Robbins, *Air America,* (New York, 1985), chapter 9; McCoy, chapter 7 and elsewhere.

4   McCoy, chapters 4, 5 and 7; Robbins, chapters 5 through 9

5   Jonathan Kwitny, *The Crimes of Patriots: A True Tale of Dope, Dirty Money, and the CIA* (W.W. Norton & Co., New York, 1987)—bank's drug connections: chapter 16 and elsewhere; bank's CIA connections: see index, p.404; McCoy, p.461–78; *The Village Voice* (New York), July 1–7, 1981; *CounterSpy* magazine (Washington, DC), November 1980–January 1981, p.30–33

6   Casey: *Los Angeles Times,* April 14, 1989, p.11, derived from the Kerry Report (see below)

7   *Cocaine Politics,* op. cit., chapters 6 and 10; John Dinges, *Our Man in Panama* (Random House, NY, 1991), passim; Murray Waas, "Cocaine and the White House Connection", *LA Weekly* (Los Angeles), September 30–October 6 and October 7–13, 1988; National Security Archive Documentation Packet: "The Contras, Cocaine, and Covert Operations" (Washington, DC, 1996)

8   *Washington Post,* November 28, 1995, p.3

9   *Drugs, Law Enforcement and Foreign Policy,* a Report of the Senate Committee on Foreign Relations, Subcommittee on Terrorism, Narcotics and International Operations, 1989, p.2, 36, 41 ("Kerry Report")

10 *Los Angeles Times,* April 8, 1988, p.12

11 Costa Rica/Hull/Cubans: Robert Parry, *Lost History: Contras, Cocaine, the Press & "Project Truth"* (The Media Consortium, Arlington, VA, 1999), p.220–223 and elsewhere; *Cocaine Politics,* op. cit., see "Anti-Castro Cubans" in index; Martha Honey, *Hostile Acts: U.S. Policy in Costa Rica in the 1980s* (University Press of Florida, Gainesville, 1994), chapters 8 to 10 and elsewhere; Martha Honey and David Myers, "U.S. Probing Drug Agent's Activities in Costa Rica," *San Francisco Chronicle,* August 14, 1991

12 *Cocaine Politics,* op. cit., chapters 2 and 3 and elsewhere; Hyde: Peter Dale Scott, *The Official Story: What the government has admitted about CIA ties to drug dealers* (Institute for Policy Studies, Washington, DC, 1999), p.28–9. This monograph is an analysis of two CIA and one Justice Department

reports issued in 1997–8 in response to the many allegations of CIA drug connections. See also *Lost History*, op. cit., passim for an analysis of the government reports.

13 Ilopango: Celerino Castillo and Dave Harmon, *Powder Burns: Cocaine, Contras and the Drug War* (Mosaic Press, Canada, 1994), p.128–139 and elsewhere; North's diary: *Washington Post*, October 22, 1994, p.11; Guatemala: Frank Smyth, "In Guatemala, The DEA Fights the CIA", *New Republic*, June 5, 1995.

14 *New York Times*, April 14, 1989, p.8; *Cocaine Politics*, op. cit., p.60–62; Customs Agent: FBI debriefing of Dennis Ainsworth, California Contra supporter, January 21, 1987, p.8, part of National Security Archive Documentation Packet, op. cit.

15 Kerry Report, p.42–43; *New York Times*, April 14, 1989, p.8

16 *Cocaine Politics*, op. cit., p.17–18

17 *New York Times*, April 14, 1989, p.8

18 *Washington Post*, March 17, 1998

19 *Whiteout*, op. cit., p.95–7; *Wall Street Journal*, November 22, 1996; *New York Times*, November 19, 1996; *Miami Herald*, November 23, 1996, p.B1

20 McCoy, p.436–60; Tim Weiner, *Blank Check: The Pentagon's Black Budget* (Warner Books, NY, 1990), p.151–2; *New York Times*, June 18, 1986; *Covert Action Information Bulletin*, (Washington, DC) No. 28, Summer 1987, p.11–12; *Los Angeles Times*, November 4, 1989, p.14; *Washington Post*, May 13, 1990, p.1

21 *Los Angeles Times*, August 22, 1993

22 *New York Times*, Nov. 14, 1993; *The Nation*, October 3, 1994, p.346; *Washington Post*, March 8, 1997

23 In the United States: Gary Webb, *Dark Alliance: The CIA, The Contras, and the Crack Cocaine Explosion* (New York, 1998), passim; *San Jose Mercury News*, August 18–20, 1996, series by Gary Webb, from which his book springs; *Cocaine Politics*, op. cit., passim; *Lost History*, op. cit., passim; *iF Magazine* (Arlington, VA), March–April 1998, September–October 1998, and other issues; *The Official Story*, op. cit., passim; *New York Times*, October 10, 1998, "CIA said to ignore charges of contra drug dealing in '80s"

24 *Eugene Weekly* (Oregon), January 15, 1999, interview with Webb

CHAPTER 25

1 Speaking as vice president in the context of the shooting down of an Iranian passenger plane by an American ship, taking 290 lives, *Newsweek*, August 15, 1988

2 *Washington Post*, December 18, 1987

3 *New York Times*, November 11, 1996, p.12

4 Author's conversation with the Cuban Interest Section in Washington, DC

5 *U.S. Aid to North Vietnam*, Hearings Before the Subcommittee on Asian and Pacific Affairs, House Committee on International Relations, July 19, 1977, Appendix 2.

6 *Los Angeles Times* and *New York Times*, March 11, 1997

7 For a discussion of this maiming, see John Pilger, "Vietnam: The Final Battle", *Covert Action Quarterly* (Washington, DC), #64, Spring 1998, p.54–65

8 Holly Sklar, *Washington's War on Nicaragua* (South End Press, Boston, 1988), p.169–70, 314

9 *San Francisco Chronicle*, April 16, 1987, p.15

10 Interview of attorney Ramsey Clark, September 7, 1999, by the author. Clark had acted on behalf of many of the claimants.

11 Interview of attorney John Kiyonaga of Alexandria, VA, September 10, 1999; he and his brother David were the attorneys for these cases; see their op-ed in the *Los Angeles Times*, April 1, 1990; see also *The Guardian* (London), July 28, 1990, p. 7; *San Francisco Examiner*, April 26, 1992, p.4

12 Interview of Elizabeth Abimershad of the IACHR-OAS in Washington, September 7, 1999. The case is Salas, et al. against United States of America, Case No. 10.573

13 Read to the author over the phone, December 22, 1999, by the State Department's Panama desk from an official press announcement

14 *The Independent* (London), February 15, 1999, p.12; Seymour Hersh, "The Missiles of August", *The New Yorker*, October 12, 1998, p.34–41; *New York Times*, October 21, 1998, p.1 and 8

15 *Washington Post*, July 25, 1999, p.F1

16 *Peacelink* magazine (Hamilton, New Zealand), March 1991, p.19; *Washington Post*, February 8, 1991, p.1 (includes Powell remark)

17 "Nato bombed Chinese deliberately", *The Observer* (London), October 17, 1999; and November 28, 1999. Also see *Extra! Update* (Fairness & Accuracy in Reporting, New York), December 1999

18 *Weekly Compilation of Presidential Documents*, March 15, 1999, p.395

19 *Public Papers of the Presidents of the United States* (GPO), *1968–69, Vol. II*, p.800

20 The Associated Press, dispatch from Athens, Greece, November 20, 1999, by Terence Hunt; *Washington Post*, November 21, 1999

21 *Weekly Compilation of Presidential Documents*, March 24, 1998, p.491

CHAPTER 26

1 *Los Angeles Times*, January 2, 1995, Assembly Bills 36X and 57X
2 Ibid., September 29, 1994; *Washington Post*, December 26, 1999, p.16
3 Speech in Austin, Texas, April 1993, unveiling her health-care campaign.
4 *Los Angeles Times*, January 2, 1995, Senate Bill 1330
5 *New York Times*, December 25, 1992
6 *Washington Post*, June 11, 1995
7 Ibid., July 5, 1996, column by E.J. Dionne Jr.
8 Ibid., May 15, 1998, p.9
9 Ibid., June 20, 1995
10 Ibid., November 30, 1995
11 *New York Times*, June 7, 1987, Section 11CN ("Connecticut Weekly Desk"), p.36 (found in Lexis-Nexis)
12 *Los Angeles Times*, September 2, 1994

CHAPTER 27

1 *The Guardian* (London), October 11, 1984; January 11, 1986, p.7
2 *Los Angeles Times*, August 26, 1991, p.6
3 Guatemala: Stephen Schlesinger and Stephen Kinzer, *Bitter Fruit: The Untold Story of the American Coup in Guatemala* (Doubleday & Co., New York, 1982), p.183; Jagan: Arthur Schlesinger, *A Thousand Days* (Boston, 1965), p.774–9; Bishop: Associated Press, May 29, 1983, "Leftist Government Officials Visit United States" (Lexis-Nexis)
4 *Los Angeles Times*, February 24, 1994, p.7
5 *Washington Post*, April 19, 1999, p.14
6 *Los Angeles Times*, April 4, 1999, p.4
7 *Washington Post*, May 9, 1999, p.1 and 22
8 Christopher Simpson, *Science of Coercion* (Oxford University Press, NY, 1994), p.4
9 *Washington Times*, July 28, 29, 30, 1999.
10 *Washington Post*, January 2, 1999; see also constitutional lawyer Floyd Abrams' serious criticism of Clinton's policies on First Amendment issues, *New York Times Magazine*, March 30, 1997, p.42–4

Index

About the Author

Williamilliam Blum left the State Department in 1967, abandoning his aspiration of becoming a Foreign Service Officer, because of his opposition to what the United States was doing in Vietnam.

He then became one of the founders and editors of the *Washington Free Press*, the first "underground" newspaper in the capital.

In 1969, he wrote and published an exposé of the CIA in which was revealed the names and addresses of more than 200 employees of the Agency.

Mr. Blum has been a freelance journalist in the United States, Europe and South America. His stay in Chile in 1972–3, writing about the Allende government's "socialist experiment", and then its tragic overthrow in a CIA-designed coup, instilled in him a personal involvement and an even more heightened interest in what his government was doing in various corners of the world.

In the mid-1970s, he worked in London with former CIA officer Philip Agee and his associates on their project of exposing CIA personnel and their misdeeds.

The late 1980s found Mr. Blum living in Los Angeles pursuing a career as a screenwriter. Unfortunately, his screenplays all had two (if not three) strikes against them because they dealt with those things which makes grown men run screaming in Hollywood: ideas and issues.

He is once again living in Washington, DC, outstandingly ineligible to renew his lapsed security clearance; indeed, because of his questionable political views, doubtlessly unhirable by any government agency or right-thinking private company, and reduced, as can be seen, to writing rather eccentric books in a desperate attempt to make a living. He therefore asks you to make your purchases of this book in multiples of ten. Otherwise, he sees no way of making it to the 22nd century.

email:bblum6@aol.com
http://members.aol.com/bblum6/American_holocaust.htm

FOR MORE GREAT BOOKS
AND INFORMATION

Award-winning Common Courage Press has been publishing exposés and authors on the front lines since 1991. Authors include

- Louise Armstrong
- Judi Bari
- Peter Breggin
- Joanna Cagan
- Noam Chomsky
- Laura Flanders
- Jennifer Harbury

- Bob Harris
- John Ross
- Ken Silverstein
- Norman Solomon
- Cornel West
- Howard Zinn
- and many others

Also available: the dynamite **Real Stories Series** of small books from **Odonian Press** including titles from Noam Chomsky and Gore Vidal.

FOR BULK DISCOUNTS CALL 800-497-3207

For catalogs and updates, call 800-497-3207.

orders-info@commoncouragepress.com

Write us at
Common Courage Press
Box 702
Monroe, ME 04951

www.commoncouragepress.com